Behavior Space

Behavior Space

Play, Pleasure and Discovery as a Model for Business Value

ALEXANDER MANU

Routledge
Taylor & Francis Group

LONDON AND NEW YORK

First published in paperback 2024

First published 2012 by Gower Publishing

Published 2016 by Routledge
4 Park Square, Milton Park, Abingdon, Oxon OX14 4RN

and by Routledge
605 Third Avenue, New York, NY 10158

Routledge is an imprint of the Taylor & Francis Group, an informa business

Publisher's Note
The publisher has gone to great lengths to ensure the quality of this reprint but points out that some imperfections in the original copies may be apparent.

Gower Applied Business Research
Our programme provides leaders, practitioners, scholars and researchers with thought provoking, cutting edge books that combine conceptual insights, interdisciplinary rigour and practical relevance in key areas of business and management.

British Library Cataloguing in Publication Data
Manu, Alexander, 1954-

  Behaviour space : play, pleasure and discovery as a model
  for business value. -- New ed.
  1. New products--Social aspects. 2. New products--
  Psychological aspects. 3. Creative ability in business.
  4. Consumers--Attitudes.
  I. Title
  658.5'75-dc23

Library of Congress Cataloging-in-Publication Data
Manu, Alexander, 1954-
  Behaviour space : play, pleasure and discovery as a model for business value / by
  Alexander Manu.
    p. cm.
  Includes bibliographical references and index.
  ISBN 978-1-4094-4684-2 (hbk) -- ISBN 978-1-4094-4685-9 (ebook) 1. Creative ability
  in business. 2. New products. 3. Product design. 4. Consumer behavior. 5. Strategic
  planning. I. Title.
  HD53.M3627 2012
  658.4'094--dc23

                          2012022759

ISBN: 978-1-4094-4684-2 (hbk)
ISBN: 978-1-03-283732-1 (pbk)
ISBN: 978-1-315-56890-4 (ebk)

DOI: 10.4324/9781315568904

Contents

List of Figures

Acknowledgements

This book began as an idea that grew with the inspired vision of many collaborators and colleagues. My thanks to John Sutherland for his insights, for his kindred spirit over the past few years and for embracing and furthering in practice the ideas and methods described in this book. To Mathew Jones, my gratitude for his articulation of the many ideas that inform the core of the Dataspace concept. Thanks to Ulla Jones, a traveling companion on the journey of understanding the value of 'play in work'; her insights have provided me with many points of departure in the reframing of the experience of work. Kelly Seagram has been a constant source of inspiration and a reliable source of wisdom; her framing of 'What Play is' has been a defining perspective for this work.

Many thanks as well to Saul J. Berman and Ragna Bell, from IBM's Global Business Services, for generously contributing their knowledge in the section *Digital Transformation: Creating Business Models Where the Digital Meets Physical*.

Special thanks to Terence Smith, Sergey Kovalyukh, Ivan Yuen and Caitlin Storey from my 2011 MBA class at the Rotman School of Management at the University of Toronto, who have contributed the conceptual framework for a new type of organization, designed to realign purpose with individual passion.

Finally, to the many organizations and individuals that embraced over the years my ToolToy concept, my thanks for making it a reality of everyday products and services, and for transforming life in the festival that it deserves to be.

Toronto, July 1, 2012

Prologue:
The Landscape is Shifting

On January 9, 2007 the world woke up to the now memorable headline: "Apple Reinvents the Phone with iPhone."[1] In a battery of announcements— one of which was the change of Apple's corporate name from Apple Computer Corporation to Apple Corporation—Steve Jobs introduced a new device, combining three products: a mobile phone, a widescreen iPod with touch controls, and a breakthrough Internet communications device with desktop-class email, web browsing, searching and maps—into one small and lightweight handheld device. The product pioneered a new user interface that took advantage of the large screen of the device, accessible by multi-touch, giving users the ability to control actions by dragging their fingers along the screen surface. This was both a software and a hardware feat, and announced a new era in the interaction between user and display based devices. *"iPhone is a revolutionary and magical product that is literally five years ahead of any other mobile phone,"* said Jobs. *"We are all born with the ultimate pointing device—our fingers— and iPhone uses them to create the most revolutionary user interface since the mouse."* The company's press release[2] of January 9, 2007 was as excited as his speech:

> *iPhone includes an SMS application with a full QWERTY soft keyboard to easily send and receive SMS messages in multiple sessions. When users need to type, iPhone presents them with an elegant touch keyboard which is* predictive *to prevent and correct mistakes, making it much easier and more efficient to use than the small plastic keyboards on many smartphones. iPhone also includes a calendar application that allows calendars to be* automatically synced *with your PC or Mac.*

---

1 Available at: http://www.apple.com/pr/library/2007/01/09Apple-Reinvents-the-Phone-with-iPhone.html [accessed: September 2, 2011].

2 Available at: http://www.apple.com/pr/library/2007/01/09Apple-Reinvents-the-Phone-with-iPhone.html [accessed: September 2, 2011].

iPhone features a 2 megapixel camera and a photo management application *that is far beyond anything on a phone today. Users can browse their photo library, which can be easily synced from their PC or Mac, with just a flick of a finger and easily choose a photo for their wallpaper or to include in an email.*

iPhone is a widescreen iPod with touch controls that lets music lovers 'touch' their music by easily scrolling through entire lists of songs, artists, albums and playlists with just a flick of a finger. Album artwork is stunningly presented on iPhone's large and vibrant display.

iPhone lets users enjoy all their iPod content, including music, audiobooks, audio podcasts, video podcasts, music videos, television shows and movies. iPhone syncs content from a user's iTunes library on their PC or Mac, and can play any music or video content they have purchased from the online iTunes store.

iPhone's Advanced Sensors   *iPhone employs advanced built-in sensors—an accelerometer, a proximity sensor and an* ambient light sensor—*that automatically* enhance the user experience *and extend battery life. iPhone's built-in accelerometer* detects when the user has rotated the device *from portrait to landscape, then* automatically changes the contents *of the display accordingly, with users immediately seeing the entire width of a web page, or a photo in its proper landscape aspect ratio.*

iPhone's built-in proximity sensor detects when you lift iPhone to your ear *and immediately* turns off the display to save power *and prevent inadvertent touches until iPhone is moved away. iPhone's built-in ambient light sensor automatically adjusts the display's brightness to the appropriate level for the current ambient light, thereby enhancing the user experience and saving power at the same time.*

Wow!

A full disclosure document, outlining for every competitor where the bar was now set, in the space of mobile communication devices. Multi-touch displays, sensors throughout the unit—capable of sensing the relative position of the device to the horizontal, thus ideal for use as a handheld gaming device—email, address books and all you can expect in multimedia. True to its track record of not disappointing users, Apple launched the iPhone right on schedule, on June 29, 2007. The rest just followed.[3]

On the date of the announcement in January 2007, Nokia was the market leader[4] in the smartphone space, holding 53 percent market share, with RIM (Research in Motion) in second place, around 40 percent in the United States. Apple Corporation held 0 percent of the market. By the fourth quarter of 2007, Nokia had 52.9 percent, RIM 11.4 percent and Apple 6.5 percent. By September 2011, the market share picture was almost reversed: RIM 11.7 percent (10.6 million units sold) Apple 18.2 percent (20 million units sold).

Meanwhile in Waterloo, Canada …

Jim Balsillie, the co-CEO of Research In Motion Ltd., makers of the BlackBerry email device, said in an interview[5] that he was not losing any sleep over Apple's efforts to disrupt the wireless market, and he could not confirm whether anyone at RIM had managed to get their hands on an iPhone. "I haven't seen one."[6]

A number of technology experts writing in the media warned RIM that Apple's assault into the wireless market is more than just the arrival of another trendy and well-designed device. It was apparent to everyone—but not to the executive suite at RIM—that the functionality of the iPhone set the bar significantly higher in terms of user experience, and the look and feel of mobile wireless devices.[7] But one had to try out the unit in order to understand how the iPhone *felt*, and how it was different than anything existing in the marketplace in that moment. Balsillie declared that he is "*doubtful the device will have much of an impact on RIM's overall sales. For one thing, the iPhone will hold little appeal for*

---

3   In June 2007, Apple announced that the iPhone would support third-party "web applications" that share the look and feel of the iPhone interface. On October 17, 2007, Steve Jobs announced that a software development kit (SDK) would be made available to third-party developers in February 2008. The iPhone SDK was officially announced and released on March 6, 2008. The App Store was launched with the release of iOS 2.0, on July 11, 2008. As of June 6, 2011, there are at least 425,000 third-party apps officially available on the App Store. By early July 2011, 200 million users have downloaded over 15 billion apps from the App Store.
4   http://www.canalys.com/newsroom/smart-mobile-device-shipments-hit-118-million-2007-53-2006.
5   http://www.thestar.com/Business/article/233390 article by Chris Sorensen for *The Toronto Star*, July 7, 2007.
6   Ibid.
7   Ibid.

RIM's core business market and its need for secure information technology systems, which RIM has been providing for years with its corporate BlackBerry email servers."

Is it remarkable that the co-CEO of a publicly traded corporation can read so little risk in the launch of a competitor's product? Or is it more remarkable that the analyst community did not ask any questions about the iPhone of RIM's leadership in the earnings call of April 2007, the first such occasion after the announcement of the iPhone was made? There are many remarkable misses in this story, and they are not relegated to RIM alone. Nokia, the market leader at the time and presumably the company with most to lose, also did not see the threat the iPhone represented. To be clear, I am not picking on one company to make a point; I am using the incumbents in the market at the time of the launch of the iPhone as a case study in missed opportunity. Both RIM and Nokia are public companies and, as such, their mistakes have affected thousands of shareholders. And so the story goes, by November 16, 2011, according to iPass, Apple was leading BlackBerry in business phones in the U.S. market.[8] The circle was now complete:

> *Apple has ousted Research in Motion's BlackBerry as the top smartphone for mobile workers, according to the latest research from wireless specialist iPass. The company's survey of more than 2,300 employees at 1,100 businesses reveals that more than 45 percent of mobile workers now use iPhones, up from 31 percent last year. BlackBerry users, however, slipped to 32 percent, down from 35 percent in 2010. Apple's iPhone is the top smartphone for mobile employees. Apple sold 17.1 million iPhones during its recent fiscal fourth-quarter results, a 21 percent hike on the same period last year.*

---

8   James Rogers, *The Street*, November 16, 2011. Available at: http://www.businessinsider.com/most-innovative-gadgets-2011-11?op=1 [accessed: November 17, 2011].

1

The Business of Behavior Space

Introduction

SO WHAT WENT WRONG HERE?

What can we learn from this? And how is it applicable to your business? This was not a mere product launch on January 9, 2007. It was the launch of a *new behavior space*. The launch of a new ecosystem in the mobile device category, an ecosystem inclusive of new behaviors, new places to play in, and new devices to play on. The San Francisco event was the launch of a new corporate strategy. It was the explicit declaration of a strategic ambition, the ambition of creating and dominating an emerging new space.

The list of what went wrong might include hubris, arrogance, ignorance—the lack of methods and practice in seeing and understanding the behavioral disruption the iPhone represented. Success builds arrogance, and hubris, but it should never build ignorance of the shifting landscape; rather it should build expertise in the analysis, understanding and riding of the shift in one's own market space. It is common for companies to miss shifts in their business landscape: Microsoft did it with the advent of the Internet, and famously IBM, after the introduction of the PC. Sam Palmisano, former COO and CEO of IBM, declared candidly: *"We invented the PC but viewed it incorrectly. We saw it as a gadget, a personal productivity tool. Unlike Intel and Microsoft, we didn't see it as a platform. We missed the shift. So the lesson to me is you cannot miss the shifts. You have to move to the future."*[1]

Indeed, one has to move to the future, fast and furious. But how? And along what coordinates? This book proposes a number of them. And it all starts with understanding the nature of the shift not in product development terms, but

---

1 [Online]. Available at: www.forbes.com/forbes/2011/0627/focus-sam-palmisano-watson-christensen-ibm-at-100_2.html [accessed: January 2, 2012].

in strategic terms. From understanding to action, the path for the incumbents might have looked like this:

- understanding the business of behavior space

- understanding the behavior context

- the design dimensions and the compelling experience imperative

- capitalizing on the need for play

- relearning work, pleasure and motivation

- make foresight a core capability and transformation a daily passion

- make unlearning a core competence

- redesigning the work experience and designing from the inside out

- redesigning the business model

1. Understanding the business of behavior space

The first lesson is that market leaders cannot afford miss the shift in the behavior context, shift that occurs every time a *new behavior space* is introduced.

Apple's press release was the precise outline of a new behavior space—a space made possible by the device itself, as well as by the ecosystem that includes the App Store, the SDK (software developer kit), the third-party applications, and a large developer community. Apple defined the blueprint for a space in which devices and their users can now behave in a new way. For any competitor the challenge was not that of competing with a device, but that of competing with a *behavior space strategy*.

In strategic terms, the introduction of the iPhone was a disruption of an existing behavior space—mobile phone calls, push/pull email messages, web browsing, music and other media on a handheld device. Each of the announced features of the iPhone was expanding the footprint of the mobile phone behavior space, thus creating a new behavior space.

Apple introduced an operating system built specifically for the mobile experience, and as soon as the device became popular, they revealed the next level of the strategy: the App Store. The device was now a mobile computing platform, capable of being customized with any number of free or affordable applications. Each of these applications *represents a different behavior*: the touch screen invites *interaction*, the music store invites *contemplation*, the email messenger invites *communication*, the Huffington Post invites *up-to-date news commentary*, and so on. The platform that allows all of these behaviors to take place is the iPhone device, which cannot be seen simply as just a "product," but it has to be understood as a platform for behavior: *a behavior space*.

Was the competition up for this challenge? The answer is no. While the iPhone behavior space strategy was transparent from the beginning, the competition failed to understand its characteristics as any different from what they were competing with already. They looked at the iPhone as being *just another device*.

Most disturbing for a public company, was the complacency of the market incumbents—Nokia and RIM—after the introduction of the iPhone in June of 2007. The incumbents focused wrongly on the volume of sets sold, and on the number of subscriptions signed each month, as measures of success in a market that by now was valuing different metrics: product desirability, ease of use, fun, and pleasure while in use. In other words, the *depth of engagement* with the behavior space, represented by the device, the applications store, and the applications themselves.

Nokia and RIM simply did not "get" the iPhone, and had a sense of exemption from competing with it. The iPhone was below them, a singular product from a new entrant in the market, and one that had no previous experience in the telecommunications industry. How can you feel threaten by this little toy? Yes, it looks clean and well designed, but it does not look like a "business device." So, for the first two years of the iPhone, 2007–2009, both companies forgot about it. When visiting one of the incumbents in September 2009, I was stunned to realize that none of my interlocutors—developers, product managers, UI specialists, strategists—had ever used either the iPhone or the iTouch. These products—a worldwide phenomenon by the time of my visit—were no more than a theory to them.

2. Understanding and responding to the emerging behavior Context

The dynamics of behavior form a system in permanent change and adaptation. A new behavior space changes the dynamic, due to both the evolving nature of the people using it, and also with the evolving nature of the device itself. The user and the device are involved in a behavior cycle; the cycle once completed by the satisfaction of a user's goals, the user is now looking for more goals to be satisfied by the device—or the technology. It is in this "looking for more" goals to satisfy that the economic impact of a behavior space is felt.

The smartphone market shifted again as soon as the Apple introduced the App Store, a move that allowed users to interact with the company in new ways, and for new reasons. The app phenomenon introduced the iPhone as a platform for behavior—more behavior possible through applications, more satisfaction gained by users, and more monetization potential for Apple and third-party application developers. And all of this was not possible yet on the BlackBerry.[2]

RIM responded with BlackBerry devices that felt like overcooked vegetable dishes, with too many ingredients that don't work together. To the original secure email device, RIM added lots of new media applications the operating platform was not designed for. It is as if someone at RIM took a look at the iPhone and said "We can do that! We can add applications on our products just like you have." Problem is that the applications of the iPhone were designed from the *inside out*, while the BlackBerry developers added them from the *outside in*. Designing from the inside would have been RIM's measure of agility, which is an organization's ability in four domains:

1. The ability to act on intelligence received from the field (from the periphery of the business, from media reports, from unfolding signal maps, from consultants, and so on).

2. The ability to unlearn legacy processes.

3. The ability to reshape legacy supply chains.

4. The ability to reframe and rethink tools and metrics.

---

2 Comparing app availability, iPhone users can do some 450,000 things that Blackberry users cannot—as of July 2011, three years after the release of the App Store.

When behavior spaces shift, it is critical that competitors shift with them. Kodak invented digital cameras, but tried to defend the film business and lost the new market to Japanese competitors. When the executive suite tries to defend and extend the old success formula after a market shifts, only bad things happen. When new products are designed with the intention of defending and extending old products, new sales do not emerge'.[3] Competitors introducing changes in the behavior context kill the pioneer, and a new demographic emerges, which holds new sources of value as prerequisites for a product's viability. The demographic that embraced mobile computing and communications is the demographic of the millennial. No longer satisfied with products that just work, the millennial is looking for products that allow for self-expression, for participation in their own community of interest, and for new and multiple layers of engagement. What the millennial is looking for is a *compelling experience* in the products and services they purchase and use.

3. The design dimension and the compelling experience imperative

The iPhone was a shift in what users find of value in a mobile device, and introduced *new sources of value* at the level of user experience. The incumbent's first task in connection to this would have been to map and catalogue the elements of the compelling experience offered by the iPhone, and then design equally or more compelling experiences on their own platforms. Equally compelling would have been a minimum—the ideal is to strive beyond competition. But for that, one needs to understand the shift of value from security as a feature, to *fun, pleasure and discovery as an attitude*. No one buys an iPhone for making phone calls or sending secure transmissions to their friends. Fun, pleasure and discovery are characteristics of the new behavior space the iPhone introduced and brilliantly expanded on. There is a long list of companies in the technology space that have often confused "features" with "value." The value is the *user experience*—the *what*—and not the how it gets to be there. The iPhone introduced a value metric in which hardware, beauty, functionality, usability and application customization all play equally relevant parts, in creating an experience that has but one headline: Pleasure. *The iPhone is pleasure objectified*.

---

3   Adam Hartung. 2011. Available at www.thephoenixprinciple.com/blog/lockin/page/2/.

4. Capitalizing on the need for play

During the Q&A session of the July 2011 RIM Shareholders Meeting,[4] one investor took center stage by giving a heartfelt speech which ended with the following declaration: *"You're letting Apple and Android eat your lunch, and those are not business devices, those are kids' games."* To this, the audience applauded wildly.

Unwittingly, this investor hit the nail on the head: Apple and Android *are kids' games, they are invitations to behavior,* and this is *precisely* why they were so immediately successful. Apple and Android devices are fun to interact with, they are pleasurable and playful. *Apple and Android products are play behavior spaces.* The iPhone pioneered the transformation of a piece of technology into a behavioral object, something that invites playful use, directs the user and responds—providing feedback—to his or hers actions. In the iPhone, play builds a bridge between pleasure and purpose. Achieving purpose with pleasure is the real value of *Play Value,* described later in this book. Play Value means empowered participation and engagement; empowerment comes in the form of the device, which allows for customization and multiple layers of use through applications. The iPhone is not a tool, and it is not a toy. It is a device for, exploration, surprise, and delight. Play for purpose. The recognition that there are times in which we need to take everything less seriously, allow ourselves to possibility, and to enjoy the journey. The rewards will come, but none more satisfying than our return to the children we always wanted to be. This is a product about *the journey.* And this is why it is so hard to compete with.

5. Relearning work, pleasure and motivation

The iPhone announced that we are entering an era of play and imagination. The status quo will not be enough anymore. To compete and occupy a place in the new behavior space of mobile computing, your organization needs to imagine and innovate *possibility.* And this does not come from work, but it comes from play. Playing with ideas, playing with possibility.

The emergence of disruptive behaviors has exposed in many organizations the widening gap between current capability and current possibility. We know what we can do, we understand what we are capable of, and we perform

---

4   Available at: http://memeburn.com/2011/07/rim-shareholder-android-and-apple-are-kids-games/ [accessed: August 2, 2011].

flawlessly within that climate. Yet rarely do we know what is possible. We rarely know how to see what is possible, and act upon what we see. Simply put, people and organizations become limited by what they look at, rather than what they see. The first iPhone released in July 2007, had 11 application icons on the home screen, and four icons on the menu bar in the lower side of the screen. A total of 15 applications. This is what was visible to the eye.

But how much was visible to the imagination? Was possibility resident in the 15 applications you can see, or in the blank display space where nothing resided? While I realize that this is by now a rhetorical question, you get the point: to compete, one needs to see beyond the visible, you need to imagine what would be there in the very near future, and to imagine, you have to suspend reality for a while, and allow yourself to enter the world of play, imagination, and magic.

Is your company culturally equipped to do this? To allow your millennial work force to be themselves, to excel at their passions and produce outcomes that they are in love with? Probably not. More likely, your workforce is told to follow pre-established routines, processes created long before they got there. Millennials[5] face disappointment when they reach the organization: raised to believe that everything is possible and the sky is the limit, these are people of ambition, purpose, and experimentation. They have grown up in an environment in which technology allowed them early participation in the culture, as well as hands on experience in the creation of a new networked society in which they feel they are in control. At least, this is what they believe. They were promised all the freedom of thought and action worthy of their aspiration, just to discover once they join the organization, that the old structures of the workplace are not as permeable to change as they claim to be. Once in the workplace, they are now part of a system that does not necessarily recognize merit, imagination, play, and the cultural and economic participation that characterized the millennials' behavior up to joining the workforce. The old structure of the organization does not see empowerment and participation as necessary attributes for the prosperity of the corporation. In such an environment, millennials become disillusioned in their work, disempowered, and retreat in passionless non-performance.

This book proposes a new model for employee-retention and job satisfaction, a model in which millennials are recognized as purpose-driven individuals, and they are given roles where motivation comes from autonomy, mastery, and purpose.

---

5   A. Manu. *Distruptive Business*. 2010. Farnham: Gower Publishing, p. 6.

One of these factors, purpose, cannot be given to employees, but instead must be instilled in them through their experiences with the organization. As my collaborator Terence Smith observes, "*a purpose-driven organization is born when employees feel an urge to be a part of the organization because they desire the pure pleasure of it.*"

This pleasure comes from an emotional alignment with the vision of the organization, its higher purpose. The vision must identify a conflict to be resolved, and paint a picture of a better future. For the millennial, the vision must engage a large enough audience from which to draw energy for motivation.

Imagine that RIM and Nokia would have immediately understood that the iPhone represented a grand conflict they needed to resolve. Grand conflicts force us to imagine their resolution, and that is an image of possibility J.F.Kennedy's "*Putting a man on the moon*" was both a grand conflict to be resolved, and an image of possibility. Terence Smith talks about images of possibility in Chapter 7, "The Organizational Dimension" of this book, where he develops the FEED-R3 model of organizational design. He proposes an organization designed around a high purpose and a high caliber conflict to be resolved. The tougher the resolution of the conflict, the more purposeful the pursuit for the organization.

A company that fails to paint a picture of a better world that can be created will fail to tap into the source of energy that humans have to resolve conflict in their lives. Without a desire for a change our present condition, we have no desire to act. Because desire for change prompts action, a purpose-driven organization benefits from designing a vision that helps people see the change they can create in the world, by contrasting the current inadequate status quo with the superior, desirable future state. When done well, the framing of this conflict can spark an emotional response from employees, and make them feel an urge to contribute to the larger effort to resolve this conflict.

6. Make foresight a core capability and transformation a daily passion

A few pages ago I asked, "*But how much was visible to the imagination? Was possibility resident in the 15 applications you can see, or in the blank display space where nothing resided?*" This question cannot be answered by the scientific method; we are not dealing here with things which impart physical forces on other things, which can in turn be calculated and a prognostication be made.

This is not about predicting the future, but about foresight. Not about natural science but about human science: the choices individuals make have much more weight on the shape of the future than any technology will by itself. So the question could have been answered by constructing foresight scenarios, stories in which the engagement between people and technology could have been imaginatively explored. Scenarios can push the limits of what is possible, can reveal limitations, and allow for value judgments that inform a foresight strategy.

Foresight seeks to discover the signals that create the patterns of emergence. Emergent behavior patterns—the seeds announcing the presence of a new behavior space—start with very simple acts that get multiplied on a collective scale. The capability to map a signal in its earliest stages, accelerates our understanding of the possibilities resident in it, and allows for the appropriate course of action to be chosen. An appropriate course of action will maximize the opportunity—or minimize the threat –for both the individual and the organization. To maximize the resident opportunity, we must first recognize the *different nature* of a new variable.

What is *different* between this cell phone and my old device? Not in the device itself, *but in my attitude, goals and expectations from it? What is different in me, and how will THIS change MY nature?*

At the strategic foresight level the incumbents did not understand what needed to be redefined, enhanced and expanded in their own business models, once the iPhone and iPad became part of the mobile behavior space. They did not see the iPhone as the change agent of the business context. This is a *failure of transformation* through imagination. The iPhone spelled a transformational moment; foresight and imagination would have spelled *where* to innovate and *what*. It is insufficient for management to focus on defending past business; they must champion and support the creation of new behavior spaces. For that to take place, management has to be of the times, and of the culture in which it operates; management needs to be the primary user-base for all the devices in the space. They need to "get it" in terms of the culture in which their products play a substantial role.

The author Arthur C. Clarke suggested that the full possibilities of any technology are often missed by the very people who invented them. Clarke calls it a "Failure of Nerve"—even when given all the relevant facts, one cannot see that "they point to an inescapable conclusion."[6] The failure to understand the meaning and implications of new behavior spaces is not solely intellectual, but also requires courage, sensitivity, and imagination as preconditions for those who want to explore the necessary strategic transformation. Robert Burgelman and Andrew Growe[7] have called this understanding *"strategic recognition"*: identifying the importance of emerging practices and approaches after they arise, but before unequivocal environmental feedback is available to make their significance obvious. *"Companies tend to develop strategies which lead them to rely on certain kinds of competencies and to engage in certain kinds of product-market areas,"* says Burgelman. *"They learn what they can do well and find it difficult to deal with new possibilities that come along unplanned."*

The new possibilities are the result of an emerging context, the development of which is not necessarily of our choosing, but rather a convergence of multiple agents, sometimes unrelated, working toward the same goals, and in the same technology spaces. Once the context has changed—no matter how imperceptible at first—an organization's strategic intent needs to change as well. When strategic intent—*where are we going and why*—is at odds with strategic action—*what are we doing and how*—the organization is in a state of strategic dissonance.[8] The premise of strategic dissonance is that in dynamic industries the alignment between strategic intent and strategic action is not likely to last, due to the speed at which change occurs. Inevitably, strategic actions tend to lead strategic intent. This divergence between intent and action creates *"strategic dissonance."* Once this state is reached and recognized, new strategic intent is needed to get out of this condition. Burgelman and Growe proposed four strategic questions that frame the challenges and opportunities faced by an organization in this dynamic. The questions are formulated around the tension between two opposing sets of data: the new context vs the organization's distinctive capabilities, and new sources of value vs business models.

- To understand the **New Context** one needs to ask: *How is the Landscape Changing?*

- To understand the **New Sources of Value** one must as: *What needs can be met, problems solved or desires fulfilled?*

---

6   Arthur C. Clarke. 1961. *Profiles of the Future*. London: Orion Books, p. 9.
7   R. Burgelman and A. Growe. 1996. Strategic dissonance. *California Management Review*, Winter.
8   Ibid.

- To understand the **New Distinctive Competencies** ask: *What new capabilities are needed to succeed?*

- To understand the **New Business Models** ask: *How are we presently structured to capture value?*

The answers to these questions reveal the taxonomy and the ontology of the emerging context; they will reveal what has emerged in the visible world, and what is the meaning of it all, the intelligible aspects of change. Asking these questions in early 2007 would have allowed the incumbents to fully understand the new landscape, have the right ambition for their possibility, and build a competent strategy toward transformation. Chapter 6, "The Strategic Dimension," presents a few practical approaches toward transformation and the creation of business models where the new meets the old, the digital meets the physical.

7. Make unlearning a core competence

Transformation requires recognition, imagination, courage, and unlearning. Change begins with unlearning, with addressing the environment of your business as though through the eyes of someone seeing for the first time. It allows for the discovery and framing of powerful questions, exploring our imagination without expectation or inhibition. Powerful questions are at the core of the creation of new standards of living. Powerful questions frame desires, and desires frame actions that we never thought possible (putting a man on the moon?). An imaginative and powerful question is very much like play; in it time and space are suspended, technology can do anything, and our goals are as free and as surprising as our imagination allows. Which is precisely why this is so hard; it exposes the truly imaginative mind from the creative imitator.

It takes time and courage to unlearn things, as we have so many things to unlearn. We needed to unlearn that we don't need to develop pictures anymore, or even carry a photographic camera. We needed to unlearn that we don't have to buy maps anymore, or carry a calculator, or listen to the radio for the weather forecast. We needed to unlearn that messages from friends can come to us at any time, in our pocket, and we don't have to rely on the postal office.

The hard part is unlearning what one's core capability used to be, and embracing a new path. For a while, most CEO's try stalling. They pretend that if they improve the processes, they will maintain revenue. Six Sigma and all that. Reducing the "productivity gap." Investing in technology. Streamlining operations. Efficiency. The trouble is that efficiency has nothing to do with flavor, taste, smell, feelings, memories, and all the transformative experiences people are looking for in their lives. People themselves—and their families for that matter—are not about efficiency. They are about life, the rollercoaster of experiences that a day represents, and the emotions that result from it. We, the people that buy stuff, want that stuff to mean something, not just to "do something." This is why we seek pleasure in our encounters with objects, spaces, foods, images, sounds and other human beings. It takes a whole lot of unlearning for an organization to be able to respond to what people really want.

8. Redesigning the work experience: designing from the inside out

Culture eats strategy for breakfast … Much wisdom is to be found in this quote attributed to Peter Drucker. It is the culture of the organization that nurtures its people, their passions and aspirations and their capacity for transformation. Without this capacity, transformation is a chore rather than a calling. Which is precisely why the incumbents had—and still have—a hard time competing with Apple. In the moment of disruption—the introduction of the iPhone as a new and disruptive behavior space—what needed to be overhauled was not a product line, but the corporate culture of the organization, and the very models that made the business successful. Once remodeled, the company could have produced hits as a *result of being*, and not as a matter of competing. But this transformation is a hard task, as it requires designing a corporation from the inside out, from the passions and expertise of the individuals to the outcomes these individuals produce.

The need for an inside-out redesign is not about a company's ability to create and innovate, but about much more: *it is about passion of the enterprise*. It is this passion that rekindles the creative fire of each individual, giving them the energy for change.

It is hard to fix problems that you are not ready to recognize exist, and this is precisely where RIM found itself in the summer of 2011 when a number of letters written by employees of the company surfaced in the media. One employee writes:[9]

> *Most of the design decisions at RIM are made by 50 something engineers, otherwise highly accomplished and credible in the field of engineering … and don't have any real background or even social sensibility for culture, design and such issues, they're woefully unqualified for the task of aesthetic judgment. The problem is not so much that they can't create a user experience with 'sex appeal" – because they could hire the right people and improve, again, it's that they don't recognize their own weaknesses in the area. They don't speak the language of "the creative process" and would probably laugh at anyone who did. Perhaps I can provide you with an anecdote; there is a folk-tale at RIM that the software engineers once brought in a foosball table – probably the most standard form of distraction and a minor symbol of authentic expression of what really is a heavy, intellectually creative process in need of … you know "breaks" and "fun" … One of the Co-CEO's summarily dismissed the idea: "not in my company." There is no room in his notion of what it means to be "professional" for t-shirts, lounging, and hip-hop.*

What RIM needed with urgency was leadership capable of:

- Cultivating and stimulating the imagination of others, individually or in groups, and translating it in user value, fitting within the culture of the times;

- Guiding, managing and inspiring others on the path of discovery and learning;

- Nurturing ideas, identifying their value and transforming them into opportunities for growth.

Now add to this mix an empowered generation—a generation that is no longer satisfied to work for pay, *but wants to work for pleasure*. A generation that is more accustomed to asking "Why am I doing this?," seeking reason for every action that they are asked to be engaged in. In Chapter 7, Sergey Kovalyukh, Terence Smith, Caitlin Storey and Ivan Yuen call this group Generation Why,

---

9   [Online]. Available at: www.businessinsider.com/ex-rim-employee-2011–6 [accessed: June 17, 2011].

a generation no longer satisfied with asking what should they do, but focused on the reason for doing. Generation Why will demand a redesign of the organization from the inside out; from the passions of the individuals to the output of the organization. Every output will be a manifestation of passion and purpose, in an organization that will perpetually supersede their previous achievement. You cannot manage Generation Why; instead you have to lead them in following their passions, mastering their knowledge and their strengths. A corporation working from the passion of its employees has at least a better chance to keep pace with the emerging context.

9. Redesigning the business model

When was the last time you redesigned your business model? How frequently do you do so? Should business models be redesigned every time we encounter a change in the context of business? The answer is again provided by Apple Corporation, an organization that functions understanding that the emerging context and its emerging behaviors are the constant, while their business is the variable:

> You've got to start with the customer experience and work backwards to the technology. You can't start with the technology and try to figure out where you're going to try and sell it ... we have tried to come up with a strategy and a vision for Apple, it started with "What incredible benefits can we give to the customer? Where can we take the customer?" Not starting with "Let's sit down with the engineers and figure out what awesome technology we have and then how are we going to market that?" And I think that's the right path to take.[10]

In a post-industrial, globally competitive economy, innovation is no longer about *serving the market*, but about making—or transforming—markets. It is no longer about adding value, but about creating value. Innovation as strategy is not about what people *are doing now*, but about *what people are about to do*. Understanding that business is in the same dynamic as the changes in behavior, requires agility and flexibility in the redesign of the business model. Compare Apple's business model in the year 2000 with the one in 2010. Each product and service introduced by Apple in this 10-year span was a redesign of their business model, a restatement of the value proposition, an expansion of the customer segment as well as a diversification of their value creating activities

---

10 Steve Jobs in a video presentation. [Online]. Available at: www.presentationzen.com/ presentationzen/2011/10/steve-jobs-simplicity-the-art-of-focus.html.

and key resources. With the advent of the App Store, third-party application developers became a key resource. The expansion of the company into retail, gave them a new distribution point not existent in the year 2000. And with iTunes, their key partnerships now include content creators for music, film, and literature. Naturally, all of these changes reflect themselves in the sources of revenue. Who would have guessed 10 years ago by looking at their existing business model, that by 2008, only five years after the introduction of iTunes, Apple will become the largest retailer of music in the US?[11] The iPhone and its associated behaviors are a perfect fit within the company's new business model. Can the same be said about Research in Motion?

The business model that made RIM successful in the mid 2000s is also responsible for its downturn. The B2B model (inclusive of enterprise, the carriers, and the income generated by secure email services) is responsible for the company's passivity with regards to marketing, and also for their attitude towards marketing as a corporate and brand function. It is apparent that at RIM, the marketing function was an afterthought. This is typical of most B2B organizations, where sales take place at a purchasing manager's level, for large volumes, and for secured periods of time. In such relationships, the drive to innovate is seen as a risk. No one wants to throw away what works so well in the present. Why change? The essence of RIM's business model has remained the same since the company turned profitable in 2005. The value proposition is still secure eMail transactions through the BB Enterprise Server. Their customer segment is small-medium size businesses, enterprises, government, and the public at large—a development that took place mostly as a result of the iPhone and Android competition, reluctantly, as it was outside the company's comfort zone. The distribution is still through mobile operators and carriers, and revenue is mainly from devices, subscriptions, software and services, as it was in 2005. While some of RIM's key activities had to change to accommodate the BlackBerry App world and third-party applications developers, this is not a redesigned business model, but a tweaking of the old model.

When not redesigning the business model as a result of changes in the context, the only option is maintaining revenue, and the organization and its employees become obsessed by numbers, focusing on the quarter-by-quarter results and not on the big picture. So you become a "technology efficiency" company and not a technology company; what this means is that you are much more concerned with timelines, reducing costs in the procurement of the

---

11 [Online]. Available at: www.apple.com/pr/library/2008/04/03iTunes-Store-Top-Music-Retailer-in-the-US.html.

smallest piece of technology, at the expense of ease of use, user-friendliness, and industrial design. At the expense of the experience of using the product and service you are providing. You start believing that *efficiency spells strategy*, and start planning strategy around the wrong objectives: manufacturing devices, large-volume orders, and sell through. These are all means, not ends. The end is a satisfied user, and that can happen only if one sees business as generated and driven by marketing. Marketing in this context does not mean "sales." Marketing means *the creation and delivery of a standard of living*.[12]

This is what the iPhone represented upon its release on July 2007: *a new standard of living. A new behavior space*. The action called upon the incumbents was to define their own behavior space strategy, formulated around the characteristics of behavior space.

CHARACTERISTICS OF BEHAVIOR SPACE

A behavior space is a platform for manifest behavior around specific goals and motivators for action, and it is composed of *value spaces*. A value space is any object or action present in a behavior space that holds *a different value proposition for the user*.

The value spaces on the iPhone (see Figure 1.1.1) are the applications present on it. The individual experience of users transforms a value space into an *Individual Value Place*. The transformation of "space" into "place" is the critical dimension necessary for a long-term relationship with a product or service. "Places" are distinctively ours, and they are unlike any other places. My "Contacts" application on the iPhone is different than your "Contacts" application on the same device. It is distinctively my own, containing *my friends* and *their contact information*. The same can be said about the iTunes application; it is distinctively mine, it is a place for the music I value. It is my musical repository value place.

The value of a behavior space for any user is proportional with the number of value spaces present within that space. Email is a value space, iTunes is another value space. They are different in value, as they are manifestations of a different *value proposition*. With the introduction of the App Store in July of 2008, the number of value spaces possible on the iPhone platform, became

---

12 McNair P. Malcolm. 1968. Marketing and the social challenge of our times, in *A New Measure of Responsibility for Marketing*, Keith Cox and Ben M. Enis. Chicago: American Marketing Association.

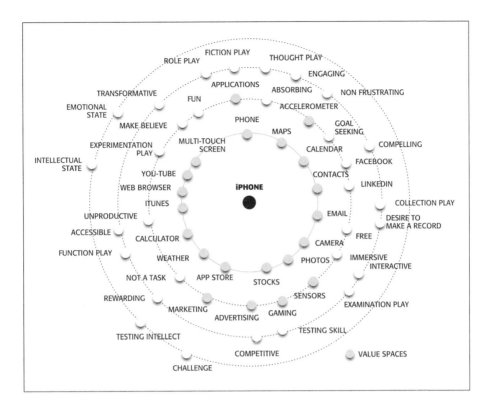

Figure 1.1.1   The iPhone behavior space

proportional with the number of third-party applications available on the App Store. To this writing, over 600,000 applications.

Each one of these applications is a window to another potential behavior space. What you will observe in studying Figure 1.1.1 is the nature of the engagement with the iPhone behavior space: it is fun, it is rewarding and it is engaging. Very much like play. It is also not a task, but rather an activity undertaken with pleasure. It affects the user's intellectual and emotional state; we are transformed while in this behavior space and as a result of each value space it holds.

Value space analysis reveals the monetization dimension of a behavior space. How many spaces are available for the manifestation of behavior? (see Figure 1.1.2) Value Place analysis reveals the personal dimension allowable in a value space; the intensity of the personal experience, the emotional, and intellectual engagement which transforms a "space" into a "place."

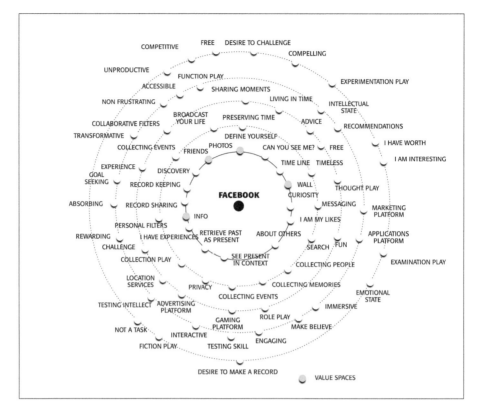

Figure 1.1.2   The Facebook behavior space

Take a look at Facebook: each of your friends is a value space, while each interaction with that friend is an individual value place. On YouTube, each video is a potential value place—in as far as it creates a compelling interaction with the viewer, and a value space in as far as the relationship potential with a large group of viewers, as in the case of viral videos.

Starbucks is a behavior space—the brand itself, the store layout, the combination of flavors, the products sold on premises—with each of the flavors being value spaces, having the potential to transform a user's experience in a very personal way, thus becoming individual value places for each user.

The space to place transformation is critical in achieving a satisfactory relationship with a product or service. In the context of behavior space, "Space" defines the dimensional realm in which material objects and events occur, objects and events directly connected to the performance of a specific goal. In the same context "place" is a particular portion of space; it is set apart from space by the specific activity that is accomplished between its boundaries. Searching for videos on YouTube is different than listening to music on iTunes.

Any place is a space, but not any space is a place. The transformation of space into place occurs when the user is *transformed by the action and interaction* with the objects present in the space. In a relationship that achieves satisfaction, the user's emotional and intellectual state is transformed in multiple dimensions. As John Sutherland observes in the Afterword to this book, we experience a transformation of our relationship with the *people* around us, with the *self*, with *ideas, objects*, with *time* and with *space*.

DEFINING BEHAVIOR SPACE

Any set of behavioral characteristics and their required media—products, systems, substances, energy—which form part of a set of actions directed toward a similar goal. Behavior space is a multidimensional construct that includes time, rhythm, motion, attention, retention, a variety of stimuli and a variety of responses. Behavior space is the ecosystem of dependencies that insure the performance of a human activity.

What I am proposing in this book is that corporations do not design products or services anymore: *they design behavior spaces*. Facebook (Figure 1.1.2) is not a product, not a technology, but a behavior space. I am a strong advocate of the idea that innovation is the creation of a new behavior;[13] *innovation is the moment in which behavior, as outcome, is being changed by invention*. Innovation is then a human activity, which resides in our motivations, and manifests itself as behavior, once we have defined that something new is the *right media for this manifestation*.

My collaborator John Sutherland insightfully observed that the product or service is simply the disruptor that enables a new behavior space to emerge. *"The size of the behavior space footprint, represents the potential value a product or service offers; the greater the value potential, the greater the monetization potential."*

How do we maximize user-engagement in the behavior space and thus expand the value potential? By creating value spaces, spaces which hold a value proposition for the user. The characteristics that compel user-engagement with a value space time and time again are characteristics we find in play behavior.

---

13 Manu, *Disruptive Business*.

Fun, curiosity, discovery, challenges, and rewards. It is my view that products and services that are economically sustainable, profitable, desired, and create vast economic benefits, are rooted in play behavior, and specifically in the concept of play value. It is play value that gives a value space individual value for the user.

This book advances the idea that play value is essential in achieving satisfaction in the engagement between users and products or services, and in this process transforming the user through new layers of pleasurable and productive engagement. By intentionally incorporating play value in products and services, the user-engagement becomes a "compelling experience" while at the same time the process for developing such outcomes is no longer the traditional design and development process, but the more complex process of experience design. Experience design is any outcome providing the stimuli eliciting responses from users, over the course of time, stimuli that transform a user motivation into behavior, the actions we engage in, or, in a much simpler language, *the pleasure of using the iPhone*. This is what both RIM and Nokia failed to understand: the behavioral dimension of the new device introduced by Apple in January 2007.

Defining Play Value

Play value is the relationship between physical and mental features—stimuli—of a product or system, elements that achieve a relationship with the user, a relationship described as fun, challenging, non-frustrating, absorbing, and rewarding. The compelling mix of these elements prompts *repeat play value*, which is the desired value of the product or service for its users. Repeat play value is the reason we keep engaging with YouTube, Facebook, Google, Twitter, iPhones, and iPads, and more. These compelling products and services are all *behavior spaces*, providing experiences that are fun, challenging, rewarding, absorbing, and non-frustrating. They succeed precisely because they never hide this fact. The hypothesis advanced here is *that the value of an object or service as a behavior space for its users, is synonymous with play value*.

In the chapters that follow, I will discuss what gives products and services value for their intended user groups, and how this value can be created, sustained, and monetized by organizations.

1.1 The Business of Behavior Space

A few years ago, my partner and I were asked to review the characteristics of the iPhone against our client's about to be released "iPhone killer." In trying to be nice but accurate as to the feel and performance of each product, my partner Matthew Jones produced what might well be the shortest report I can recall. It read:

> *Just like the iPhone, but* without the pleasure.

If you ever used an iPhone, the preceding statement makes sense, and it does not need any further explanation. On the other hand, for someone that has never used the device, it will take a lot of doing to explain how important the *"without the pleasure"* finding really is, in the context of business, user interaction and product development.

It has been more than a decade in which products have moved from *noun* to *verb*; from the tangible of the device to the process—the element of the experience—leading to beneficial outcomes. Organizations in the consumer product space must now design *benefits* and not just simply products. They innovate and design new behavior spaces and because of that, they design "experienced" outcomes. The outcome is compelling, useful, and sustains or creates a new way to experience life. You talk about it. You remember it. You share it with your friends. It transforms you. The scope of industrial design has also shifted from "devices" and the physicality of user interactions, toward "feeling:" toward the experience of the design. Or *how do I feel doing this? How does this make me feel? Would I come back to this experience? Would I tell others about it? Did this change me? Am I transformed by this interaction? Am I satisfied or unsatisfied by this experience?* The iPhone is not about "how does this feel in your hand?" but about "how does this *make you feel?"*

Measuring satisfaction in this new experience is not only a subjective metric, but one deeply rooted in the understanding of people's motivations, their goals, and desires. This understanding does not come from empathy or immersion. It comes from *the condition of being humane*. It comes from understanding people. Their life, their goals, and desires and what gives them pleasure. It comes from understanding the experience of life. The pleasures of life come from experienced emotions. These are the moments when life is worth living. And this is what Apple is delivering first and foremost: *moments of pleasure*. Pleasure achieved through play, discovery, and engagement. Pleasure achieved from transcending one's current condition.

INNOVATION, BEHAVIOR SPACE AND PLAY

I mentioned in the Prologue that I advocate innovation not as a process but as an outcome which is experienced by users.[14] An outcome that is new and transformative, an outcome that holds value for the user as well as value as an action that can generate an economic exchange. In other words, a business value. Value is implicit in the media we use, only if you or I are willing to exchange things against it; it exists only if it can trigger behavior, which in turn creates action. It is this action that holds the potential of sustaining the user's interest in the device, application or the service you are providing. It is also this action that is monetized; *technology cannot be monetized, only behavior can*.

I illustrated[15] the connection between people's desires, goals, and motivation and the success of the products and services we innovate, in order to provide a working tool—the innovation behavior map—to developers and product strategists, a tool that invites for understanding, planning, reflection and at the same time allows for auditing the performance of any innovation. When using this tool on a variety of examples of products and services, it became apparent that the key to sustaining interest is the ability to determine and maintain, in a dynamic and synchronic way, what is the value of the "thing" as media to its users. The individual value of a product or service for a user is what I termed a value place. In other words, once I launched a bar of soap, how do I maintain and increase its value for users? How do I compel users to keep using my product and find renewed satisfaction in the relationship? How do I make Dove "My Soap"? When asking these questions it becomes clear that the user needs a transformative experience. Adding more moisturizer in the soap—a physical transformation—might not accomplish this goal. An experience at the intellectual level as well as the emotional level might engage the user with the brand. What is needed is a transformation of the relationship between users and Dove soap, by transforming the relationship users had with the object, as well as with the self, and the people around them. And so it was that Unilever created the Dove Campaign for Real Beauty.

---

14   Ibid., pp. 19–20.
15   Ibid., pp. 9, 19–20.

The Dove Campaign for Real Beauty was launched in 2004 worldwide, and included advertisements, video, workshops, events, the publication of a book, and the production of a play. The central concept of the campaign was the celebration of the natural beauty of diversity; all women are beautiful, and the beauty resides in their uniqueness as people and contributors to other people's lives:

> *Imagine a world where every girl grows up with the self-esteem she needs to reach her full potential, and where every woman enjoys feeling confident in her own beauty. Imagine the world of possibilities we can open up by helping to build self-esteem in the people we love most. Our movement is building a world where women everywhere have the tools to inspire each other and the girls in their lives. We'll give you opportunities to mentor the girls in your own life, as part of a community of women from all over the world. Are you ready to take action?*[16]

In the context of the innovation behavior map illustrated here (Figure 1.1.3) a *dynamic* dimension means that the object which is media—the product or service—provides a compelling experience time and time again, by tuning the action components —either the Relationship or the Satisfaction modes—to provide a stimulus that is rooted in a context valuable to the user.

The *synchronic* dimension means that behavior cycles, once completed, demand new compelling experiences to sustain the business; these experiences are altered by the context just created by the previous behavior cycle. Once we can navigate our interaction with a mobile device by using our fingers, we will demand a new experience, a new dimension of interaction from devices. It is a "Now what?" moment in which we expect more. Our desires, goals and motivations change, and this change is an opportunity to define a new space for our behavior. Synchronicity means launching the iPhone at the precise moment every Apple user was ready to engage in the behavior of using it.

---

16 [Online]. Available at: www.dove.ca/en/Social-Mission/About-the-Movement.aspx [accessed: November 8, 2011].

The Behavior Cycle Map

In the moment a product or service is introduced to the marketplace, it has value as media[17] for a target demographic—only in so far as it is capable of creating an experience that includes a relationship between the user and the product. This experience results in satisfaction or dissatisfaction; satisfaction will ensure a continuation of the relationship between user and product, while dissatisfaction will result in abandoning the relationship. The action of using the product in the first place is the result of behavior, and behavior is rooted in the user's motivations, informed by goals and generated in desire. It is the human desire for knowledge that sets the goal of higher education, which in turn creates the motivation for attaining that goal through available means— media—be they books, institutions or Google.

The innovation behavior map (Figure 1.1.3) illustrates the individual behavior space of a product or service. When trying to determine the value of any product or service for its users—in other words the value as a medium for the satisfaction of purposeful objectives—we must look at where it all starts: everything starts in desire, which establishes goals, which establish motivation. Motivation needs capabilities for action –the means– and when motivation finds means, we engage in behavior. Behavior involves action. The action is manifest, visible, tangible, consuming energy, specific to the act, and involves a relationship between user and product, with satisfaction being the only relevant metric of that relationship. If the means do not do the job—there is no beneficial result at the completion of the interaction– the relationship is not satisfactory. A satisfactory relationship transforms the user—he or she has accomplished the goals which started this cycle—and transforms the medium into something of value to the user.

Every media we use to satisfy our goals meets the conditions 1 to 6 (in Figure 1.1.3) in the moment of use, but does not necessarily meet conditions 7, 8 that lead to 9, the value of the thing as media.[18] You may use a tool and the tool does the job, but you may not be satisfied in your relationship with the tool and thus, the tool has no value as media for you. You are unlikely to use it again. Conversely, you may encounter immediate satisfaction in the relationship with the object, satisfaction that can have a variety of stimuli: the shape of the tool, the way it performs, the way it interacts with the user, the way it provides

---

17 'Media' is used in this diagram to represent the means—tools, ideas, spaces—by which we achieve a purpose.
18 Manu, *Disruptive Business*, pp. 19–20.

feedback, the way it allows for mistakes and for their correction, the way it allows for solving challenges, and so on. Each of these moments of satisfaction create a pleasurable and transformative experience with the tool, an experience that you will repeat; the tool has become media for you. As expectations change, conditions 1, 2, and 3 change, with the result of a new medium (4) being required.

The need for business model transformation comes from the changing nature of the desires, goals and motivation of your user-base (1, 2, and 3). Humans perpetually seek media for a better self, and perpetually seek the next means to achieve the best self. Understanding the behavior cycle of a product or service as inclusive of the elements depicted in Figure 1.1.3, is to understand that products and services are behavior spaces in a perpetual dynamic.

Using behavior space as a strategic tool is to ask what is it that humans seek when deciding to use or not to use a new product or a new service. What is the primary question this new product or service has to answer? In my view there is a single question products and services are answers to, and

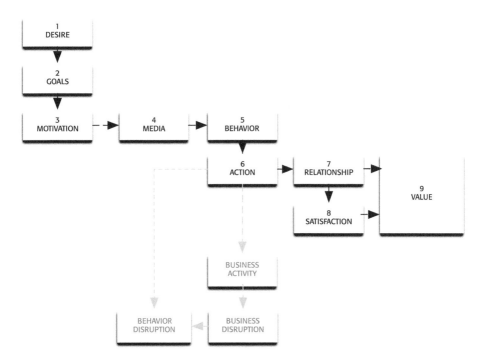

Figure 1.1.3   Behavior cycle map

that question is, "How is *this* (product or service) media for me?" "How does this product help me satisfy my goals, help me achieve my objectives?" We ask this question every time we encounter a disruptive media, as we seek to understand in what measure this "thing" can become a capability for us to progress forward, to achieve more efficiency, to achieve more pleasure in life. How can the *automobile* satisfy my motivating goals? How can *this mobile device* mediate my relationship with life, my environment, my friends, my work? *How is this a medium for me* is the question that every behavior space has to answer. The success or failure of a product or service is proportional with its capability of becoming the means—the media—by which motivating goals are satisfied (Figure 1.1.4).

Behavior Space and Business

The ultimate capability of a business organization is the knowledge of initiating, managing, and monetizing the creation of culture. In this dynamic, the role of a business organization becomes to create the tools, objects, and services through which people can manifest what they want, who they are and who

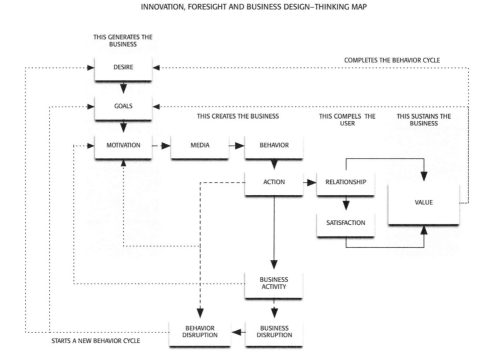

Figure 1.1.4   Behavior space as business

they want to become. In this view, all innovation is aspirational. I proposed earlier that innovation is behavior—as outcome—changed by technology. YouTube, the AppStore, the Kindle, and iTunes are some of the manifestations of this definition. The innovation of YouTube is not in technology, but in people's engagement with it. The innovation of YouTube is a behavior; when behavior engages technology in an innovation outcome, we have a *disruptive business model*. This is not about a product or a service, but about the creation of culture, the creation of a disruption in the human behavior space (Figure 1.1.5), a disruption that has meaning for humans as it provides value, becoming a new source of value that changes the dynamic of life, giving us a new capability for the satisfaction of our new goals. It follows that the ultimate capability of a business, is the knowledge of initiating, managing, and monetizing, the creation of culture in the human behavior space.[19]

The purpose of business organizations is to deliver the capability of a particular technology to a desired behavior. An organization's capability to

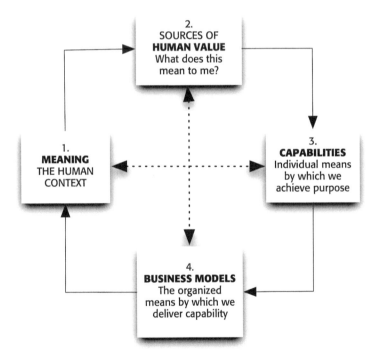

Figure 1.1.5 The human behavior Space

19 Manu, *Disruptive Business*.

meet this desire directly contributes to the success of their products and services in the marketplace. A business is an organization created for the purposes of providing the means by which people receive the capabilities empowering them to achieve their purpose. From publishing, to telecommunications to the automotive industry, all organizations fit this definition. They create and provide *media for you* to become something else, a better self. As transformation is the key to growth, then the capabilities for transformation are culture-creating. This applies to everything from soap, to computers and iPhones. Any company that knows what its true social purpose is essentially creates products for transformation.

To initiate the creation of culture—the things we do every day, the habits we form around products and services—one must understand that each product or service is an answer to conscious or subconscious goals residing in human motivation, and also understand that motivation starts in desire. It follows that the growth of any business is tied to the size of the behavior space footprint it can create, and the number of engagement opportunities present in that footprint. Reframing and rethinking innovation not as a process, but as a dynamic system of behavior, adds to the task the notion of synchronicity, the capability to continually respond—as a business organization—to the *constant human desire for a better experience of life*. And this is precisely where the iPhone excelled. It constantly repurposed the engagement with its users, becoming the poster child of business as the creation of culture:

> *… it can hardly be denied that the major part of human energies have been devoted, from earliest times, to this enterprise of using the resources of the world to satisfy our inexhaustible wants, or of making out of the world something that corresponds to our desires. Having moved from the realm of needs to the realm of wants, from desiring to live to desiring to live well (that is, better and better), and having acquired the uniquely human propensity to attempt things that we did not know quite how to achieve, we should not be surprised that the best energies have been spent on this enterprise. Indeed, to be 'intelligent" means to be a creature not merely of needs that must be satisfied, but of wants that are imagined, chosen, and pursued. Needs are limited and are related to some notion of bare existence. Wants are inexhaustible because they are related to no fixed condition of things. Michael Oakeshott*

Value Spaces: Business Growth in Behavior Space

The strategic business question for any corporation is: *"What is the **question** to which **your product is the answer**?"* To this question, a precisely defined answer is purported to show a clear understanding of the market space.

The trouble with the precise answer is that it may narrow the true monetization potential of any technology. I will use an example from the appliance industry to illustrate this point. If you are in the business of washers and dryers, it is not a motor-based appliance that you should be trying to monetize, but the revenue generating opportunity of the behavior space a motor appliance creates. When you look at what you produce and market with the lens of *behavior spaces*, the revenue potential of your organization expands: you are no longer seeing your business as the manufacture of washers and dryers. You are seeing it as the *behavior space of fabric care*; in this space, washing laundry is just one of the behaviors we engage in. The products—the washer and the dryer—are simply platforms that enable a behavior. More behaviors one is associated with in the same space equals more monetization potential.

This simply means that a *strategy of maximization* will see the business organization control all the engagement points present in the behavior space of fabric care, maximizing user touch-points and maximizing revenue generation. The idea here is to create revenue extraction triggered by behavior, rather than the onetime sale of a washing machine. Let's examine the potential of this idea a bit further: the size of the behavior space footprint is equal to the number of actions—and the needed capabilities (products)—that the user needs to be engaged with, in order to effectively accomplish the stated goals in a behavior space. In the case of fabric care, the behavior space footprint includes some of the following: water, electricity, detergent, fabric softener, washing machine, drying machine, iron, and ironing board.

All of the items above contribute to the value of the experience of fabric care. Each is a touch point between a user and a product, for a needed capability in the given behavior space. The *value potential* of the behavior space of fabric care is the sum of all the products and interactions present in the space, which carry a value proposition to a user. The greater the footprint of the value space under your control— being the producer and distributor of all products that are required for attaining the goals of the behavior space— the greater the monetization potential. Imagine that in your laundry products division you are manufacturing and marketing washing machines, but you are

NOT manufacturing or marketing dryers. Can you imagine Gillette marketing shaving machines, but not marketing shaving gels and foams? Seems absurd, right? If you were not making dryers it will be like an open invitation to other manufacturers to introduce a competitive touch point—and their own value space—in the behavior space of fabric care. Absurd or not, this is precisely what is happening already as appliance manufacturers have allowed others to monetize user behavior in the laundry behavior space, by not making or marketing detergent, not making or marketing softeners, not making or marketing irons, not making or marketing … and so on.

If you are an appliance manufacturer, your quick reaction to this might be:

> *Detergent is NOT OUR BUSINESS! We are in the motor appliance business.*

Which brings us back to: "*What is the question to which your product is the answer?*" While you explore the in-depth answers to this question, what will quickly become apparent is that you are in the business of fabric care. This is why people do laundry, because they care for their clothes and because they love clean, fresh fabrics. *Clean, fresh fabrics is precisely your business.* A business that includes in its behavior space the provision of a number of capabilities inclusive of electricity, water, detergent, washing machine, dryer, softener, and ironing implements. In other words, *the complete value space*. In any business, *growth* is achieved from the monetization of the value space, and not from the sale of individual products. What are the possible value space extensions in this case? Here are just two examples.

VALUE SPACE EXTENSION 1: NEW DETERGENT

There is a first natural extension in the provision of detergents. To add more value—tangible savings as well as a must have status for a growing segment of consumers interested in efficiency and ecology—the detergent needs to be in itself a new behavior—creating a new disruption in the behavior space — and for that, the appliance maker might want to look at a paradigm shifting solution that will remove dirt from fabric. This solution needs natural ingredients, and the capability of cleansing without the need of a long wash cycle. This means less rinsing. A reduced cycle results in less energy being needed, as well as in substantially reduced water consumption.

VALUE SPACE EXTENSION 2: WATER TREATMENT TECHNOLOGY

To enhance the performance of the new detergent, water needs to be made more soluble (softer). Soluble water results in better detergent performance, faster rinsing times with less water being used, and also reduced scaling with the corresponding reduction in maintenance costs. The environmental aspect of the opportunity—especially in areas where water availability is at a premium—is also the area where more growth, and subsequent value space extensions can be anticipated in the years to come.

THE ULTIMATE BENEFIT AS A STRATEGIC OBJECTIVE

"People don't want to buy a quarter-inch drill bit. They want a quarter-inch hole." This is what management guru Theodore Levitt was frequently advising his students at the Harvard Business School. This quote[20] helped product development methods and capabilities navigate from needs to wants for the past couple of decades. For a time, this was appropriate and gave development teams the freedom to explore the bigger picture. But Levitt was famously wrong: people do not want a quarter-inch hole—the immediate —people may want a painting hung on the wall. This is the *ultimate benefit*. The world according to Levitt was a place full of quarter-inch holes, and that has no benefit to anyone. The challenge of creating behavior spaces is in imagining and defining new business opportunities that start with mapping and understanding user behavior, in search of the ultimate user benefit. People want clean clothes, fresh food, to belong, to have peace of mind, to be entertained, and so on. The washing machine, the fridge, the cell phone, movies, music, and books, are just the means toward these ultimate benefits.

1.2 The Behavior Context of the Millennial Economy

To create and deliver benefits and behavior spaces instead of products, we need to master the stimuli that make humans respond by engaging in action. This is what organizations do—they create the stimuli; the stimulus can be an idea, a space, a form, a new function, a piece of written communication, a visual experience, or an audio experience. It could also be a flavor, a sensation, a way one feels at a particular moment in time. When you create an experience you aim to carve that moment in time. At its best, *experience design is time carving;*

---

20 [Online]. Available at: http://hbr.org/product/marketing-malpractice-the-cause-and-the-cure/an/R0512D-PDF-ENG [accessed: January 2, 2012].

nothing more, and nothing less, than defining, at one moment in time, the best circumstances for the way we experience life. The best means to reach our goals. To be seen, to be heard, to be remembered.

The human behavior space is goal-driven (Figure 1.2.1); as our goals change with our accomplishments, new behavior patterns emerge, which in turn give rise to new motivations, and new goals. It is in the meeting of beneficial goals that humans find value; the benefit of the *felt* experience of satisfaction, the experience of pleasure, the experience of being. *Seeking satisfaction through experience rather than performance through interaction with objects and spaces* is the higher calling of experience design. To achieve this, it all comes back to understanding humans. Not consumers, not users, not demographic targets, but simply the human being, as all human action is instigated by the desire for, and in the pursuit of, something. As Bertrand Russell[21] puts it, *"Desire in behavior is like force in mechanics."*

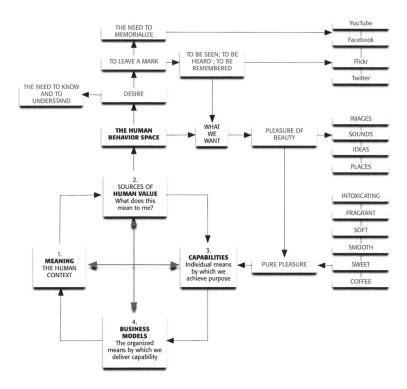

Figure 1.2.1   The human behavior space2

21 Bertrand Russell. 1921. *The Analysis of Mind*. [Online]. Available at: www.gutenberg.org/ebooks/2529. Released 2001.

Here are the goals directed by desire:

- **Basic desires for the nourishment of the body and the pleasure of the individual:** in this category we seek the qualities of smooth, soft, shiny, sweet, fragrant, intoxicating, beauty, and pleasure.

- **Motivating desires for the growth of the individual:** in this category we seek to participate, to leave a mark, to maintain, to enhance, to actualize, and to propagate the self.

- **Ultimate desires for the nourishment of the mind:** in this category we seek knowledge, understanding, and hope.

PLEASURE AND DESIRE AS ECONOMIC CONTEXT

Human life is a quest for a higher life experience. As we move from experience to experience, we learn, and we transform ourselves, and in this process our goals transform as well. We now seek softer than before, faster, sweeter, more beautiful. All in the quest for pleasure, as a smooth and soft beautiful object is just the manifestation of pleasure in a tangible form. As Santayana[22] has observed, "beauty is pleasure objectified." Beauty is value positive and intrinsic; beauty is pleasure regarded as the quality of a thing.

What about the connection between desire, pleasure, and the economic system? While Adam Smith in *"The Wealth of Nations"* gave us the *"how,"* *"where"* and *"what,"* in defining beauty and pleasure, George Santayana brings to the understanding of the economic system the *"why"* of these exchanges. This might provoke you: the economy is driven by the human desire for pleasure in all its forms; the system is a response to the necessities of the senses. Basic materials, transportation, energy, utilities, consumer staples, consumer cyclicals, technology and telecom are nothing but the supply chain of desire. To verify this, just open the business section of today's newspaper and peruse the names of some of the companies mentioned in the headlines. You might find the names Future Shop, Netflix, British Airways, Honda, Saab, Rio Tinto, General Electric, and others. What keeps these companies in business? Is it the uniqueness of their product or service, or is it the fact that our motivations dictate our behavior to purchase these products and services? I believe it is the latter. It is due to our desire for the pleasure of comfort in transportation

---

22 George Santayana. 1896. *The Sense of Beauty*. [Online]. Available at: www.gutenberg.org/ebooks/26842. Released 2008.

that Rio Tinto exists to supply Honda and Saab with iron ore and bauxite. It is our desire for the pleasures of multimedia entertainment that give birth to Netflix and ensure its business continuity; it is the same for Future Shop where we purchase our video and audio equipment. It is our desire to know and to understand that created aircraft capable of defying gravity, and our seeking of new places to explore and enjoy that keeps tourism alive. I can go on, but for now I urge you to look at the newspaper and decide for yourself.

Motivation and Ambiguity

In discussing the compelling motivators for human action, illustrated in Figure 1.2.2, one will quickly observe that they share a common trait: they are not measurable; they are all ambiguous.[23] Ambiguity is a fertile ground for interpretation and for diversity in products and services. Ambiguity is also where the largest differentiator is to be found in the un- measurable attributes that transform an object into a desired product for the individual.

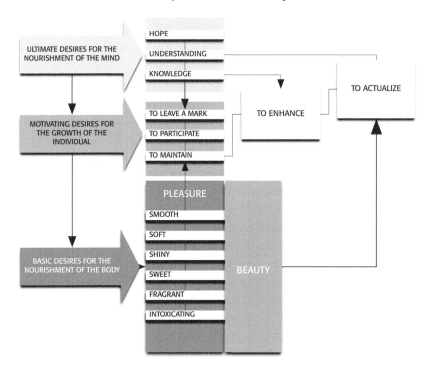

Figure 1.2.2   Compelling motivators for action

---

23 Manu, *Disruptive Business.*

In other words, the unmeasurable attributes that give any media value for the individual user, transforming a value space into an individual value place.

It is in this ambiguous domain of "value" that most products succeed or fail; some fail because their value is temporary and accidental, as they were designed from the "outside in," from the form of the object to its interactive features; others succeed because their value was the very starting point of the design process. They were designed from the "inside out," from the value proposition outward, from the desired outcome to what makes the outcome.

The starting point matters as it defines more than the process, it defines the nature of the experience users will have with the product. The question is not "what features can the iPhone technology support?" but *"what would people use their iPhone for?"* What behaviors are we ready to engage in now that we have a platform to do so? What transformations will take place in us, now that we can behave in new ways? These are all questions that define the relationship building features one will design in the device, and the touch-points of user satisfaction.

The Millennial Economy

The addition of "millennial" to the word "economy" is not just a matter of syntax; it is a necessity, as we must look at the "millennial economy" as a human behavior space in which the rules and the metrics we used for so long in the economic system differ. The economic measures we learned to use do not apply to the economy I label here as belonging to the millennial generation. We are just at the beginning of creating the tools to adequately measure the valuation of millennial behaviors in economic terms. We are good at valuing the hardware of the system but poorly equipped so far to value its software; the depth of engagement. It is the engagement in a behavior space that creates the revenue extraction opportunity.

And so it is that in January of 2011, Goldman Sachs[24] invested $450 million in Facebook, at a $50 billion dollar valuation. Yes, that's right, $50 billion dollars, or $30 billion more than the valuation of Nokia, $42 billion more than the valuation of RIM, and $29 billion more than the valuation of Yahoo. The news kept the financial press as well as the technology press busy with speculation

---

24 [Online]. Available at: www.bloomberg.com/news/2011-01-03/goldman-sachs-investment-in-facebook-may-draw-sec-scrutiny-on-disclosure.html [accessed: January 17, 2011].

running rampant around the wisdom of valuing any company at 25 times revenue (at the time of the investment, Facebook's revenue was rumored to be about $2 billion, although the company does not release financials). Some have called it "crazy," citing that fundamental value is a multiple of the revenue, and 25 times revenue makes no sense. Analyzing the potential of a company is done by looking at the proprietary technology they hold, at their market share and its profit margins, all solid indicators if the company in question sells physical assets, where the exchange of value between user and the business is manifest in terms of money against a product or a service. This metric does not apply when evaluating a *phenomenon*. Is Facebook a technology? Is it a traditional product or service? Can Facebook be understood in terms of future potential by traditional financial analysis?

No. **Facebook is a behavior space.** The real question should be *"what is a behavior space worth?"*

A behavior space is very much like a unique place, with its distinct geography, climate and ecosystem of relationships. Think of places; they are the sum of people's interactions between themselves as well as people's interactions with the physical surroundings, the fixtures of places, buildings, parks, objects ... A place is about identity, about groups that embrace time and space in the same way, and at the same location. Some places create social phenomena, which in turn strengthen the image they have in the mind of their inhabitants, and further imprint the identity of the individual with the identity of the place. A space is empty. *Places are populated.* Individuals are about place before they are about anything else. How many times have you met a stranger and asked, "Where are you from?" And how many times was the answer "I am from Paris" just the beginning of a longer and more expansive conversation with your new friend, about Paris. So what is Paris?

Paris is a behavior space. Paris is a city as well, but that is just geography and country administration. Behavior spaces are not just locations; they occupy dimensions in the mind, in the heart and in the gut. They are about memory, a memory that cannot be transplanted anywhere else. Behavior spaces are about activity; an activity that cannot be transplanted elsewhere. They are about status, a status that cannot be achieved by "other" places. Behavior spaces are about self-possibility.

And so, how much is Facebook as a behavior space worth? A place that has a population of 840 million and growing, with each one creating content, sharing it and then creating some more? I have the strange feeling that, from the perspective of the past, and with the tools of the present, we are not equipped to valuate at this time places of possibility. When we will retool our mindset and create new metrics, do not be surprised if Facebook's valuation at $50 billion dollars will seem comically low.

The trouble in valuating Facebook as a business is that we lack the tools to do so. We are adept at measuring the book value of any business based on inventory, accounts receivable, the value of real estate and so on, all measures that refer to the past but not to the future. We lack the tools to valuate behavior in economic terms. Behavior is not a raw material, and yet it is *behavior that gives value to raw material*.

Facebook's valuation is a wakeup call that we need new metrics to evaluate the economic value of manifest behaviors, the behavior that we can see and document, as well as *retrieved behaviors*, behaviors that are now possible due to new spaces being created. To valuate behavior spaces we need a good measure of foresight and signal mapping.

Foresight, Behavior Space and Behavior Retrieval

The essentials of a foresight valuation are:

- **The dynamic ecology of behavior**—understanding that behavior is a dynamic that migrates with new technology enablers—and

- **The understanding of signals in the emerging context.**[25] Signals have multiple dimensions of opportunity, all present to a viewer at the same time. Some dimensions are precise, some are undeniable, some are intuitive and some are just sensed. Let's use as a signal the Timeline feature introduced by Facebook in the summer of 2011. Once we observe a new behavior signal, we need the imagination to anticipate its future growth. Take a look at Figure 1.1.1 again. What is undeniable? What do you sense?

- **Precise** (the dimensions of the opportunity are exact, accurate, and detailed). What do you see? Picture, maps, books, lists of places,

---

25 Manu, *Disruptive Business*, p. 39.

highlighted experiences that took places yesterday or years ago, a repository of memory.

- **Undeniable** (the potential for high impact is visible, but not detailed). Which of these placeholders in Timeline holds the potential for high impact? How would this impact your business? In how much time? Where else can Timeline go, what other forms of content will be added in the very near future?

- **Intuitive** (the opportunity can be defined, but it has multiple manifestations). A signal usually appears at the periphery of your business space and migrates towards the mainstream, where it reaches its maximum possibility and economic opportunity. How will Timeline change marketing communications and advertising? How would it change the collection and preservation of individual memory?

- **Sensed** (there is awareness of possibility in the signal; it has multiple strategic opportunity directions, yet undefined). The field of maximum opportunity is reached when the market is maximized by both the low cost of the technology, and the *retrieved behavior*— posting moments as memory as an everyday action—becoming manifest behavior, an activity of everyday life. An activity in which 2 billion people will engage in, every day.

Facebook was initially a behavior at the periphery of business, having as users only students. It became mainstream once other users retrieved the behavior associated with Facebook, and became regular users. Facebook is much more than an application on the Internet, and much more than a company monetizing their user-base by generating revenue from advertisers. Facebook is a behavior space on which thousands of other behavior spaces will be built, and millions of value places will be monetized, with Facebook extracting revenue from each one of them. Imagine this business as the largest—and the most desired—city in the world, where people interact, congregate in places, have conversations, open businesses, entertain, create, consume, and have every transaction they can dream about, and then imagine that you can charge a small tax on every one of these interactions, every one of these businesses.

Mark Zuckerberg has been talking about Facebook becoming the first trillion-dollar company, and I think he has all the ingredients to do it. It is also conceivable that Facebook *will be* the Internet.

The first trillion-dollar company will be the organization capable of collecting and interpreting the largest amount of user data, and making use of it in ways beneficial to the consumer or to other businesses. And this organization looks more and more like Facebook. This capability is not only tied to data aggregation and analytics, but to the ability to understand individual user's needs, and have the foresight to suggest products and services the user might find of benefit. This also suggests that the future of marketing will be preemptive; *awareness*, one of the pillars of the profession, will be replaced by the *proactive creation of goods and services*, using the information embedded in the vast amounts of data collected from users, through the creation of a space that successfully retrieves behavior.

In connection with this—and as a measure of the company's foresight—consider Google's purchase of YouTube in 2006. This was a declaration of understanding behavior space retrieval and its specific dynamic: the speed of behavior retrieval compresses the time frame between a "precise" signal and a "sensed" signal. *The degree to which a technology retrieves latent behavior is the rate by which a sensed signal becomes precise.* So how many users does YouTube have today? Daily?

The ultimate strategy must be focused on the sensed signal: at its intended penetration, what value will YouTube represent and what are the constituent components of this value—in other words "where will the value come from?" The answer is simple, and it is connected to the massive behavior data gathered by the actions (retrieved behaviors) that YouTube enables: *the value of YouTube is the value of the behaviors it has successfully retrieved. YouTube is a retrieved behavior space.*

Once mastering the analysis of data collected by the voluntary engagement of users on the sight, the sky is the limit for the business opportunity that the collected data can generate. Spending $1.65 billion dollars on YouTube might be the smartest investment Google has made to date.

According to this metric, the value of Facebook is proportional with the value of the behaviors that Facebook retrieves. And with Timeline, the company just added another behavior space and more retrieval. More behavioral retrieval—

actions one can engage in, the depth of the engagement and the duration of the engagement—more opportunity for monetization of these actions. Note that the duration and quality of the engagement, plays a large role in transforming Facebook from a space into an individual value place. Once in a value place, the user will engage at a different depth, with more sincerity and more disclosure. The quality and quantity of the disclosures made by users increases the economic value of Facebook.

Summing up Facebook as value and potential monetization opportunity:

- It is the largest repository of personalized trust recommendations systems around every type of content.

- It acts as a cohesive reputation system, whose precision increases with every transaction or peer to peer action.

- It represents a collective taxonomy which is the sum of users' preferences, transactions, likes, and dislikes.

The above makes the case that Facebook might be the first data-enabled organization—an organization that uses data as the material for product and experience development, as well as for monetization. More on data-enabled organizations in Chapter 8.

1.3 Play Value and Compelling Experience

I described earlier play value as the relationship between physical and mental stimuli of a product or system, stimuli that prompt the user to engage in a relationship with the system. To achieve length and depth of engagement, this relationship has to be *fun, challenging, rewarding, non- frustrating, engaging and absorbing*. Play value is what compels us to go back time and time again to YouTube—it is fun, it is absorbing, it is rewarding the challenge of searching for the video clip we are in need of at that moment. The value of our engagement with YouTube—in this example– is synonymous with play value. Make the search results any less relevant, and you have a decreased reward which will make the engagement a lot less fun.

With the iPhone, Apple did not invent a technology, but new ways of engagement with the possibilities of technology, for any number of desired and beneficial outcomes. The device is a window into behaviors that, most likely, the user never thought she/he had. Each engagement with the device brings about more satisfaction, deepening the relationship between user and device. We marvel at the simplicity and beauty of the industrial design, and yet the aesthetic of the iPhone moves beyond the realm of the form into an aesthetic of relationship. What we appreciate is the permanent transformation of our relationship with and through the device. We are transformed by each application we use, by each relevant bit of information that changes our relationship with the present.

Transforming a piece of technology into a behavioral object, something that invites use via stimuli, directs the user, and responds—providing feedback—to his or her actions is very much what a good toy does. Toys are perfect examples of behavioral objects;[26] by themselves they mean and do nothing. They are designed for "relationships," for the experience of use, and not simply for their movable parts or form aesthetics. The functionality of a toy resides in its potential for creating a relationship, either between user and toy, or amongst users, and this might well be the development brief for the iPhone. When we intentionally add elements for behavior to any object or system we are purposefully transforming that object into a behavior space.

TRANSFORMATION IN BEHAVIOR SPACE

It is this transformative attribute that makes the experience of using the iPhone compelling, and it is also transformation that maintains the relationship with the device and results in satisfaction. My collaborator John Sutherland observed that what a disruptive behavior space does well is a transformation in the relationship between the user and his/hers life domains. Every successful behavior space disruption will modify the relationship between the user and *people, objects, ideas, time, space,* and the *self.* A calendar reminder transforms the user's relationship with time. Email, Facebook, Twitter transform the relationship with people as well as with the self. A GPS navigation application transforms the user's relationship with space. A newsfeed application transforms the relationship with older forms of mass media. Netflix transforms a previous relationship with Blockbuster (and transforms Blockbuster ...). And so on.

---

26 Ibid., p. 78.

The iPhone is the archetype of a behavior space in which the user-engagement is redefining the platform itself. The same can be said about Facebook, Twitter and YouTube: every time we engage with these spaces, the experience is improving slightly our most recent experience with the same space. We are engaged in a dynamic and synchronic behavior cycle, with a behavior space that transforms as we seek to transform ourselves, through the tasks that we accomplish in a free and fun manner (see Figure 1.3.1).

The iPhone is an invitation to bring play into "serious" life, reuniting the accomplishment of goal-oriented tasks, with the experimentation and self-expression of play.

The human relationship with tools is instrumental in nature—the interactions we perform with our tools are goal-oriented, finite, and focused on accomplishing a task. Play objects—toys—engender affinity-based relationships, in that we identify and engage emotionally with such objects,

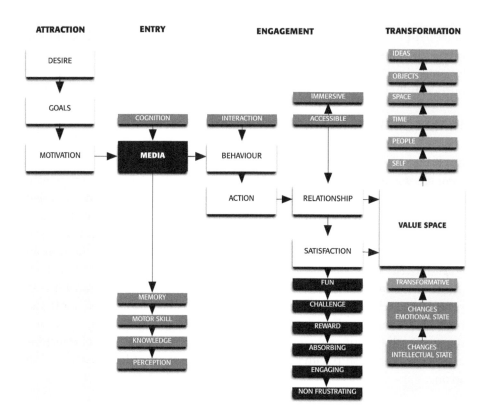

Figure 1.3.1   Behavior space transformation

and express our inner selves through the actions we perform with them. Such actions are not goal-driven but exploratory. The questions that drive our interactions with play objects are, "What else can this object be?" and, "What else can this object do?" "How else can this object make me feel?" In exploring the answers to these questions, we employ our imagination. By imagining and experimenting, latent needs and possibilities are revealed in both the object and ourselves. The unique interactions that a person has with a play object, make the object deeply personal and closely connected to the identity of that person. In this way, qualities of emotion, self-expression, identification, and connection are all latent within a play object. These are the transformative qualities of objects, spaces and ideas, and they transform the individual because they are compelling in their engagement.

COMPELLING EXPERIENCES

What is a compelling experience? What compels you? Is it a story? Is it an emotion? Is it a favorite flavor? Is it a smell? Is it a favorite piece of music? Or is it all of the above. We all have experiences; what makes an experience compelling is *surprise and delight*. The pleasure of the unexpected. The pleasure of returning to a long-forgotten moment in life, just by listening to a few bars in a song. A compelling experience is the magic in everyday life. You might recall from the prologue that Steve Jobs introduced the iPhone as "a revolutionary and magical product" and indeed, it had all the qualities of a magic trick: it produces objects on the screen, it makes them disappear, it restores them and transforms them. A compelling experience is a journey designed to alter your emotional and intellectual state. The designer is in charge of defining the stimulus, while hoping for the appropriate response on the part of the user. More powerful the stimulus, more powerful the response.

Sweetness is a compelling stimulus. And so is salt. They are both stimuli which elicit a response on our part. The response is subconscious and unstoppable. We cannot plan our reaction to the stimulus of sweetness; we respond instinctively. Our response is either in pleasure or in pain. In delight or in disgust. The stimulus in question—be that sugar, sounds, people, light, and so on—changes the nature of the behavior space in which we find ourselves. In a movie theatre the lights dim slowly, allowing you to enter the story by removing you from daily life. To the stimulus of darkness we respond "*Yes, I am ready now to enter this story*" —you are ready to enter the behavior space that the movie will construct.

Anatomy of a compelling experience

The strategy firm Doblin, under the leadership of Larry Keeley, has described (1997) compelling experiences as having three stages, two transitions, and six attributes. The stages are Attraction, Engagement, and Extension, with Entry and Exit as transitions. Expanding on Keeley's original work, I have adapted these stages to the concept of behavior space and added the nature of the stimuli that will engage user experience as well as defined the nature of the experience as illustrated in Figures 1.3.1 and 1.3.2.

- **Attraction**: to attract someone to something you have to provide the stimuli. The stimulus is first in the domain of the senses, and presents itself as data. The senses are the apparatus that most resides in our deep motivations, and our desire for pleasure in all its forms. We are attracted to soft and smooth materials. We are attracted to shiny surfaces. We are attracted by fragrant smells and by intoxicating substances. We are attracted by beauty, and intellectually, we are attracted by hope. Human beings are hard-wired and not very complicated when it comes to motivational stimulus. It is only a matter of *how much* and not a matter of "Why?" Would you engage in *this behavior* for $1,000 dollars? How about for $1,000,000 dollars? The stimulus—the amount in this case—engages the behavior

- **Entry**: in entering an experience, perception and cognition are the primary operators. We experience the world with our perceptual apparatus but also engage our *apperceptive* faculties. Apperception is the memory of our experiences with people, places, and objects, and it is apperception that gives expression and meaning to our moments of experience. We enter experiences through our cognitive ability, our memory of similar experiences from the past, our memory of shapes of objects that are familiar. Our senses of feel, touch, and smell are heightened, as we try to gain understanding of this new moment of experience. We store these moments in our memory, we rank these memories using our knowledge and our sense of values. One experience is better than another; one moment in time has more value than another.

- Perception is how you see the world and none of us sees the world the same way at the same time. What does this mean for the experience designer? It means that we need to provide stimuli which are familiar to the eye, yet advanced just enough to inform the user that they are new. It means we give familiar names to new capabilities: we call a pocket data transmission device a "cellular phone." In time, we change our understanding of its capabilities and call it a "smartphone." The reality is that the device is not a phone, and it is not smart. But we crave the familiar, as without it everything "new" will be meaningless.

- **Engagement**: behavior space is a construct that combines the attributes of a compelling experience, with the characteristics of play value. It is play value that maintains the engagement in the experience, and it is play that ultimately gives value to the experience itself. We will not immerse ourselves into an experience in a compelling way, if some of these characteristics of engagement are not present: it must be fun, challenging, rewarding, absorbing, engaging—at the physical and intellectual level—and non-frustrating. These are dimensions of value in behavior space which affect our intellectual and emotional state, transforming the space into a temporary playground. Our place to learn about ourselves, about others and about a new relationship with our immediate

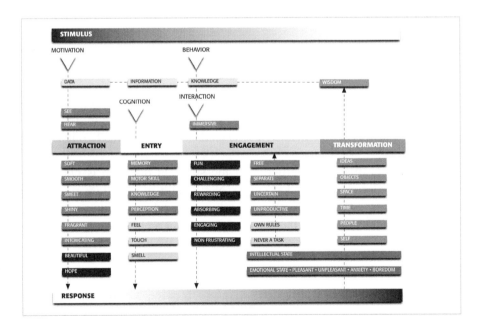

Figure 1.3.2   Compelling experience map

ecosystem—time, space, objects, and so on. Fun, challenge, reward, absorbing, non-frustrating. Does Facebook do these things? Yes. What is the challenge in Facebook? *To maintain your relevance.* What is the challenge of Twitter? *Deciding what to post. Participation. Perpetual renewal of content. To be seen and to be heard.* The ultimate challenge and reward of Twitter is that it makes you feel you are part of the context.

What is the nature of the engagement we have with and on Twitter? And how is it different than the characteristics of play? Take a look at this list:

A free engagement: by which the entry in the Twitter behavior space is not obligatory;

- **Separate**: by which the Twitter behavior is circumscribed within limits of space and time, defined, and fixed in advance;

- **Uncertain**: by which the behavior space suspends ordinary laws and establishes new legislation, which alone counts;

- **Unproductive**: by which the aim is not to create goods or any formal elements of wealth;

- **Governed by rules**: by which the space suspends ordinary laws and establishes new legislation which alone counts; and

- **Never a task**: by which there are no tasks to be accomplished and benchmarks to be measured against. You are there in a voluntary capacity, for an activity performed for its own sake. Just like play.[27]

And how is this listing different if the space in question is not Twitter but YouTube, Google, Starbucks, Zynga, Netflix and more? They are all play behavior spaces, where play value alone counts, and where the individual's transformation is a matter of the depth of the engagement.

---

27 Multiple sources describe play as free, separate, uncertain, unproductive, governed by rules and never a task, notably Roger Caillois. 1961. *Man, Play, and Games.* New York: Free Press of Glencoe.

The empowerment and participatory behavior that are the essence of people's engagement with YouTube, are not manifestations of technological innovation. *They are manifestations of innovation as the creation of a behavior space.*

BEHAVIOR SPACE, EXPERIENCE AND PLAY VALUE

In a behavior space play value means participation and engagement, two equally important behaviors that ensure the user's compelling experience with a product or service. Participation and engagement are the values of the iPhone and its compelling qualities for its users. The iPhone is not a device; devices are tools, and on tools we act with our hands. The four stages of experience in behavior space (Figure 1.3.3) are not all present when we are using a tool. We are not *attracted* by a hammer; we need a hammer to accomplish a very specific task, to a very specific end state, which is visible and clearly defined. There is no emotional engagement when we use a tool to its ends. As such, hammering a nail is not a compelling experience. By contrast, we are *attracted* by a toy. We do enter the experience as a conscious declaration that from this moment forward, until we exit this experience, we will separate real life goals

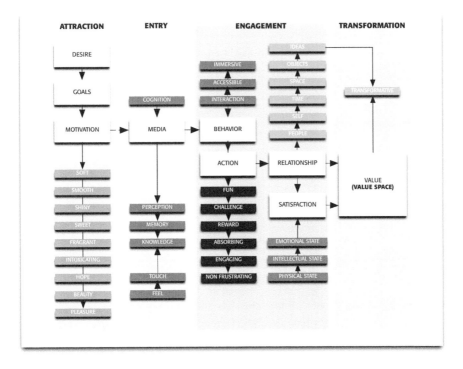

Figure 1.3.3   Compelling experience behavior space

from the very rewarding nature of this temporal relationship with this toy/ space/product. What allows for engagement, is a sequence of actions in which the physical nature of the thing itself—let's say a teddy bear—is less relevant than our emotional participation in the engagement. How is this different than engaging with the iPhone, the iPad, on YouTube or Facebook?

The iPhone is closer to a toy, as while engaging with toys we act with our imagination. The whole being needs both as a condition of self-actualization. We may choose to call the iPhone a "device," but its nature is closer to a *toy*—it is a device for exploration, surprise, and delight *through play*.

2

The Design Dimension

2.1 Tools, Toys, and ToolToys

To create a compelling experience with products and technology, we must look at a new conceptual model—one that places play value at the core of the creation of experiences. By designing with play value and interactivity as the experience providers, we create the benefit of the best toys: they are fun, engaging, challenging, rewarding, non-frustrating, and the value of the experience is both repeatable and cumulative. Play should not be seen here as a trivial activity, performed by hands and objects, but as a highly spiritual activity dependent on imagination and creativity more than on any artifact. The artifact for play is the human brain. Hands don't play. The mind does.

The slow acceptance of the personal computer in the early 1980s was partly due to the adult's inability to engage in play. A child would have recognized immediately the "benefit" of the activity, and the play character and play pattern of the device. When something loses its play nature, it becomes a chore. And a chore does not entice the user to engage in the activity. The device needed to engage us is what I called a ToolToy.[1]

I coined the term ToolToy in 1989 to emphasize the importance of consciously reexamining the process of product and experience design in the context of an improved conceptual and behavioral model in which play, and the values it represents, have a pivotal role. In an early definition, I described a ToolToy as *a product that satisfies the requirements for a functional tool and gives the user the pleasures associated with toys.*

The basic passage of any artifact from tool to toy must be placed in the context of educational psychologist Abraham Maslow's famous Theory of Human Motivation (1943). His theory proposes that humans must satisfy a

---

1   A. Manu. 1995. *ToolToys: Tools with an Element of Play*. Copenhagen: Danish Design Centre.

series of needs in order to achieve healthy and fulfilled lives. Beginning with basic physiological and safety needs, the hierarchy then extends to latent but permanent needs such as love/belonging, esteem/status, and self-actualization. While referencing Maslow, I must point out that I do not subscribe to the interpretation that Maslow places needs in a hierarchy, with some necessarily seen as more important than others. In my readings of his arguments I could not find any such "hierarchy of needs," but rather a sequence of goals which humans strive for. It is in this striving that goals become needs and for the fully functioning human being, needs are rarely hierarchical but rather synchronic and dynamic. They relate to each other and are equally important to the human spirit. And so it is with tools and toys: we act on tools with our hands, and on toys with our imagination. The whole being needs both as a condition of self-actualization.

The form and function journey of any tool involves the creation of its purposeful and functional shape first, and then the addition of elements unrelated to that function.[2] Some of these elements are decorative, as in surface treatments or engraving, while others identify the tool by the individual user or owner, such as crests or trademarks. Look at any history of swords, and you will see the transformation described above. The journey from tool to toy—and particularly from tool to ToolToy—involves adding to function and image a third element: behavior.

Toys are a perfect example of behavioral artifacts. By themselves, they mean and do nothing. They are designed for "relationships" or for the "experience of," and not simply for the aesthetics of form or practicality. The functionality of a toy resides in its potential for creating a relationship, either between it and the user, or among users. It is here that we can find a new product development brief that takes into consideration the relevance of play behavior and its continuation in adulthood, in the context of all cultures, and with specific regard to the creation of artifacts and environments.

When we intentionally start adding elements of manner and relationship— behavioral play characteristics—to any object or system that contains elements of purpose (that is, any object that must help human beings to do things), we are transforming a tool into a ToolToy, as is with Swatch watches, Nike shoes, the Apple OS X operating system or Smart cars. Tools are designed for what we do with them; ToolToys determine *the way we do it*—our physical technique, involving our physical prowess as well as our imagination.

---

2   A. Manu. 2006. *The Imagination Challenge*. Berkely: New Riders, pp. 81–2.

ToolToy is the re-examination of the process of design from the perspective of a behavioral model in which play and the values play represents have a major role. In this model form follows the spirit of the user. Form becomes what the users need it to be in this moment. This is a paradigm in which what makes a product useful and practical is not its features, but its *purposeful relationship value*—an integrative construct that results from a development model using the basics of play behavior as its starting point. Accordingly, purposeful relationship value is the result of a process in which:

- motivation for play (mindset) leads to behavior

- behavior leads to action

- action leads to function

- function leads to form

- form leads to engagement, and

- engagement at multiple levels of experience creates relationship value.

ToolToys are a manifestation of Relationship Value. Methodologically, ToolToy is the development of physical models that translate the characteristics of play value into product or system features. It is a model in which any product is seen as the transformative experience between a human being, and a behavior space constructed for the purpose of that specific relationship.

And this brings us back to toys, as perfect examples of objects constructed for experiential and transformative relationships. In the case of toys, the old design dictum of "form follows function"—a dictum in which function was seen as primordial—is turned on its head, and replaced by a form that performs functions according to the spirit of its user.

This is a framework in which the aesthetic of a product is not the result of the harmonious composition of its physical elements, but the stimulus that provokes a response in which engagement is essential. It is the aesthetic of what one can do with a product and how one does it. This is the aesthetic of the iPhone and the reason for its mass acceptance and success. The iPhone is not a "what is" product, but a *What could it be?"* relationship, full of discovery, pleasure, and wonder. The iPhone is not a tool. *The iPhone is a ToolToy.*

The ToolToy framework emphasizes the importance to organizations involved in marketing products, of consciously reexamining the process of product development from the perspective of an improved conceptual and behavioral model, in which play and the values it represents, has a pivotal role. Look around you: what fits this bill? Your iPhone? Facebook? YouTube? Google?

ToolToys are products that satisfy not only the requirements for functional tools, but also give to the user pleasures associated with toys. ToolToy is not simply a descriptive term for a thing or product in which the lines between function and emotion appeal blur. It is a model to be applied in the shaping of new behavior spaces that respond to new values generated by emerging contexts.

SATISFACTION, PASSION, AND VALUE

Because they create physical objects, designers think of needs as having tangible shape and product design tries to anticipate and meet the solid, mechanical needs of users. Wants, in contrast, are felt to be ephemeral and intangible, if not a kind of self-indulgence, unrelated to good design. Yet, human wants can be profound. Human beings crave love and esteem; beauty and pleasure. Needs only partially describe behavior, because priorities are juggled to maximize overall satisfaction. A woman will skip lunch to buy a new dress for a date, even though food is theoretically more important than the social esteem purchased with a dress. In an affluent society, physiological needs are not experienced as pressing. Most people already possess all the requisites of physiological or safety well-being. In such a world, physical performance alone no longer has the impact of novelty. Sometimes without realizing it, users seek products that answer higher social and personal expectations. This is where the ToolToy fits in, as a product that continues to maintain physical performance while also addressing emotional needs. If a business organization trivializes or ignores the emotional needs of users it will fail to meet the competitive challenge of the new multi-use products offered by competitors. For product developers, ToolToy offers a new terminology for discussion of a broad range of fresh issues; for the corporations using design, ToolToy expands the design briefs with the recognition that "consumer satisfaction" is not necessarily linked to buying more products, but with the satisfaction of relationships that are created in the behavior space in which the product functions.

QUALITY OF LIFE

For the purpose of drawing a line in establishing the demographic for ToolToy behavior spaces, I place this line at peoples living in societies where electricity and water are used for physiological and safety reasons but also for leisure activities. In affluent societies there is a multitude of choices as far as products designed for an identifiable need. Competition is based on price and quality in an overcrowded market. On the other hand, new product introductions are aimed more and more at desires and want, thus at satisfying the social and/or the personal needs of the user. The market for this type of product is identifiably larger, as there are more wants per same number of consumers as there are needs. A simple explanation of this statement may be the fact that within any individual there is a perceived limit of what constitute products addressing physiological and safety needs, but an unknown—and always growing—number of personal and social needs. In Chapter 4 of this book, Michael Oakeshott addresses this point very eloquently when he writes *"Wants are inexhaustible because they are related to no fixed condition of things."*

Affluence and "quality of life" are neither interchangeable nor equivalent. Satisfaction means an increasing number of elements that must be considered when developing new products that perform in behavior space. More and more of these elements have very little to do with the product's function. As stated before, we do not buy an iPhone because we need to make phone calls. Affluence depends not only on material wealth but also on subjective satisfaction. There is apparently plenty of room for choice in designing a life of affluence. Satisfaction is not necessarily linked to buying more products, or with replacing them with more trendy models. Replacement of objects with a newer model is not an automatic impulse of all consumption. Objects that satisfy the whole person who uses them on many levels, such as ToolToys, will be preserved and permanently rediscovered, not replaced. The ToolToy approach, then, does not bring about more consumption and a demand for the latest style. Rather, it is seen as promoting objects of lasting value, capable of satisfying both the inner and outer person over time. Users have emotional needs as well as physical ones, and products that meet both these needs at once will prove of enduring value.

2.2 Play Value and ToolToys

Webster's Dictionary defines tools as *"an implement for manual work; an instrument for achieving any purpose."* Tools are products designed and manufactured in response to a perceived need, capable of achieving a stated purpose.

Thus:

- A chair is a tool in as much as it achieves the purpose of supporting the human body at preset heights and for set activities.

- The coffee maker is a tool in as much as it achieves the purpose of extracting a liquid from a solid.

- A vacuum cleaner is a tool in as much as it achieves the purpose of retrieving by suction particles of unwanted matter and collecting them for further disposal.

The previous examples reveal that the main criteria in the design of tools is functionality, or the achievement of the stated purpose. For general users, a product's function as a tool is the most important feature. The manner in which such purpose is achieved—comfort in the case of the chair, taste in the case of the coffee maker, and ease of use in the case of the vacuum cleaner, is secondary to function and clearly not part of the commonly used definition of "tool."

Webster's Dictionary defines toys as *"a thing for amusement only; lightly, without seriousness; plaything; flirt; game, etc."* I mentioned in an earlier section that toys have always tried to respond to the desire for play, and the measure in which they have successfully fulfilled that desire, is proportionally related to the achievement of an activity that is:

- engaging

- fun

- absorbing

- challenging

- rewarding

- non-frustrating and

- has "repeat-play value."

More of the above "activity goals" being satisfied, the better the toy is—"better" in this context meaning the universality of the toy's appeal, and the lasting "play value" of the same toy form over centuries. The "activity goals" are the first criteria used in judging the play value of any toy type product, as they are practical responses to the main objective—which is the satisfaction of the need to play. Thus, play value can be considered the *primary functional characteristic*.

There are, however, other characteristics that enhance the functionality— and subsequently the play value—of toys. They are mostly concerned with the structural value characteristics of the object and the manner in which these contribute to the achievement of a host of secondary—but not less important— toy objectives,[3] such as:

- the functional value

- the experimental value

- fantasy value

- multipurpose value

- the material value

- the educational value, and

- the spatial value.

Using LEGO building blocks as an example, we can produce the following listing of its "toy characteristics":

---

3   Multiple sources describe toy characteristics and objectives, notably:
      Erik Erikson. 1977. *Toys and Reasons: Stages in the Ritualization of Experience*. New York: Norton, 1977.
      Johan Huizinga. 1938. *Homo Ludens: A Study of the Play Element in Culture*. Boston: Beacon Press, 1971.

- A LEGO building block is a toy in as much as it achieves through its normal operation an activity which is engaging, fun, rewarding, non-frustrating while providing the user with any combination of functional, experimental, fantasy, multipurpose, material, educational, or spatial values.

Not surprisingly this definition fits perfectly the iPhone—and all the Android offerings as well—Facebook, Google, YouTube and more. This is not a forced fit; read the definition again and recall your latest interaction with the aforementioned brands. This is naturally leading us to the definition of ToolToy, as a combination of appropriate Tool and Toy characteristics.

DESIGN DEFINITION

The iPhone is a ToolToy in as much as it achieves the user's purpose through means that are engaging, fun, rewarding, non-frustrating and with "repeat-experience value" while providing the user with any combination of Functional, Experimental, Fantasy, Multipurpose, Material, Educational, and/or Spatial values.

The above description could be rephrased in many ways as long as the core criteria remains intact; that is, the ToolToy performs by blending function with playful engagement. The desire to possess the ToolToy is consistent with the human need for balance between rationality and passion.

TOOLTOY PROPERTIES

ToolToys are much concerned with achieving a harmony between the rational element in human nature and the passionate element, specifically between the functional value of the object and its emotional value. Emotions are something nobody can copy. Hence the primary property of the ToolToy: the flawless blending of characteristics that appeal to both the rational and the passionate/emotional elements in human nature. To satisfy its marketing and design definitions as well as provide stimuli to perceptions, a ToolToy must have properties that fall in all the categories illustrated in Figure 2.2.1. Some categories may not apply to specific product areas, while some may apply only in part.

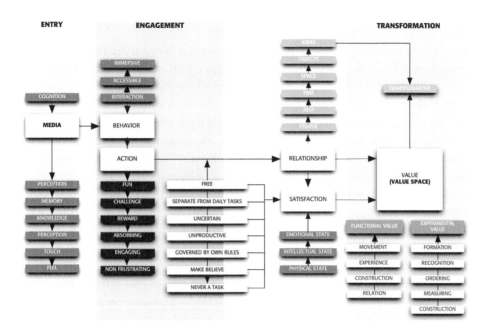

Figure 2.2.1   ToolToy Behavior Space

A ToolToy meets human needs at every level. Its physical tool aspect is flawless, without frustration to the user. As a tool, it provides effective powerful performance with long-term reliability. It is comfortable and convenient in use, and offers every precaution to ensure user safety. If fashion or status are significant aspects of the use of a particular product, then the ToolToy playfully address these issues with sensitive long-term solutions. A ToolToy approach to design recognizes that users have social needs. Finally, a ToolToy must offer personal meaning to its users. An object that offers a witty association or surprise, provides a moment of pleasure beyond the scope of its ordinary use. ToolToy forms are appealing for their simplicity, which makes them easily understood and appreciated by the viewer. Like toys, ToolToys avoid unnecessary visual complexity.

The deliberate multi-sensory appeal of ToolToys is one of the most significant ways in which they demonstrate toy values. A ToolToy seeks to involve as many of the user's senses as possible. Its initial appearance invites handling, so that the user becomes involved with its other sensual qualities, whether the satiny texture of the finish, or the aroma of fresh paper wafting from a new book. The urge to handle the product is an important learning experience. As in play, tactile feedback increases the impact of the learning experience, by rewarding an action with a pleasurable "response." We see people habitually *push* buttons and *run* their hand over the corner of a surface while visiting a store. The pushing of buttons is a conscious action, premeditated and with scope: that of testing the features—or the tool—side of the product. The running of the hand over surfaces is an unconscious action, one that looks for the satisfaction of the ambiguous compelling motivators and the desires associated with the toy side of the product. As in childhood, we cannot recognize a form just by simply looking at it; we have to touch it, we have to "see it" with our hands. If a product offers an attractive appearance, multidimensional sensory feel, and emotional connection to the user's personal life, then its value can hardly be surpassed. ToolToys reward all handling with immediate response. With sensory confirmation, the user's test of performance gains satisfaction and meaning:

> **Marketing definition:** *A ToolToy is any product that satisfies the physiological and safety needs as well as the social and/or the personal needs of the user by blending in its performance function with emotion.*

The goal of any human being is to be whole within yourself, and this goal requires complete self-recognition. Human beings are emotional, social, comical beings as well as logical, practical ones. The desire to possess a ToolToy is consistent with the human need for balance between rationality and passion. When the two principles are blended, a momentary harmony is achieved. While product details and specifications may be influenced by future technological advancements, the basic rules for the development of any ToolToy are not transitory; they reside in the timeless characteristics of the tools and toys that have been part of human civilization since the beginning. ToolToy is a tool for life in all its complexity.

And so is the iPhone.

> *Beauty is pleasure regarded as the quality of a thing. This definition is intended to sum up a variety of distinctions and identifications which should perhaps be here more explicitly set down. Beauty is a value, that is, it is not a perception of a matter of fact or of a relation: it is an emotion, an affection of our volitional and appreciative nature. An object cannot be beautiful if it can give pleasure to nobody: a beauty to which all men were forever indifferent is a contradiction in terms.*[4]

---

4   George Santayana. 1896. *The Sense of Beauty*. [Online]. Available at: http://www.gutenberg.org/ebooks/26842. Released 2008.

3

The Play Dimension

3.1 The Case for Play

Play, imagination, and innovation are very closely linked. Play is an attitude, an approach to life that asks imaginative questions and acts out on instinct the qualities and impulses of the natural self. Imagination is the formulation of concepts not present to the senses—a vital act of the mind at play, as the player combines his self with the surrounding environment to conceptualize things that never existed before. These concepts, artifacts, interventions that result from imaginative play may be innovations upon what has existed before, or they may be inventions that create a "new" category of artifact.

The definition of play and the understanding of its role in human life, is changing from superficial and extraneous to vital and wholesome. Play has long been understood to serve an important function in the development of young bodies and minds, but once physical maturity is reached, play's purpose seemed, for a long time to fade into the background, and thus play came to be regarded as the provenance of children—leisure and entertainment the provenance of adults. Ritualized and formalized play and games became another segment of industry, and those authorized to play within that business framework (the professionals, the Tiger Woodses of the world) are not so much freely playing as they are acting out a specific role.

So what is the difference between work and play? Why are the two activities separated? How can the most fulfilling aspects of the play experience be translated into a productive working role? And why is this necessary?

"Innovation" and "Creativity" are the business buzzwords *du jour*, and publications and educators look to the design industry for guidance on what these terms mean, and how to apply them. "Design thinking" is the married name that business and design has chosen for itself. What publications and educators seem to overlook is that the innovative outcomes, the true disruptive innovations and game-changers, these breakthroughs do not always emerge from within their established systems. Any system which restricts, constrains, or discourages self-directed play is detrimental to the self-directed, passionate innovator. The self-directed passionate innovator is the key figure of the twenty-first century in terms of business success. And if these people are to grow and to flourish, we must understand their core capabilities, what is it that they do differently from others, and nurture those traits from early childhood. Little do we realize, we are already beginning to do this. The Millennial generation entered the workforce almost 10 years ago bringing with them a different set of expectations due to their unprecedented experiences growing up. This generation came of age in a digital context, where sharing and trading information is more important than monetizing capital and purchasing from others. Social networks are explicit, and distance is no hindrance to friendship. Collaboration and creation are the name of the game, as the mutability of digital goods lends itself to cheap, easy hacks, and playful interventions. Reciprocity, changeability, transparency.

Now imagine mapping that set of expectations onto the hierarchical order of the traditional business, and it is easy to understand why those Millennials who innovate from outside the traditional hierarchy are leading the game, and changing the economy. Successful businesses will not attempt to map one paradigm onto the other superficially, but will instead tear apart and rebuild their businesses to support passion innovation.

Business has a lot of unlearning to do in the new generational and economic reality, and the people with the least unlearning to do—the Millennials—are poised to capitalize upon the possibilities existing in the changing landscape.

DEFINING PLAY

Roger Caillois[1] writes that it is to J. Huizinga's credit that he has masterfully analyzed several of the fundamental characteristics of play and has demonstrated the importance of its role in the very development of civilization. First, he sought an exact definition of the essence of play; second, he tried to clarify the role of play present in or animating the essential aspects of all culture: in the arts as in philosophy, in poetry as well as in juridical institutions, and even in the etiquette of war. Summing up the formal characteristics of play we might

---

1   Roger Caillois. 1961. *Man, Play, and Games*. New York: Free Press of Glencoe.

call it a free activity standing quite consciously outside "ordinary" life as being "not serious," but at the same time absorbing the player intensely and utterly:

- Play proceeds within its own proper boundaries of time and space according to fixed rules and in an orderly manner.

- Play promotes the formation of social groupings which tend to surround themselves with secrecy and to stress their difference from the common world by disguise or other means.

There is also no doubt that play must be defined as a free and voluntary activity, a source of joy and amusement. A game which one would be forced to play would at once cease being play. In effect, play is essentially a separate occupation, carefully isolated from the rest of life, and generally is engaged in with precise limits of time and place. There is place for play: as needs dictate, the space for hopscotch, the board for checkers or chess, the stadium, the racetrack, the ring, the stage, the arena, Facebook, YouTube, and so on. Nothing that takes place outside this ideal frontier is relevant.

WHY WE PLAY GAMES?

Caillois proposed a number of motivators that answer this question. We play games because of:

- The need to prove our superiority.

- The desire to challenge, make a record, or merely overcome an obstacle.

- The hope for and the pursuit of the favor of destiny.

- Pleasure in secrecy, make-believe, or disguise.

- The search for repetition and symmetry, or in contrast, the joy of improvising, inventing, infinitely varying solutions.

- Solving a mystery or riddle.

- The satisfaction procured from all arts involving an instrument, mechanism, and so on.

- The desire to test our strength, skill, speed, endurance, equilibrium, or ingenuity.

- Conformity to rules and laws, the duty to respect them, and the temptation to circumvent them.

- The intoxication, longing for ecstasy, and desire for voluptuous panic.

These attitudes and impulses, often incompatible with each other, are found in the unprotected realm of social life, where acts normally have consequences, no less than in the marginal and abstract world of play. Here we have to do with an absolutely primary category of life, familiar to everybody at a glance right down to the animal level. In reading these characteristics, we can see at a glance that play is a thing on its own, even if language possesses no general concept to express it. Play cannot be denied. You can deny seriousness, but not play.[2]

THE PLEASURE OF PLAY

Play helps to develop a wide range of skills and abilities that translate into other areas of life. The challenges of play stimulate physical and mental skills. Play comprising intellectual activity widens knowledge. Through listening, observing, and collecting, play offers the opportunity to develop new interests, and to define and differentiate existing ones. In playing, unlike as in formal education or most work, all of the senses and abilities, both physical and mental, are used at once in a coordinated effort. A child running on a field and carrying a ball while others give chase, may be formulating mental strategies for flight while experiencing the purely sensual exhilaration of motion. Play brings together into a new trial relationship, the complex abilities and aspirations of human beings, and affords a testing ground for individual abilities that may have been previously unsuspected. Abilities and actions gain meaning from their integration into a single activity. As a "combined activity," play increases meaning in life and the pleasure of being.

Where does the pleasure in play come from? It comes from the exercising of our freedom, it comes from the excitement of exploration, and from the thrill of discovery. It comes from feeling no limits to our possibilities to be who we

---

2   Multiple sources discuss play behaviour theories and the need to play, notably David L. Miller. 1970. *Gods and Games: Toward a Theology of Play*. New York: Harper & Row.

truly are: curious and shy children who while at play, can hide and seek, can pretend, and can achieve the supernatural of being just ourselves. In play we are not measured against the metrics of our day to day life; we are measured against our imagination.

PLAY BECOMES BUSINESS

As Huizinga noted in *Homo Ludens*,[3] a play-element had entered into business competition at an early stage. Statistics stimulated it with an idea that had originally arisen in sporting life, the idea, namely, of trading records. The statistics of trade and production could not fail to introduce a sporting element into economic life. There is now a sporting side to almost every triumph of commerce or technology: the highest turnover, the biggest tonnage, the fastest crossing, the greatest altitude, and so on.

Business becomes play. This process goes so far that some of the great business concerns deliberately instill the play spirit into their workers so as to step up production. The trend is now reversed: *play has become business*.

WHAT PLAY IS[4]

"Play" is not toys. It's not games, pranks, or jokes. Play is not entertainment. It is an attitude, a state of mind that correlates strongly to the feeling of empowerment, to one's individual sense of implicit worth as a human being. Anything, any object, system, or concept can be played with. The idea that nothing is sacred is fundamental to the play attitude. But that does not mean play is disrespectful. Indeed, the concepts and artifacts we hold most dear can be the best places to begin playing. Think of a child encountering an object for the first time. Let's say it is a rock, a fist-sized piece of quartz. The child picks it up, touches it, turns it over in his hands. He holds it up to the light. Maybe he smells it or touches it briefly to his lips. He weighs it, feels its heft in his palm. He tosses the rock in the air and catches it, throws it or drops it to the ground, just to see what happens. Is the child being disrespectful of the rock? This curiosity, this impulse to discover what the rock is and what the rock could be to him, is a reverent activity. It is simultaneously serious and playful. Through this play, the child conceptualizes and schematizes the rock and, understanding

---

3   Johan Huizinga. 1938. *Homo Ludens: A Study of the Play Element in Culture*. Boston: Beacon Press.
4   I am grateful to my collaborator Kelly Segram who contributed this precise, fresh and thought provoking definition of play, its attributes and outcomes.

the rock's basic properties, the child begins to innovate. He imagines the rock enlarged to the size of a mountain, or ground down into sand. He imagines it polished as a gem or splintered into sharp pieces. He changes its color with his imagination. The rock becomes more than what it is, it becomes everything it could possibly be, because the child has picked it up and played.

This capacity for play, to see the "everything," all the possibilities around, within, and because of that object (which could just as easily be an idea, or a system, or any other perceptible entity) is inherent within the person playing. No one instructed this child or granted him permission to conduct his investigation. But even more importantly, he was never disallowed or discouraged from this investigation, either. It has been theorized that play activities are engaged in when basic needs are satisfied and humans experience an excess of energy, that play is essentially an expression of a surplus.

SELF-ACTUALIZATION THROUGH PLAY

The processes of identity formation are dynamic and ongoing. The results of this ongoing process provide the basis of the "self" that is actualized in play. In play, the construct of identity, the center of the self, finds expression. By engaging in freely chosen (albeit largely structured) leisure activities from which one might opt in or out at any time, the human re-establishes their agency and individuality, in essence, their identity. No one else will play with the chunk of quartz in exactly the same way as the child I described. His imagination, his ideas of what the rock could be, the situations and contexts and variations he can conceive for this rock will be unlike anyone else. His associations and imaginings are free, but they are informed by everything he has chosen for himself through his process of becoming who he is. His knowledge or lack of knowledge of geology, his fantasies of battle, his urge to pitch the rock like a fastball towards an unseen opponent, these factors all depend upon his values and experiences—everything that came before this encounter.

In his actions and choices while playing, he experiences the joy of self-expression, of utterly being himself.

There are different types of play activities, playing with others and playing alone. Both are expressive of identity. A large component of one's identity itself may be the quality of willingness or eagerness to exploit play opportunities or create play opportunities. The degree to which a persona is likely to engage in play is an important quality for designing play experiences and should be taken deeply into consideration. Also, the type of play experiences to which a certain personality is inclined is very important. Questions which might determine this quality:

Do you like to play with others or play alone?

Do you initiate play on your own? With others?

Are you likely to join play with others upon invitation? Without invitation?

What inspires you to play when you are alone?

Are there environmental cues, object cues?

What social cues inspire you to play?

Overall, the willingness to initiate play or participate in play may manifest itself differently according to the inner "state" of the individual, and how the individual allows his "state" to be influenced by situational context.

WORK AS DEPLETIVE, PLAY AS RESTORATIVE

The idea of recreation as "re-creation" of the self (ones identity) after the self is subverted through externally directed work—this principle is dependent, it seems, upon a dichotomy existing between work and play. A highly play-motivated individual, who is likely to create play opportunities, is not likely to cease this behavior even under circumstances of external direction.

Once play opportunities and behavior are engaged consistently, the individual's identity is perpetually expressed, and the self is continuously actualized. There is therefore no need, for this hypothetically actualized person, to recover the self in "recreational" activities, quite the opposite—the freely chosen activities are further explorations of the actualized self.

The dichotomy is somewhat erased, in that the subject no longer experiences a depletive effect on the self through externally directed work. Identity depletion (loss of the self's "center") can happen outside work as much as during work activities. Any time the self-worth, the centeredness and belief of implicit worth and stable identity is subverted in the individual, is when the depletive effect occurs. This can happen in a toxic work environment or in a toxic interpersonal relationship.

"Toxic" in this sense means depletive to the self-worth of the individual.

Once the depletion occurs, it is then necessary to have a restorative experience, a "re-creation." If the individual has a stable and well-centered identity and sense of worth, they are less likely to be depleted and more likely to self-actualize and express this identity through a play mindset, in effect they are so certain of self that they will add their self (their personal touch) to every encounter. In this sense, the inherently depletive value judgment assigned to the nature of work, and the inherently restorative value judgment assigned to the nature of non-work, are inaccurate.

DEPLETION AND RESTORATION

Depletive and restorative experiences are possible in both work and non-work contexts. Play, as self-actualization and identity expression, can be accomplished regardless of situational or environmental contexts; it depends instead upon the "spiritual" state of the individual. Depletion of self-worth and identity, likewise, can occur regardless of context, and is dependent upon the inner state of the individual.

Fulfillment, in terms of maximizing self-actualization and minimizing self-depletion, is dependent upon achieving a state of secure identity within the individual.

Because identity is dynamic and ongoing, and because self-actualization is an episodic experience, the individual that is adept at play also understands the state of their identity, the self, some may call it the "soul," and are able to express this identity freely and restore it when it becomes depleted.

These processes may not be consciously practiced, but they are happening in that individual. Self-actualizing and depletive experiences are thus repositioned as being properties of the inclinations of the individual. It is possible to provide restorative outlets for individuals, but it is impossible to provide a consistently self-actualizing environment. Taking advantage of the opportunity for self-actualization, and the likelihood of doing so, is a personality quality very much akin to the inclination to play.

Seeing play through this lens enables behavioral understanding, and paves the way for increasing self-actualization, and thereby, quality of life. To the need for play there is no external "cure." One can subcontract work, but not play.

Play on.

3.2 An Imaginary Dialogue with George Santayana about Pleasure and Play

AM: In your book "*The Sense of Beauty*" published in 1896 you broke quite a few conventions regarding the study of aesthetics, and advanced the idea that beauty does not reside in objects, but in the individual's sense of beauty and in the individual's desire for pleasure. Are humans in a perpetual quest for beauty?

GS: *To feel beauty is a better thing than to understand how we come to feel it. Beauty is a value, that is, it is not a perception of a matter of fact or of a relation: it is an emotion, an affection of our volitional and appreciative nature. In the second place this value is positive, it is the sense of the presence of something good, or (in the case of ugliness) of its absence. It is never the perception of a positive evil, it is never a negative value.*

Further, this pleasure must not be in the consequence of the utility of the object or event, but in its immediate perception; in other words, beauty is an ultimate good, something that gives satisfaction to a natural function, to some fundamental need or capacity of our minds. Beauty is therefore a positive value that is intrinsic; it is a pleasure. These two circumstances sufficiently separate the sphere of aesthetics from that of ethics. Moral values are generally negative, and always remote. Morality has to do with the avoidance of evil and the pursuit of good: aesthetics only with enjoyment.

Finally, the pleasures of sense are distinguished from the perception of beauty, as sensation in general is distinguished from perception; by the objectification of the elements and their appearance as qualities rather of things than of consciousness. The passage from sensation to perception is gradual, and the path may be sometimes retraced: so it is with beauty and the pleasures of sensation. There is no sharp line between them, but it depends upon the degree of objectivity my feeling has attained at the moment whether I say "It pleases me," or "It is beautiful."

This pleasure must not be in the consequence of the utility of the object or event, but in its immediate perception; in other words, beauty is an ultimate good, something that gives satisfaction to a natural function, to some fundamental need or capacity of our minds. Beauty is therefore a positive value that is intrinsic; it is a pleasure. Every idea which is formed in the human mind, every activity and emotion, has some relation, direct or indirect, to pain and pleasure.

AM: What role does the practical play in our sense of beauty? Does something beautiful need to have a practical proposal to a human being, or is the pleasure gained from it enough?

GS: *A beauty not perceived is a pleasure not felt. Beauty is pleasure objectified. All pleasures are intrinsic and positive values, but all pleasures are not perceptions of beauty. The philosophy of beauty is a theory of values. Values spring from the immediate and inexplicable reaction of vital impulse, and from the irrational part of our nature. Preference is ultimately irrational.*

AM: What is your definition of beauty?

GS: *Beauty is pleasure regarded as the quality of a thing. This definition is intended to sum up a variety of distinctions and identifications which should perhaps be here more explicitly set down. Beauty is a value, that is, it is not a perception of a matter of fact or of a relation: it is an emotion, an affection of our volitional and appreciative nature. An object cannot be beautiful if it can give pleasure to nobody: a beauty to which all men were forever indifferent is a contradiction in terms.*

AM: You note that humans take pleasure—find beauty—in the multiplicity of things, stars being a prime example of "multiplicity in uniformity." What is beautiful about the stars?

GS: *The infinity which moves us is the sense of multiplicity in uniformity. Accordingly things which have enough multiplicity, as the lights of a city seen across water, have an effect similar to that of the stars, if less intense; whereas a star, if alone, because the multiplicity is lacking, makes a wholly different impression.*

AM: What role does apperception play in our experience of the stimuli of the world around us?

GS: *In the perception of the object, a notable contribution is made by memory and mental habit, the value of the perception will be due, not only to the pleasantness of the external stimulus, but also to the pleasantness of the apperceptive reaction; and the latter source of value will be more important in proportion as the object perceived is more dependent, for the form and meaning it presents, upon our past experience and imaginative trend, and less on the structure of the external object.*

Our apperception of form varies not only with our constitution, age, and health, as does the appreciation of sensuous values, but also with our education and genius. The more indeterminate the object, the greater share must subjective forces have in determining our perception; for, of course, every perception is in itself perfectly specific, and can be called indefinite only in reference to an abstract ideal which it is expected to approach. Every cloud has just the outline it has, although we may call it vague, because we cannot classify its form under any geometrical or animal species; it would be first definitely a whale, and then would become indefinite until we saw our way to calling it a camel. But while in the intermediate stage, the cloud would be a form in the perception of which there would be little apperceptive activity, little reaction from the store of our experience, little sense of form; its value would be in its color and transparency, and in the suggestion of lightness and of complex but gentle movement.

AM: In a moment of perception, our apperceptive forms—the images and emotions we have stored in our memory—combine with new images and emotions which in turn give value to the moment of perception. Does the APPERCEPTIVE create meaning in the PERCEPTIVE?

GS: *The beauty of landscape, the forms of religion and science, the types of human nature itself, are due to this apperceptive gift. An object which stimulates us to this activity, therefore, seems often to be more sublime and beautiful than one which presents to us a single unchanging form, however perfect. The way in which the human figure, for instance, is depicted, is an indication of the way in which it is apperceived. The arts give back only so much of nature as the human eye has been able to master. Imagination, in a word, generates as well as abstracts; it observes, combines, and cancels; but it also dreams.*

AM: So it is apperception, the memories of our experiences of thing or place, that give the thing or place "expression"?

GS: *Expression then differs from material or formal value only as habit differs from instinct in its origin. Physiologically, they are both pleasurable radiations of a given stimulus; mentally, they are both values incorporated in an object. But an observer, looking at the mind historically, sees in the one case the survival of an experience, in the other the reaction of an innate disposition. This experience, moreover, is generally memorable, and then the extrinsic source of the charm which expression gives becomes evident even to the consciousness in which it arises. A word, for instance, is often beautiful simply by virtue of its meaning and associations; but sometimes this expressive beauty is added to a musical quality in the world itself. In all expression we may thus distinguish two terms: the first is the object actually presented, the word, the image, the expressive thing; the second is the object suggested, the further thought, emotion, or image evoked, the thing expressed. What constitutes the individual expressiveness is the circle of thoughts allied to each object in a given mind. The expressiveness of everything increases with the intelligence and knowledge of the observer.*

AM: You wrote that "play may be our most useful occupation" and further that in a society most of the imaginative and liberal pursuits of humanity are better suited to be labeled as "play" rather than work. What meaning do you assign to the dichotomy between play and work?

GS: *There is an undeniable propriety in calling all the liberal and imaginative activities of man play, because they are spontaneous, and not carried on under pressure of external necessity or danger. Their utility for self-preservation may be very indirect and accidental, but they are not worthless for that reason. On the contrary, we may measure the degree of happiness and civilization which any race has attained by the proportion of its energy which is devoted to free and generous pursuits, to the adornment of life and the culture of the imagination. For it is in the spontaneous play of his faculties that man finds himself and his happiness.*

Work and play here take on a different meaning, and become equivalent to servitude and freedom. The change consists in the subjective point of view from which the distinction is now made. We no longer mean by work all that is done usefully, but only what is done unwillingly and by the spur of necessity. By play we are designating, no longer what is done fruitlessly, but whatever is done spontaneously and for its own sake, whether it have or not an ulterior utility. Play, in this sense, may be our most useful occupation.

4

The Bridge

In the section that follows, Michael Oakeshott's concern is a very simple question: what does it mean to be human? Do we strive for the satisfaction of practical needs—like all other animals—or are we, human beings, about something more. What do we pursue in life and why? In Oakeshott's view, life is the pursuit aimed at satisfying desires. If we realize that, then we engage in it with pleasure, see the journey as an adventure and thoroughly enjoy it for its own sake. Just like a game. But to play the game well, we must know we are "in the game." We are all players, seeking and using the resources at our disposal for the provision of our quest to satisfy our wants. And in this play that is life, we are engaged in an activity that is not frustrating, has no limits, and brings us satisfaction when our wants are at hand. In providing the rationale for a life at play as well as an excellent summary of why humans need play, Oakeshott does not pass judgment on this activity.

He just makes lists, for the accuracy of the record.

4.1 Work and Play

MICHAEL OAKESHOTT

Without pretending to be scientific about it, the world may be imagined to be a vast collection of existences—things and substances of various compositions and kinds—each of which is what it is, and moves, changes, grows, or decays as it does by reason of its relation to other things: things existing in various ways by, and in some cases, at the expense of, or on, other things. This image is sometimes called the economy of nature, and it is sometimes said to have a "balance" or equilibrium of needs and satisfactions. Human beings are recognizably part of this economy of nature. They are also what they are, and they move, change, grow, flourish, or decay as they do by reason of their relation to other things. Like the lion, the rosebush, or the iceberg, a human being has needs such that, if they are not supplied by his environment, he perishes.

Nevertheless, it has also been recognized that human beings have some characteristics that, at least partly, distinguish them from the other components of this natural world. The chief of these characteristics is commonly denoted by the Latin word sapiens, "intelligence." Homo sapiens: human beings distinguished by something called intelligence. What "intelligence" means here is the ability and the propensity not merely to accept what the world happens to offer in satisfaction of needs but to seek for what it does not immediately offer, to adapt, to use, to appropriate, and to invent: the propensity to choose and to determine for ourselves what our relationship to the world shall be. And in this process, needs are replaced by wants. Indeed, to be "intelligent" means to be a creature not merely of needs that must be satisfied, but of wants that are imagined, chosen, and pursued. Needs are limited and are related to some notion of bare existence. Wants are inexhaustible because they are related to no fixed condition of things.

Human beings, then, are distinguished as creatures of wants. It is as a creature of wants that a human being has acquired, not only other characteristics that have been said to distinguish him (his disposition to make things, to fabricate, and his invention and use of tools), but also his peculiar attitude toward the world around him: both positive and intelligent. This world—the whole of it, all its components without exception—he is disposed to think of as material for satisfying his wants. It is something to be used; it is something upon which he may impose his own purposes. It is something to be subjected to himself. It is almost an enemy to be conquered, and having been conquered, to be exploited.

Now, it is not to be supposed that this attitude to the world was acquired all at once. In bygone times there were sacrosanct trees that might not be used for firewood and holy animals that might not be slaughtered. And there are peoples (in India, for example) who have been more hesitant than we have been to acquire this view of the world, or (at any rate) hesitant about letting it become a dominant attitude. The ancient Romans, oddly enough, had a much more reverent attitude toward at least the earth than did the ancient Greeks (who regarded it much more as an enemy to be subdued). But by and large, the human race has come more and more to take the attitude that understands the world as material for satisfying wants.

Of course, human history has not been confined to this enterprise of doing and making, of using the resources of the world in order to achieve that sort of human happiness which comes from satisfying its inexhaustible wants. Other activities have been discovered that we shall come to later.

Moreover, there have always been some recognized limits to this enterprise. What we call morality is, in part, a refusal to take this attitude to other human beings, a refusal to regard them (like the other components of the natural world) simply as materials to be used. But it can hardly be denied that the major part of human energies have been devoted, from earliest times, to this enterprise of using the resources of the world to satisfy our inexhaustible wants, or of making out of the world something that corresponds to our desires.

Some people have tended to think of this enterprise as mainly or fundamentally a matter of physical exertion. But this is an obvious mistake. It has been an enterprise of immense thought and intelligence. In order to master the world and to use it for the satisfaction of human wants, we have had to learn from nature. And the knowledge that has made possible our current mastery of the world, knowledge of the qualities of the different components of the world and of their eligibility to be used in satisfying our wants, has been accumulated over thousands of years. The inventiveness of human beings has devised new means for exploiting the natural resources of the world-tools and machines of all kinds; and materials have been contrived by human beings out of combinations of natural materials in order to satisfy new wants. And all this knowledge and these skills have been handed down from generation to generation in an appropriate sort of education—an education in "useful knowledge," as we call it—knowledge that enables us to use nature to satisfy our wants.

Having moved from the realm of needs to the realm of wants, from desiring to live to desiring to live well (that is, better and better), and having acquired the uniquely human propensity to attempt things that we did not know quite how to achieve, we should not be surprised that the best energies have been spent on this enterprise. Every success, every want satisfied in this enterprise, must be only a prelude to a new adventure. For how could this process be halted? Only by ceasing to have wants or by having wants that we choose not to satisfy. But many wants demand recurrent satisfaction, and it would be almost a contradiction to imagine refusing to give thought to how they might be satisfied better or more easily. And while men have often exercised choice, it has usually been a choice between which of their wants they will seek a satisfaction for now and which satisfactions shall for the moment be postponed.

It is only the odd and rare individual who has made a choice to do with wants—to turn back to needs. It is not, then, surprising that this effort to achieve the sort of happiness that is to be had from satisfying human wants should have come to be regarded as "the great business and occupation of life" (as an eighteenth-century writer put it), and that it should have been given a name: "*work*."

"Work" is a continuous and toilsome activity, unavoidable in creatures moved by wants, in which the natural world is made to supply satisfaction for those wants. It is something from which animals are exempt, except those who have the misfortune to be harnessed to human enterprise, and it is something unknown to a creature of mere needs. Indeed, "work" is so far typical of the human species that it is reasonable to add it to the epithets by which we distinguish it: *Homo sapiens* is *Homo laborans*—a "worker."

The mastery of the human race over its natural environment has not, of course, been a uniform process. There have been periods of rapid advance, periods of relative stagnation, and even periods when useful knowledge about the world has been forgotten and skills have been lost. Wood, stone, and iron each were used and experimented with for long periods before even their simple uses were discerned. We happen to live at a time when this process has been quite remarkably accelerated. And we know enough to be able to see the beginning of this acceleration about four centuries ago. There began to emerge at that time two beliefs that have gradually gained a firm hold upon us.

First, it came to be believed that "work" (this activity of exploiting the natural resources of the world for the satisfaction of human wants and the attitude towards the world that went with it) was not only typical of mankind but was our proper attitude and occupation. Indeed, it came to be believed that this ought to be the exclusive attitude and engagement to which all else should be subordinated. This belief, that human activity ought to be directed towards promoting what John Locke called "the advantages and conveniences of life," and that the human mind ought to concern itself exclusively with gathering together and putting in order the sort of knowledge this enterprise demanded—useful knowledge—is a moral belief, that is, it is a belief about how we ought to spend our lives. And, as the normal way of thinking about moral obligations was to understand them as the commands of God, the first defense or justification of this belief was an attempt to show that this is what God commanded.

One of the earliest arguments was biblical. God, it was said, as recorded in the book of Genesis, had given to mankind the natural world and everything in it; he had imposed no restriction whatever upon its exploitation for the satisfaction of human wants; and he had commanded mankind to use this gift. The natural world existed to serve human purposes. The sin of Adam modified this situation only to the extent that, instead of all our wants being automatically answered by nature, we were condemned to "work," to toil and pain, in order to satisfy them. Thus the proper pattern of human life was understood to spring from a divine gift, a divine command, and a divine penalty.

Now, this moral belief began to be partnered, about four centuries ago, by a second belief of a different sort—namely, an immense optimism about the success of this enterprise of compelling the natural world to satisfy human wants. It was believed that if we only set about it in a really determined manner, if we bent all our energies and intelligence to it, if our efforts were un-relaxed, the human race in a relatively short time would actually achieve, perhaps finally achieve, the sort of happiness that is to be had from the satisfaction of wants.

Wants might proliferate; indeed, they surely would. But if we worked hard enough and intelligently enough, they would all be certainly satisfied. An all-out, organized assault upon nature would be followed by success. Idleness and inefficiency in exploiting the resources of the natural world were not only sinful, they were also foolish. This, perhaps, was the dream of a generation that was not only full of energy and fascinated by an enterprise in which it thought of itself as a pioneer, but whose imagination more readily embraced satisfactions than the new wants those satisfactions would generate. But it is the dream we have inherited; this is the tide that carries us along. It informs all our politics; it binds us to the necessity of a 4 percent per annum increase in productivity; and it is a dream we have spread about the world so that it has become the dream common to all mankind.

Since the sixteenth century, when the dream first began to take hold of European peoples, there have been some ups and downs of confidence. The nineteenth century was, in some respects, a notable period of depression and anxiety. What was called the Law of Diminishing Returns indicated that the work devoted to satisfying wants must become progressively less effective;

and Malthus announced the depressing but undeniable truth that, if left to themselves, the number of those seeking satisfactions for their wants must increase faster than the supply of those satisfactions. But these thoughts, which greatly depressed the Victorians, have inspired us with fresh energy, and I suppose that at no time in the history of the world has mankind been more determined to devote itself to exploitation of nature for the satisfaction of its wants, less dismayed at the proliferation of wants to be satisfied, or more confident of success. This enterprise, I have suggested, is as old as the human race, as old as our emergence as creatures of wants rather than of needs. What is comparatively new is the faith and fervor with which it is pursued and the manner in which all else tends to be regarded as subordinate to the happiness that comes from the satisfaction of wants.

And yet there is something lacking in this happiness and something unsatisfying to human beings in this satisfaction. A creature composed entirely of wants, who understands the world merely as the means of satisfying those wants and whose satisfactions generate new wants endlessly, is a creature of unavoidable anxieties. If he is temporarily successful he may forget these anxieties; but he is in the position of a man who has mortgaged his future in a huge hire-purchase debt. And this has often been recognized, and not only during the last four centuries of our history when it has become particularly noticeable.

I do not mean merely the observation that this sort of happiness entails work and that work, because it is painful, is something less than wholly desirable. This has always been recognized. In the biblical story "work" itself is recognized as a defect, a punishment, a curse. I mean something much more than this. I mean the recognition that to be a creature of wants—of desires that cannot have more than a temporary satisfaction because each satisfaction, however easily achieved, leads only to new wants—is itself a curse, a condemnation to a life in which every achievement is also a frustration. It is not only that everything that is produced in satisfaction of a want rapidly perishes, or that many wants demand recurrent satisfactions, but that the satisfaction of every want generates a new want that in turn calls for satisfaction. Doing, and the attitude to the world it entails, is (as the hymn says) "a deadly thing." It is an activity of getting and spending, of making and consuming, endlessly.

Now, it has always been recognized that the life of a creature of wants is frustrating and unsatisfactory. And wherever this sort of life has tended to become predominant—as in the modern world—this recognition has become more acute. Rousseau, for example, went back behind the biblical story and imagined a condition in which mankind had not yet discovered wants; it had only needs that the world satisfied easily and for the asking, and that consequently did not generate the attitude towards nature in which it is regarded as something to be conquered and used. Rousseau knew well enough that mankind could never return to this imaginary condition, but, because the frustration of wants was absent from it, he imagined it as a kind of Golden Age.

Further, many of the great religions (including Christianity) have, among other things, offered believers relief from the treadmill existence of the creature of wants in a very different view of the world and of the proper human activities. They have taught the happiness that comes from not having wants. But apart from all this, and in spite of the fact that "work" and the satisfaction of wants has usually engaged the greater part of the attention of mankind, there is another form of activity, peculiar to human beings, that does not suffer from the defects inherent in "work" and the satisfaction of wants: "*play.*"

The complete character of a human being does not come into view unless we add *Homo ludens*, man the player, to *Homo sapiens*, intelligent man, *Homo faber*, man the maker of things, and *Homo laborans*, man the worker.

I have used the word "work" in a wide sense, to stand for the activity of satisfying wants in a world like ours that can be made to satisfy wants but does not do so automatically. I shall also use the word "play" in a wide sense, to stand for an activity that, because it is not directed to the satisfaction of wants, entails an attitude to the world that is not concerned to use it, to get something out of it, or to make something of it, and offers satisfactions that are not at the same time frustrations.

This, indeed, is what we usually mean by "play." A game may, of course, be a contest for a prize, but this is always regarded as incidental. In its proper character a game is an experience of enjoyment that has no ulterior purpose, no further result aimed at, and begins and ends in itself. It is not a striving after what one has not got and it is not an assault upon nature to yield the satisfaction of a want. Moreover, it is on account of these characteristics (which we emphasize when we say: "the game's the thing") that a game appears as a "free" activity. It may have rules of its own, and it may be played with energy and require effort, but it is emancipated from the seriousness, the purposefulness, and the alleged "importance" of "work" and the satisfaction of wants.

"Play," in short, stands for something that is neither "work" nor "rest." It is an activity, but not an activity that seeks the satisfaction of wants. For this reason, Aristotle called it "non-laborious activity"—activity that nevertheless is not "work." It is a "leisure" activity, not only because it belongs to the occasions when we are set free (or set ourselves free) from "work," but also because it is performed in a "leisurely" manner. A "leisurely" manner does not mean merely "slowly"; it means, "without the anxieties and absence of cessation that belong to the satisfaction of wants."

To try to understand and to explain the world, or any part or aspect of it, obviously entails an attitude towards the world that is not one in which it is regarded as material that can be used to satisfy wants. The aim of work is to change the world, to use it, to make something out of it; the aim of explanation is to illuminate the world, to see it as it is. The aim of work is to exert power over the hostile world, to subdue it, and to extract from it what may be useful for satisfying wants; the aim of understanding is to discern the intelligibility of the world. The aim of work is to impress some temporary human purpose upon some component of the world; the aim of explanation is to reveal the world as it is and not merely in respect of its potential to satisfy human wants.

It is, then, in the thoughts of philosophers, of scientists, and of historians that the great explanatory adventures of mankind are to be found. Philosophy, science, and history are different adventures into this realm of understanding and explanation. In pursuing any of them we are emancipated from the whole attitude towards the world that looks upon it as material for satisfying wants and from the anxieties that belong to this attitude. I have not forgotten that I said that using the world for the satisfaction of wants is a mental activity and that it requires thought and knowledge-knowledge of the different qualities and characteristics of the components of the world. What I want to suggest is that this knowledge should not be confused with scientific knowledge, and that winning this sort of knowledge is not to be confused with the scientific enterprise of understanding and explaining.

Of course, the thoughts about the world that scientists have had and the discoveries that they have made are often eligible to be used for the exploitation of the resources of the world for the satisfaction of human wants. But science itself is a great intellectual adventure of understanding and explaining that is free from the necessity of providing useful knowledge. What we have here are two entirely different attitudes towards the world: the one concerned with truth and error, the other with what is useful or useless; the one concerned to understand the world and the other concerned to discover how the world works in order to make use of it.

Philosophy, science, and history are, then, activities that belong not to "work" but to "play." In pursuing them or in reading the thoughts of those who pursue them we are not, strictly speaking, "working" but "playing." The activity of the poetic imagination is perhaps even more securely insulated from any liability of being confused with the satisfaction of wants than these explanatory activities. It is also less likely to be corrupted by it. The practical imagination of the statesman or of people in business that sees what use the world can be put to, and that foresees the condition of things that will appear when they have imposed what they imagined upon the world, cannot be confused with the poetic imagination. The practical is a dream to be followed by an effort to make it come true; the poetic is a dream enjoyed for its own sake. The world for the poet is not material to be used for satisfying wants, it is something to be contemplated. Poets allow the world to form itself around them without any urge to make it different from what it is. Poetic imagination is not a preliminary to doing something; it is an end in itself. It is not "work." It is "play."

To the ancient Greeks, who thought about these things, this seemed to be much more clearly the case with what they called the "musical arts," the arts of poetry, dancing, music, and acting. They therefore distinguished these (which belonged to the Muses) from other arts—the arts like sculpture and painting that seemed to them to have so great an element of using the materials of the world that they qualified to be understood as crafts rather than arts and that were given not to the Muses but to a god of "work." But I think we have risen above this distinction and can recognize in the activity of the painter and the sculptor, no less than in that of the poet and the dancer, the emancipation from the "deadliness of doing" that distinguishes art from "work."

My main point has been to suggest that, apart from "work," the activity of using the world to satisfy human wants, mankind has devised or stumbled upon other activities and attitudes towards the world, the activities I have grouped together as "play." It is in these activities that human beings have believed themselves to enjoy a freedom and an illumination that the satisfaction of wants can never supply. It is not *Homo sapiens* and *Homo laborans*, the clever users of the resources of the world, but *Homo ludens*, the one engaged in the activities of "play," which is the civilized one.

The gifts these activities offer us are easily recognizable. But the activities themselves are vulnerable and easily corrupted. Our way of living has generated an enormous pressure not merely to make the satisfaction of wants the center of our attention but to subordinate all other activities to it. This way lies corruption of "play."

Instead of regarding "work" and "play" as two great and diverse experiences of the world, each offering us what the other lacks, we are often encouraged to regard all that I have called "play" either as a holiday designed to make us "work" better when it is over or merely as "work" of another sort. In the first of these attitudes the real gifts of art and poetry and of all the great explanatory adventures are lost. They become mere "recreation" — "relaxation" from the proper business of life. In the second attitude, these gifts are corrupted: philosophy, science, history, poetry are merely recognized for the useful knowledge they may happen to supply and are thus assimilated into the so-called great business of human life-satisfying human wants.

The point at which this corruption is most likely to appear, and where it is most dangerous when it does appear, is in education. In these days when the satisfaction of human wants is taken to be the only important activity, those who devise our systems of education are apt to find a place for all that I have called "play" only if they can regard it as "work" of another sort. In this situation, generations may be deprived of that acquaintance with the activities of *Homo ludens* that was once thought to be the better part of education. But, as it happens, we have a defense against this barbarity, an old way of thinking about these things that has not quite gone out of fashion. The word "school" we are apt to associate with "work," and often with acquiring the sort of useful knowledge and skill without which the "work" of satisfying wants is ineffective. But the word itself means exactly the opposite. It comes from a Greek word *skole*, which means "leisure" or "free time." A school was understood to be a place where one was introduced to those activities and attitudes towards the world that were not concerned with satisfying wants, where one was introduced to those activities of explanation and imagination that were "free" because they were pursued for their own sake and were emancipated from the limitations and anxieties of "work."

This way of thinking about education reappeared among the Romans in the expression *liberalia studia*, "liberal studies" or studies liberated from the concerns of practical doing, studies concerned with all the activities that belong to "play." There must, to be sure, be a place for learning how to use the resources of the world for the satisfaction of human wants. But we are fortunate if we are not encouraged to confuse the two quite different experiences of the world. And if we are allowed to pursue our "liberal" studies undistracted by what does not belong to them, we may thank the survival of an ancient tradition of education for our good fortune.

ACKNOWLEDGEMENT

Michael Oakeshott, the distinguished political philosopher who died in 1990, taught at the London School of Economics from 1951 to 1968. The typescript of "Work and Play" is part of the Oakeshott archive at the LSE Library and is reprinted with their permission. The article was first published by First Things Magazine, *in issue 54 of June/July 1995, 29–33.*

5

The Business Dimension

5.1 Unleashing Play in Business

Do you often feel in the course of daily activities that you are not yourself? That your actions do not mirror your spirit, the core of who you are, and that you are engaged in a repetitive series of motions that do not originate within you? A feeling often felt by most adults, and yet rarely by children. Children at play are free. Adults at work are constrained by job descriptions and the expectations of others. The question "How am I not myself?" was first made popular by the movie "*I Love Huckabees*" (also known as "I ♥ Huckabees") and immediately captured the imagination of a wide millennial audience. We all ask of ourselves at times, "What am I doing now that I don't really want to do?" "What would I do now if I had the freedom to be myself?" We play because we need to explore our own boundaries for freedom, to discover pleasure, and to explore. We play because we need to discover how it does feel to be ourselves. And so to the question "How am I not myself?" the answer is:

> *I am not myself anytime I do stuff that I don't want to do, for reasons that are not mine, in a place not of my choosing, and for reasons outside myself. To re- become me, I need the freedom to be who I am, and for that I need play as a condition of being.*

PLAY BEHAVIOR AS OPPORTUNITY

It is important to list here a few contextual elements that make the past decade—2002–2012—strikingly different from the decade that preceded it, specifically when looking at the domain of triggers and releases for play behavior in adults. The following shaping events have taken place in the cultural, social, and technology domain, through the introduction of new products and services, which provide new triggers for play behavior while at the same time being platforms for their release:

Google: responding to our natural curiosity, to the desire to know and to understand.

Massive online communities: from *World of Warcraft*, to *Sim City*, Second Life, Facebook, Flickr, LinkedIn, Twitter—a new medium for social interaction for adults, as well as a medium for playing with new personas and avatars.

Massive blogging: allows the adult to express and explore in an unprecedented way, allowing for in-depth broadcasting of personal feelings.

Remix and participate: YouTube and Wikipedia being just prime examples. An unprecedented level of participation in the shaping of culture, even if in most cases in trivial detail (triviality being just a matter of time before it becomes culture).

Xbox, PlayStation, Nintendo: play systems have emigrated from the basement into the living room. Significantly, fathers and sons, mothers and daughters, are playing the same games.

A new mythology: *Star Wars*, *Harry Potter*, and *The Lord of the Rings* have been the dominant mythology of the past decade and they continue to linger in other media forms. This is significant as all three are attractive to both the imagination of the adult as well as that of the child.

Personal Mobile devices: from cell phones to MP3 players and Smartphones, the majority now own and carry an electronic device capable of storing, receiving, and transmitting data. In effect, all these people are caring a game controller at all times.

The opportunity: the enablement of having personal information and connections at one's fingertips anytime and anyplace, allows individuals to manifest their "full persona"; we are ready for a "show and tell" at all times, and also ready to play any game or contest proposed on the devices we carry. In this full persona mode people are at their most imaginative, creative, and productive selves. They are ready to be who they really are, wherever they are.

To place the opportunity in the larger behavioral context we need to review a few things about play theory, mostly to get comfortable with the idea that play is not a trivial activity relegated to children, but an ingrained behavior in all human life, and especially in the life of adults. You will note in the pages that follow that play theories are generic, and do not necessarily indicate children as the instigators or beneficiaries of the behavior. Rather, they suggest that children use play in order to lean about life, which further suggest that *play is life*.

A few notable contributions will substantiate the view of play as life. Franz Alexander published in *The Psychoanalytic Quarterly* (April, 1958) under the title, "A Contribution to the Theory of Play." The observation that "the essential feature of play is that during true playfulness the solution of a problem is not imperative." Play, therefore, is a non-utilitarian form of behavior, which is characterized by *"a pleasurable activity for its own sake."* Does this describe accurately the time we spend on Facebook? Or YouTube? Is YouTube not an activity pleasurable for its own sake? And when mentioning YouTube, we are no longer dealing with a fringe group of people, engaged in a fringe activity. This is now a mainstream activity. Both Facebook and YouTube are mainstream activities that are undertaken for the pleasure of the activity itself. Rarely do we look for utility in this activity—utility seen here as a return, either in the form of financial rewards or other extrinsic rewards. These activities are undertaken for their intrinsic value. And yet, we do not call this activity "play," as adults are rather shy at admitting that they like to play. We give it no name, or at times we create special verbs like "googling," "twitting" or "blogging." These are just three placeholders for an activity otherwise described as play:

> Play is one of the important sources (though not the only one) of man's culture-building faculty by which he changes the world according to his own image.[1]

> *(Franz Alexander, 1958)*

In *Beyond the Pleasure Principle*[2] Sigmund Freud explains how the daily actions and thoughts of the individual are motivated by the search for pleasure, with the aim of lowering the moments of tension in life, which are seen as

---

1   [Online]. Available at: http://www.pep-web.org/document.php?id=paq.027.0175a [accessed: January 4, 2012).
2   Sigmund Freud. 1920. *Beyond the Pleasure Principle*. Standard Edn 1990. W.W. Norton & Company.

un-pleasurable. By engaging in play, an activity that has meaning only unto itself (how many times have you failed to explain to others what Facebook is about?) the individual seeks to lower this tension. The function of the pleasure principle and the purpose of play intertwine: play functions to satisfy "the pleasure principle."

It is in play that we excite the deep-seated curiosity that fuels our questions and produces greater insight. We inherently understand what it is to learn through play and yet, we have systematically discouraged imaginative pursuits and play, except in extremely controlled circumstances such as professional sports or the arts. Our schools teach the limits and rewards of rational behavior, encouraging tactics and logic, rather than strategy and play. Without play, the imagination withers away. We can remedy this loss through the recovery of our imagination. A recovery that begins with unlearning.

5.2 Re-Tooling the Organization or What Is It That the Millennials Want?

Organizations and people around the world are currently struggling to see and interpret what is in front of them. A fundamental transformation is occurring in the way we create, value, and exchange knowledge. This is fueled, in part, by our changing relationship with technology, as well as our rapidly shifting social values. Our technology is becoming smaller, faster, and smarter, and its integration will soon be ubiquitous—determining different ways of living, learning, communicating, building, or destroying. And each development is rapidly succeeded by something faster or more powerful, receding as quickly as it emerged. As we struggle to keep up with the accelerated pace of change— discarding fax machines as quickly as we adopt Bluetooth—we also struggle with the implications of our actions. We know that these implications will affect everyone. What is more relevant, and more challenging to articulate, is *how*. What kinds of ideas will we choose to inform our current choices and future decisions—such as the technologies we use and the relationships we foster?

The terms of engagement are also changing. People are no longer passively accepting a new technology, idea, product, or service as it was originally intended. Rather, we are increasingly encouraging and empowering each other to participate in the creation and exchange of knowledge, experience, skill and ideas—our social capital.

The platform of technologies currently on the threshold of emergence, require a different capability to carry through on their promises because the nature of the promises has changed. Rather than asking "What can this do?" we must ask "What else can this be?" The focus of this new capability is not on what technology can do, but on *what we can do with it*. And in order to stretch to meet our ultimate capabilities, we must have the courage to be what we dream—as individuals, businesses, and organizations. While our social institutions may restrict and discourage the cultivation of courage or curiosity—as might be too invested in maintaining the status quo—our desire for it as people is real. And so is our passion.

To see possibility and create a space where possibility can emerge, we must become seers ourselves, engaging in the story that translates the information around us into imaginative potential. However, sometimes our vision and capability is clouded by expectations, habits, or fears, and we are unable to comprehend or adapt to what something means. This "new thing" on the horizon is meaningless—we don't know how to see what it represents, what it could be, how it will affect us, or our friends or families. How do we rediscover this capability in ourselves—as individuals, organizations and societies? I propose that imagination is the key.

We must allow for the opportunity of a new narrative, as stories create a space where anything could be possible. *When our mind is at play, we do not worry about the logical constraints of reality.* We all become the narrators of possibility, participating and performing as the story unravels.

As noted before in this book, it has been a common tendency to define play as the opposite of work, which is why adults have a hard time accepting play as an instrument for change. Blanchard[3] described a model of human activity drawn from anthropology that shows a more accurate relationship between play and work, and also represents an illustration of the aspirations of the baby boomer versus those of the Millennial, with respect to both play and work. Blanchard's model (Figure 5.2.1) has two integral dimensions, *pleasurability and purposefulness*. Work has a purposeful goal, whereas leisure does not. The four quadrants of his model illustrated here encompass the full range of human activities. Each quadrant is a descriptive of play and work behavior spaces, containing motivators and actions.

---

3   K. Blanchard. 1995. *The Anthropology of Sport: An Introduction.* 2nd Edn. Westport, Connecticut: Bergin & Garvey Publisher, Inc.

Quadrant A (playful work) defines occupations where one does a job that is also satisfying and rewarding. Learning, acting, directing, conducting, professional sports, playing music, art activities, designing, and so on.

Quadrant C (not-play work), on the other hand, includes types of work that are not enjoyable, but are done due to obligations or financial necessity (assembly line, data entry, retail, office administration, and so on.

Quadrant B (playing at leisure) includes those leisure activities that people devote deliberate effort to, usually over extended periods of times, such as serious hobbies or avocations. These activities include watching movies, reading, having sex, eating, listening to music, sports, travel and more. These are activities in which people grow intellectually and emotionally. These are activities in which we explore becoming the best of ourselves in non-measurable ways, just for the pleasure of it.

Quadrant D (not-play leisure) includes those times or activities, technically defined as "leisure," when we find ourselves bored, dissatisfied, and with nothing to do. Mostly doing nothing, waiting for something to do, watching TV, being non-engaged emotionally or physically.

The model applies readily to the adult world of work and leisure, but also appropriately describes school settings (for both children and adults) when you consider school to be a "job." While doing "the job" we are not ourselves. According to Rieber, Smith and Noah[4] the goals for work (Quadrants A and C) are external to the individual, whereas the goals for leisure (Quadrants B and D) are internal. A person who attains maximum pleasurability (in either Quadrant A or B) could also be described as being in a state of "flow." Flow theory, developed by Mihályi Csíkszentmihályi (1979; 1990), derives its name from the way people describe a certain state of happiness and satisfaction. In Csíkszentmihályi's[5] characterization, flow has many qualities and attributes, the most notable of which are: optimal levels of challenge; feelings of complete control; attention focused so strongly on the activity that feelings of self-consciousness and awareness of time disappear. So flow is very much like play.

---

4   L.P. Rieber, L. Smith and D. Noah. 1998. The value of serious play. *Educational Technology*, 38(6), 29–37.
5   M. Csíkszentmihályi. 1979. The concept of flow, in *Play and Learning*, ed. B. Sutton-Smith. New York: Gardner Press, pp. 257–74.

What is significant in understanding the gap between the Millennial and the baby boomer generations (C to B) is the expectation of migration throughout the quadrants (Figure 5.2.1). While the baby boomer dreams of migrating from C to the lower levels of A, the Millennial's expectations are to perform in B, and at *worst*, migrate to the *higher levels of A*. This difference in expectations manifests itself in behavior and further increases the gap between the two groups. What is a dream for the baby boomer is seen as *a right* for the Millennial. And at times, due to these vastly different attitudes, the two groups *cannot hear each other*, let alone understand each other. And what is more, the make-up of the two is vastly different in the experience leading to expectations: the baby boomer grew up in an atmosphere of respect for elders, in a household and later a workplace, in which his/her own voice was not "seriously considered."

Migration through play and work behavior spaces How do we build a bridge between these two groups? By constructing a behavior space in the organization where the generations can meet, work and collaborate. By giving them both the same purpose. By rebooting their imagination around the same set of principles, with the goal of reclaiming play as an ageless and indispensable condition of every human being: a way of life in which every product, every service and every system is a festival.

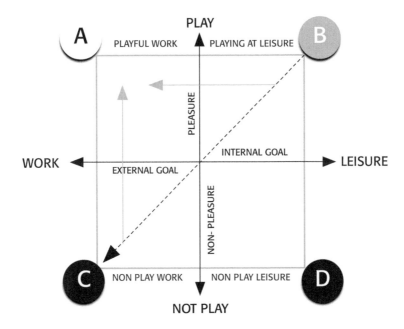

Figure 5.2.1   Migration through play and work behavior spaces

RE-TOOLING PRINCIPLES: RECLAIMING PLAY, A MANIFESTO

- We believe that play behavior dominates human consciousness and defines human values.

- Human values drive behavior and coherent human action.

- Latent imagination and creativity are embedded in play behavior.

- Play generates new ways of combining ideas, patterns of ideas, images, and concepts.

- Play behavior transforms these concepts into useful and practical ways of enabling purposeful human action that improves the human condition.

- We believe that play is ageless, and while "at play" people are just people: themselves.

- Play is the ideal conduit for communication between people; communication creates connections and encourages collaboration.

- Collaboration is key in the exploration of possibility and in achieving productivity and competitiveness.

- We believe that play is freedom, and that freedom is a precondition for exploration, imagination, and discovery.

- People thrive while at play as they pursue to discover the best of themselves, in mastery.

- Mastery gives the confidence for self-discovery and the multidimensional expression of who we truly are.

- We believe all of the above to be conditions for the self-satisfaction of individuals.

- Play is life. It is the sum of our spirit of being alive.

So far, so good. But reclaiming play for the baby boomer cannot be an easy task without a great deal of unlearning.

5.3 Unlearning as Distinctive Competence

UNLEARNING WORK

There are things one can learn, and there are things one needs to master. Play is something we need to master—the missing and essential element that complements what we learn as work. It is the continuous learning and unlearning of very simple things—play patterns—that lead to the mastery of simplicity. Imagine Tiger Woods. Now imagine his "job description." Essentially it would read very much like this: "*Put the ball in the hole.*" But his job requires both strategy and tactics. What is the strategic goal? Put the ball in the hole. How does this happen? Tactical execution. The tactical execution is play. Strategy and tactics—as in imagination and creativity—are blended when you play. In this free activity of make-believe, with no time limits, play as tactical execution requires imagination. Before swinging the club, most expert golfers will visualize every aspect, from the plane of the club to the landing zone and the roll of the ball. All of this requires imagination and the ability to adapt as quickly as conditions change. In play, conditions change all the time, requiring one to adapt, re-imagine, unlearn, and learn again. In effect, this is really the primary dynamic of life: markets, industries, societies, ecosystems all change constantly, requiring us to constantly re-imagine, unlearn, and learn, again and again. In order to meet the demands of our dynamic modern economy and society, we must learn how to unlearn.

LEARNING TO UNLEARN

Learning is at times about limits, and limits stop us being imaginative about possibility. Unlearning opens us up to the new: We had to unlearn that music is meant to be listened to while sitting in a chair or being in a group of people. We had to unlearn that we need to be connected to the wall while talking on the phone. We need to unlearn in order to believe in possibility, in order to explore unseen opportunities. We need to unlearn in order to believe that it is normal to have a camera on your phone, to allow our latent behaviors to be revealed. We need to unlearn what is it that people really want.

Unlearning needs to become an essential competence of organizations and individuals, and their capabilities to shape and participate in the creation of the future, will be directly proportional to the speed of their unlearning. We need to be swifter in abandoning rules and limitations, moving beyond the safety of what we know. But letting go of what had served us for a long time is tough, and this is why unlearning is the big fear. It takes time and courage to unlearn things, as we have so many things to unlearn. We need to unlearn the way we teach, the way we learn, the methodologies and everyday technologies we use, the markets for which we develop products and services, and the vocabulary we use in describing what we do. Time and courage are prerequisites, and so is the *will* to unlearn.

Our energy for transformation comes from the *will to transform*; this is where passion is generated, in the *will to do something*. Finding the time to do something is an intellectual exercise. It can be said about courage that one can force himself to ignore danger, and this is also an intellectual exercise. Having the will to transform is much more than an intellectual pursuit; it takes place deep in our spirit as people, and deep in the spirit of the enterprise.

I wrote earlier in the introduction that I attribute to both RIM and Nokia's failure to compete with the iPhone the failure to unlearn the spirit of their enterprise, the very culture that had allowed them to be so successful for so long. Failure to unlearn brings with it the failure to redesign yourself from the core ingredients of your best people and their attributes.

WHAT WOULD HAPPEN IF I DID THIS?

How does unlearning increase possibility? In the conventional workplace you become an extension of the space/tool/material. You are given tasks with rules and outcomes, and are never allowed to ask, "What would happen if I did this?" If you take anything that you have learned and unlearn it, take it apart, and deconstruct it—if you play with it—you will discover something completely new. By reclaiming play as a serious pursuit, we intensify the unlearning process, creating a platform for those new possibilities to exist. It is in play behavior that we can find the freedom that feeds the imagination.

When both a behavior space and an ecosphere of play—the people close to you that make group-play possible—are absent, play becomes inhibited. The result is a resistance to spontaneity and discomfort with fantasy. We equate playfulness with looking silly, or foolish, and make a conscious effort to avoid these labels through careful control or repression.

The redesign of an organization around an ecology of imagination, creativity, and innovation starts by reclaiming play as an ageless and indispensable condition of every human being, in everyday actions and at any time. Play is as essential to the imaginative adult as it is to the development of the child. It is in play that we have made our greatest discoveries. Tim Berners-Lee has stated that he was "just playing" on his new NEXT computer and exploring the possibilities of hypertext, when he invented the World Wide Web. His ability to play generated one of the most significant tools to shape the human experience.

The ecology of play allows and encourages us to maintain our natural curiosity, to chase silly questions, to get excited, and dream of impossible goals, while forgetting all the metrics that rule life outside this space. The ecology of play is the ecology of possibility, which incubates imagination and creativity.[6] And creativity starts by creating an *image of possibility*. J.F. Kennedy's "*Putting a man on the moon*" was such an image of possibility. My collaborator Terence Smith talks about images of possibility in a later chapter of this book, where he develops the FEED-R3 model of organizational design. He proposes an organization designed around a high purpose and a high-caliber conflict to be resolved. The tougher the resolution of the conflict, the more purposeful the pursuit for the organization.

THE DIVISION BETWEEN WORK AND PLAY

While play behavior has historically dominated human consciousness and defined human values—in exploration, innovation or invention—society has systemically removed play from the equation by manufacturing and maintaining a dichotomy between work and play.

> *work: activity involving mental or physical effort done in order to achieve a result, such activity as a means of earning income, a task or tasks to be undertaken.*

> *play: engage in games or other activities for enjoyment rather than for a serious or practical purpose.*

> — *Compact Oxford English Dictionary of Current English,*
> *Third Edition*

---

6   A. Manu. 2006. *The Imagination Challenge*. Berkeley: New Riders, p. 83.

We have all been participants and accomplices in this organized death of imagination after childhood, by removing play from everyday life and work. In doing so, we have created regulated channels where play as profession is subcontracted to specific adult groups—professional athletes, actors or musicians. They are socially allowed to play, though it is not without a cost to the rest of society. How much of what we feel passionately about—the things that inspire or excite our curiosity and imagination—is found in our daily jobs? For many of us, a gap exists between our role as outputs in an organization, and our role as humans. As adults, we must retrieve our imagination, integrating it into work by redefining what work can be.

WORKPLACE REDESIGN

The work setting is one of the most controlled environments that we experience and share. By deconstructing the barriers in our work habits and work ecologies, we can see patterns emerge. In our jobs, do we create or do something in a new way, or do we return to something familiar that has worked for us in the past? Is your workspace an office where every cubicle is placed in a grid? Do you see your co-workers' faces or are you looking at the back of their heads? Do you see what your colleagues are working on and can you easily share your work with them? Do you feel engaged with them and with the surrounding space? Question every aspect of your past and present work ecologies. And be prepared to leave what you find behind. Asking these questions will direct you toward the beginning of your unlearning.

PLAYING THE GAME

As Huizinga observed, there is a game side to almost every commercial effort or technological achievement: business is play. And the most successful players of this game are those who can also imagine the opposite: play is business.

The play element has long been part of business competition—specifically the competitive aspects of play that focus on setting records and proving one's superiority or merit. These aspects are at the core of the "need to play," a need as pronounced in adults as it is in children. The desire to challenge, to be the best at something in a demonstrable way—establishing a record or overcoming an obstacle, for instance—emphasizes the play and game elements in economic and social life. President Kennedy's desire to send a man to the moon inspired the nation to play with the challenge of his dream—to actively explore the "impossible." Flexibility of mind, inventiveness, improvisational skills, ambition, intuition, and focus are some of the qualities shared by people who are effective facilitators of change. These qualities are encouraged through an engagement in play activities and by the freedoms promoted by play: freedom from expected utilitarian results and repression. Every play activity we engage in is a one-of-a-kind laboratory for our instincts, insights, and intuition.

We create the freedom to work the way we need to, on whatever we desire. It is a space separate from the constraints of our "regular" lives, where we set our own time and direction in the serious exploration of possibility.

> *To feel beauty is a better thing than to understand how we come to feel it. Beauty is a value, that is, it is not a perception of a matter of fact or of a relation: it is an emotion, an affection of our volitional and appreciative nature.*[7]

---

7   George Santayana. 1896. *The Sense of Beauty*. [Online]. Available at: http://www.gutenberg.org/ebooks/26842. Released 2008.

6

The Strategic Dimension

6.1 The Emerging Context, Dissonance, and Strategy

What are we to make out of the permanent changes in our context? Well, the first task is mapping the emerging context on a regular basis; without an accurate data set we cannot focus on the implications of any particular data point.

The current emerging context data set of the mobile networked society (see Figure 6.1.1) is the first tool we must use in setting any path for transformation. The context reveals the new behavior spaces and their sources of value, while the new sources of value inform us as to the distinctive capabilities needed to successfully compete in the behavior space of our business.

TOOLS FOR EMERGING CONTEXTS

In *The Global Village: Transformations in World Life and Media in the 21st Century*,[1] McLuhan and Powers proposed a new "right brain" creative model of communication. This model demonstrates the dynamic and synchronic nature of change, which is triggered by the creation of a new artifact, and the "all-at-oneness character" of that transformation—as illustrated by the positive and negative consequences of television's impact on mass culture. The authors contended that any new technology will emphasize some of our senses and functions, while at the same time obsolescing others, even if temporarily. In this process, a person retrieves his or her latent behavior, namely the will "to worship extensions of himself as a form of divinity." McLuhan proposes the concept of the "tetrad"—a tool that could predict what society might do with a new invention, and whether it should accept or reject the artifact's future effects through a series of questions that result in experimental and alternative shapes of the future.

---

1   Marshall McLuhan and Bruce Powers. 1992. *The Global Village: Transformations in World Life and Media in the 21st Century*. Oxford: Oxford University Press.

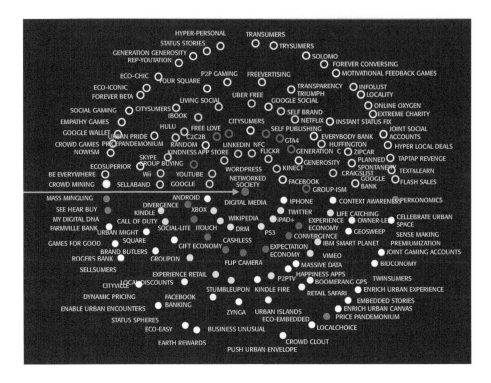

Figure 6.1.1   Emerging context data set

The questions are:

- What does this artifact enlarge or enhance?

- What does it erode or obsolesce?

- What does it retrieve that had been earlier obsolesced?

- What does it reverse or flip into when pushed to the limits of its potential?

The Behavior Cycle Map (Figure 1.1.3) is a complementary tool to this question set, as it places the "artifact" — the medium in question — in the context of the motivators and the associated behaviors it generates. Each of these questions can be answered by analyzing one or more of the attributes of the behavior cycle.

These questions are a reflection of McLuhan's belief that all media forms are extensions of our senses, bodies, and psyches, in the way that a hammer is an extension of our hand and a book is an extension of our memory and ideas. As such, they intensify one thing in a culture while obsolescing something else. They also retrieve a phase or factor long ago pushed aside—a behavior retrieval—and undergo a modification when extended beyond the limits of their potential. For example, the cell phone intensifies the capability of one person's voice reaching another's at any time, and in time will obsolesce location-bound telephones and landlines. At the same time, the cell phone reverses our freedom from location by making us perpetually accessible to others, and it retrieves the fundamental desire of being seen and heard by others. McLuhan wrote:

> *As an exploratory probe, tetrads do not rest on a theory but a set of questions; they rely on empirical observation and are thus testable. When applied to new technologies or artifacts, they afford the user predictive power; in this sense as well, they may be viewed as a scientific instrument. Once again, insofar as the tetrads are a means of focusing awareness of hidden or unobserved qualities in our culture and its technologies, they act phenomenologically.*

McLuhan's tetradic analysis acts as a lens through which we seek the deeper meaning and impact of a signal—foreseeing what it may mean in the future, by recognizing its past and present implications.

DISSONANCE AND THE DATA SET

The strategic questions framed in 1996 by Robert A. Burgelman and Andrew S. Growe and mentioned earlier in the text map the challenges and opportunities faced by an organization in this dynamic. The questions are formulated around the tension between two opposing sets of data: the new context—the new data set as illustrated in Figure 6.1.1—vs the organization's distinctive capabilities, and new sources of value vs existing business models. The data set indicates that a majority of the data points are behavior spaces concerned with social participation, engagement and empowerment, collaboration and mobility (see Figure 6.1.2). They further suggest that one's location and real-time activity has status value, and hence *social capital value*. The data set points to a context defined as SoLoMo: social, local, and mobile.[2]

---

2   More on SoLoMo at http://outspokenmedia.com/internet-marketing-conferences/the-solomo-revolution-social-media-local-search-mobile-search-collide/.

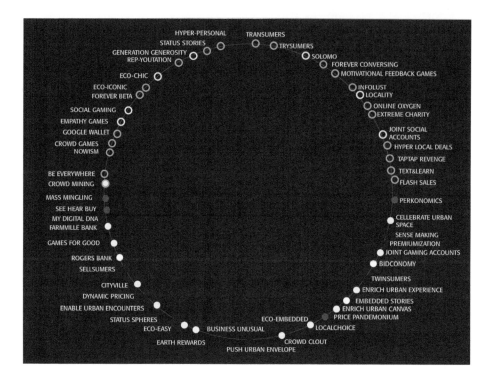

Figure 6.1.2   New behavior spaces

STRATEGIC DISSONANCE

Burgelman and Growe described a diagnostic tool that is of great necessity for companies faced with a shifting landscape. So we have a new behavior space introduced in our business context, but our strategy does not change. We are, by all accounts, at dissonance with our context, and with no practical tools to redress the situation. The premise of "Strategic Dissonance" as a planning tool is that strategic intent lags behind strategic action due to the speed at which change occurs. The context is being reshaped everyday by new players and new entrants in the market, as well as by the creation of new behavior spaces that the organization has little control over. These changes in the context—the shifts in the landscape—are in effect new behavior spaces, and new behavior spaces bring with them new sources of value.

Any new data point means a new demographic whose values have been changed by new behaviors—Figure 6.1.2 illustrates new behavior spaces by the summer of 2011—while the organization is stuck in a strategy that does not recognize the shift. What we need is a set of tools that recognize the dynamic nature of change, as well as the synchronic dimension, which is our ability to respond to the new sources of value with new distinctive competencies. According to Burgelman and Growe, *"the first cause of dissonance is the divergence between the industry's new competitive landscape and an organization's distinctive competencies to succeed in it."*

The second cause of dissonance is the divergence between what customers value and old business models. Existing structures often reflect current leaders' beliefs about historical success in their organizations or field. Emotional attachment deeply influences the leaders' perceptions, leading to hesitation to change strategies when the consequences are not completely clear. The lack of will to transform, and the imagination to do so is the major cause of dissonance. The faster we recognize the changes in context, and the nature of the new sources of value, the faster we can redesign our organization and provide a distinctive competence. But competence is not enough, as our old business model does not account for the new value propositions we must now focus on. So the forth element is the redesign of the business model. The statement "This is not our business" must be replaced with *"we will make this our business"*, by designing a new business model which contains the new sources of value as a focus point.

As SoLoMo defines the nature of the behavior space, now we can formulate the questions that will allow the organization to remain relevant in this emerging context. The questions seek to align the context with our competences and the value with our business models. Figure 6.1.3 illustrates a dissonant strategy, while Figure 6.1.4 illustrates the strategic balance achieved when answering the questions.

- **Emerging Context**: *How is the Landscape Changing? How will the social and physical infrastructures of SoLoMo help our organization reach and retain their customers, define new market segments, and create new revenue opportunities?*

- **New Sources of Value**: *What is the meaning of value in the Social Local and Mobile society? What do millennials consider essential and important in this context? What desires do they need fulfilled? What are the characteristics of the SoLoMo behavior space? What, therefore, are the characteristics of the organization that will best respond to this dynamic?*

- **New Distinctive Competencies**: *What new capabilities are needed to succeed? What are the market issues, that when addressed, will create frictionless growth and hence superior margins? What future do we envisage and plan for?*

- **New Business Models**: *How are we presently structured to create, renew and deliver value in SoLoMo? What key value activities do we need to be engaged in? What are the key business model issues that will determine our ability to develop a ubiquitous business model?*

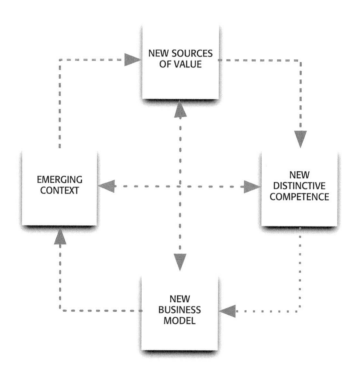

Figure 6.1.3   Strategic dissonance

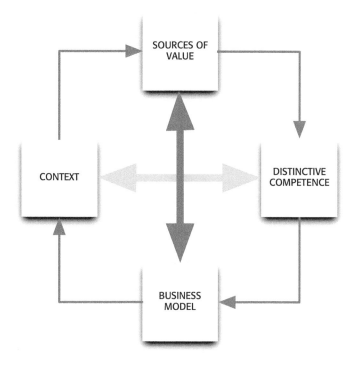

Figure 6.1.4   Strategic balance

The emerging context is that of a society in which every person, object and space is both a link and a holder of information. Later in this book I refer to this context as Data Transfer Behavior Spaces—spaces where digital data resides on mobile devices, can be transmitted and received, and can be managed. The social, local and mobile society made possible by data transfer behavior is the sum of the lifestyles of its participants, and the participants are in a constant state of searching for media to navigate it, for media to engage with from play to work, learning to knowledge, entertainment and leisure. Thus the challenge of SoLoMo for organizations is *not about technology, but about strategy*.

As we participate in the SoLoMo space, we create new norms for new social interactions, which in turn lead to new forms of engagement, new forms of exchange, which in turn, create new behavior spaces. This is the dynamic system ecology of behavior. And this dynamic makes the case for a dynamic strategy, a continuum of strategic repurposing, in which the context is at all times aligned with the organizations core competence and business models (Figure 6.1.4).

The dynamic elements of this model imply that we permanently scope the emerging context for changes and we permanently tweak or redesign our distinctive competencies and business models (see Figure 6.1.5). The scope of this permanent redesign is to make sure that strategic action does not lead strategic intent, but they are in balance at all times. In Burgelman's view, "Companies tend to develop strategies which lead them to rely on certain kinds of competencies and to engage in certain kinds of product-market areas. They learn what they can do well and find it difficult to deal with new possibilities that come along unplanned."

Which is what happened with RIM at the moment of the introduction of the iPhone. The introduction of the iPhone should have been the trigger for changes in RIM's strategic intent. But that would have required strategic recognition, the recognition of the complexity of the threat that the iPhone represented for all incumbents in the field of mobile communication. Now we have mapped the context, the new source of value and our competencies (Figure 6.1.6). Next step is *transformation*.

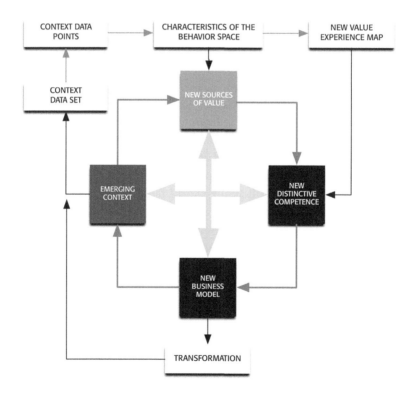

Figure 6.1.5   Strategic balance and dynamic transformation

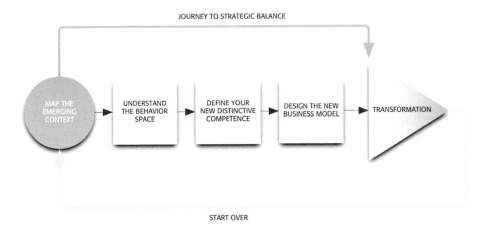

Figure 6.1.6   Path to strategic balance and transformation

6.2 Digital Transformation: Creating New Business Models where Digital Meets Physical

SAUL J. BERMAN AND RAGNA BELL

Individuals and businesses alike are embracing the digital revolution. Social networks and digital devices are being used to engage government, businesses, and civil society, as well as friends and family. People are using mobile, interactive tools to determine who to trust, where to go and what to buy. At the same time, businesses are undertaking their own digital transformations, rethinking what customers value most and creating operating models that take advantage of what's newly possible for competitive differentiation. The challenge for business is how fast and how far to go on the path to digital transformation.

THE NEW DIGITAL AGE

In every industry, business leaders realize customer expectations have created tremendous pressure to change the way they set their strategies and run their organizations. Yet, because they have to manage existing, often traditional, offerings and operations, new requirements to incorporate information and interactivity quickly drive up costs and complexity.

The IBM 2010 Global CEO Study found complexity, in fact, to be the biggest challenge facing CEOs today. However, in that same study, the ability for technology to mitigate complexity was also clear: technology was second only to market factors as a force for change.[3] This digital transformation study explores the opportunities and challenges arising when business and operating models that leverage information, customer and partner interactivity need to be integrated into existing organizational capabilities.

Business leaders have long used information technology to improve productivity and efficiency, reach new markets and optimize supply chains. What's new is that customer expectations have also changed. People everywhere are using social networks to find jobs and restaurants, lost friends and new partners—and, as citizens, to achieve common political goals. They are using the Internet for entertainment, shopping, socializing, and household management.

How can businesses best respond to this shift? How can they take advantage of the opportunity to innovate, differentiate, and grow? And how can they do all this cost efficiently, leveraging and optimizing the newest information technologies as part of their overall physical operations? In our analysis of leading companies and our work with clients, we have found that companies with a cohesive strategy for integrating digital and physical elements can successfully transform their business models—and set new directions for entire industries.

These companies focus on two complementary activities: reshaping customer value propositions and transforming operating models using digital technologies for greater customer interaction and collaboration. To do so, they are building a new set of capabilities that allows them to progress along both dimensions.

FORCES FOR BUSINESS CHANGE

Chief among forces for transformation are the surge in devices for mobile connectivity, such as smartphones and tablets, and the creation of social networks, such as Facebook and Twitter. Both of these developments are

---

3   Capitalizing on Complexity: Insights from the 2010 global chief executive officer study. IBM Institute for Business Value (May 2010). [Online]. Available at: http://www-935.ibm.com/ services/us/ceo/ceostudy2010/.

creating an exponential explosion in data, which, in turn, requires business analytics to make sense of the information and take full advantage of it.

Businesses have always looked at new information and digital technology in terms of what it can do for them—for example, greater profitability and expanded customer reach through online shopping. Now, customers also have a range of new choices, many of which are beyond the purview of business. Decisions about what to focus on or buy are increasingly informed through social networks, where personal and business contacts, product selections, home video clips, favorite news items, even real-time location coordinates, are shared instantly and widely. People who reach out to their personal networks for advice on the latest generation of washing machines are also likely to use smartphones or other devices to check their professional networks for views about business procurement choices. The habits of consumers—such as seeking independent information and advice before making a purchase—have become the habits of business buyers.

MOBILITY SHIFTS TIME AND LOCATION FOR CUSTOMER ENGAGEMENT

Mobility has eliminated the boundaries of space and time. Customers are always connected, and companies can interact with them at any time. The implications cannot be overstated. With information about products becoming as important as the products themselves, almost every company is now in the business of creating and delivering "content"—information that is personal, relevant, and timely when accessed by the customer.

SOCIAL NETWORKING IS GROWING UP

With 2 billion people connected to the Internet, social media is quickly becoming the primary means for communication and collaboration.[4] Young people may have spearheaded the changes, but people of all ages have joined the virtual revolution: 89 percent of the millennial generation uses social networking sites, but so do 72 percent of baby boomers. And the gap is closing.[5]

---

4   Internet usage statistics: The Internet big picture. Internet World Stats. [Online]. Available at: http://www.internetworldstats.com/ stats.htm.
5   Gautam A. Parasnis and Carolyn Baird. From social media to Social CRM: What customers want. IBM Institute for Business Value (2011). [Online]. Available at: http://www-935.ibm.com/ services/us/gbs/thoughtleadership/ibv-social-crm-whitepaper.html.

The scale of social media impact can be staggering; real-time information amplifies the network effect.[6] For example, when Michelle Obama makes a public appearance, her fashion choices are relayed instantaneously by fashion bloggers who compete to identify the sources of her shoes, dresses and accessories. These blogs include links to stores and designers that sell those items. The First Lady's economic impact on the fashion industry has been calculated at 2 percent per day in stock valuations of clothing companies associated with her. Over a year, stock appreciation came to $2.7 billion for the 29 companies tracked, or $14 million for each of her 189 public appearances.[7]

For today's digital native, waiting by a phone for a call is as puzzling a concept as a rotary dialer. Conversely, a time traveler from the 1970s would find it challenging to assimilate today's continuous flow of digital activity and data. As much information is now being generated every two days, according to former Google CEO Eric Schmidt, as existed between the dawn of civilization and 2003.[8] Demand for video, as well as constant connectivity, is expected to double the amount of mobile data traffic every year through 2014.[9]

> *In today's digital age, almost every company is in the business of creating "content."*

FROM INDIVIDUALS TO BUSINESSES TO INDUSTRIES

The forces of mobility, social media and hyper-digitization ripple from the individual through entire industries, as connected customers and employees move past traditional boundaries. Whether they buy from them or work for them, people are letting businesses know just what they want and need. This

---

6   IBM's retail consumer study surveyed over 30,000 consumers in 13 countries. The study showed that between 78 percent and 84 percent of consumers rely on their social networks when searching for new products, irrespective of what those products are. Forty-five percent turn to friends and relatives and some 37 percent turn to other external sources for product advice. Only 18 percent rely on the advice of retailers and manufacturers for product buying decisions. See Melissa Schaeffer. Capitalizing on the smarter consumer. IBM Institute for Business Value (2011). [Online]. Available at: http://www-935.ibm.com/services/us/gbs/thoughtleader-ship/ibv-capitalizing-on-the-smarter-consumer.html.

7   Catherine Rampbell. Does Michelle Obama's wardrobe move markets? *New York Times* (October 18, 2010). [Online]. Available at: http://economix.blogs.nytimes.com/2010/10/18/does-michelle-obamas-wardrobe-move-markets/.

8   M.G. Sigler. Eric Schmidt: Every 2 days we create as much information as we did up to 2003. TechCrunch (August 4, 2010). [Online]. Available at: http://techcrunch.com/2010/08/04/schmidt-data/.

9   Hyperconnectivity and the approaching zettabyte era. Cisco (June 2010). [Online]. Available at: http://www.cisco.com/en/US/solutions/ collateral/ns341/ns525/ns537/ns705/ns827/VNI_Hyper-connectivity_WP.html.

disruption is pushing all industries toward the digital end of the physical-digital continuum (see Figure 6.2.1). Even where offerings and points of engagement are primarily physical, as in agriculture or consumer white goods, business channels and customer relationships are being reshaped.

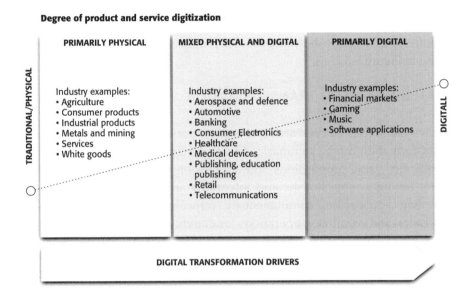

Figure 6.2.1   Digital transformation drivers are pushing industries along the physical—digital continuum
Adapted—Source: IBM Institute for Business Value Analysis.

TRANSFORMING THE BUSINESS

What do businesses need to do to get ahead of the widespread forces for change in our digital age? Key areas include reconfiguring the customer value proposition (what is being offered) and reshaping the operating model (how it is delivered). Up to now, most organizations have focused on one of these areas through a set of specific c initiatives. Each has its own set of challenges and opportunities:

- Products and services, information and customer engagement can be reshaped using the new capabilities for mobility, interactivity, and information access. The challenge then becomes how to monetize these new customer value propositions.

- The operating model can be realigned so that customer preferences and requirements inform every activity in the buying and selling chain. Doing this requires integrating all business activities and optimizing how data related to those activities is managed and tracked. What are the business requirements for achieving the topmost level and full scale of benefit?

Both sets of issues are best addressed in progressive stages of transformation, as seen in Figure 6.2.2.

STRATEGIC PATHS TO TRANSFORMATION

We have found from our research and client experience that the strategic routes to transformation can be summarized by three basic approaches. One focuses on customer value propositions and another on transforming the operating model. Taking a more holistic and integrated approach, the third combines those two approaches, simultaneously transforming the customer value proposition and organizing operations for delivery.

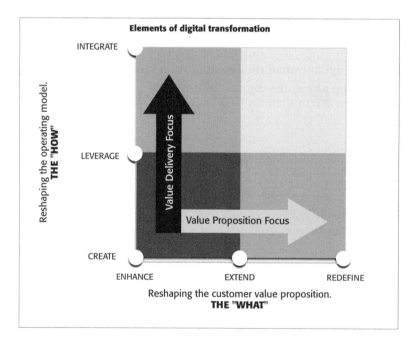

Figure 6.2.2   Most companies focus on either creating digital value propositions or operating models
Adapted—Source: IBM Institute for Business Value Analysis.

In today's increasingly digital world, even companies in the primarily physical industries will not start their digital transformation journey from "zero." Instead, most organizations are already finding ways to use digital information by providing interactive websites, improved customer service or enhanced customer experiences. Similarly, they are creating basic operating capabilities such as online channels or digital supply chain tracking. From this starting point, a company's strategic approach to transformation typically follows one of the three paths shown in Figure 6.2.3.

The best path for a particular company depends on its strategic objectives, industry context, competitive pressures and customer expectations. In industries where the product is mostly physical and customer requirements for information are not yet advanced, such as minerals and mining, companies may want to begin digital transformation with operations (Path 1). In others, such as financial services, where new revenue-based services can be offered online and through mobile devices, an initial focus on the customer value proposition will provide immediate benefits (Path 2).

However, many companies, indeed entire industries, need to redefine customer value propositions and operating models simultaneously, or in near tandem (Path 3), to succeed in digital transformation. Organizations that are able and eager to do so are in a unique position to seize industry leadership:

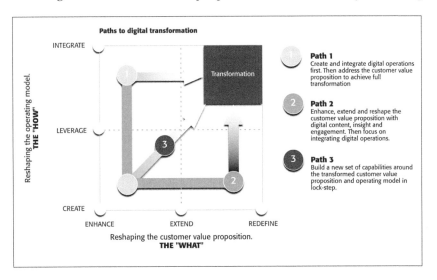

Figure 6.2.3   Digital transformation requires strategic development of the value proposition and the operating model

Adapted—Source: IBM Institute for Business Value Analysis.

Many companies find they need to focus on both their customer value proposition and operating model.

RESHAPING THE CUSTOMER VALUE PROPOSITION

Using information and analytics, organizations can reshape the customer value proposition on three levels by enhancing, extending or redefining the value of the customer experience (see Figure 6.2.4). Three stages in reshaping the customer value proposition.

Enhance products and services for a better customer experience. In all industries, companies augment traditional products with features and services that differentiate their brands on the basis of new types of information and interaction. Automotive companies like Volvo or BMW, for example, enhance their customers' automotive experiences by providing digital media access and enhanced security features, such as sensors that detect activity in blind spots. The Danish toy manufacturer, Lego, best known for its interlocking plastic blocks, has created new robotics products with the help of virtual communities that allow customers to compete in company design challenges.[10] Macy's, the U.S. department store, recently showcased a fitting room with a mirror that digitally captures the reflection of a shopper trying on a new dress or other clothing. Then, with a push of a button, the customer can add a pair of shoes or a scarf to the image, "see" an accessorized version of her outfit and send the digital image to her friends for real-time opinions.[11]

Extend offerings for new revenue streams. The next step is to find new ways to monetize these features, adding new revenue streams by extending traditional products and services through the use of digitally delivered services, content or information. In some industries, such as media and entertainment, companies must entirely replace lost revenue streams. For others, supplementary revenue is the primary benefit. Telematics, for example, provides automakers with revenue potential for everything from emergency response services and traffic and congestion alerts to advanced diagnostics and in-car applications tailored to the driving experience. Drivers who pay for "MyFord Touch" can adjust volume

---

10 For more information on Lego interactive robotics design, visit http://mindstorms.lego.com/en-us/Default.aspx.

11 Thad Rueter. Macy's offers a virtual fitting room in its NYC flagship store. Internet Retailer (October 12, 2010). [Online]. Available at: http://www.internetretailer.com/2010/10/12/macys-offers¬virtual-fitting-room-its-nyc-flagship-store.

Reshaping the customer value proposition

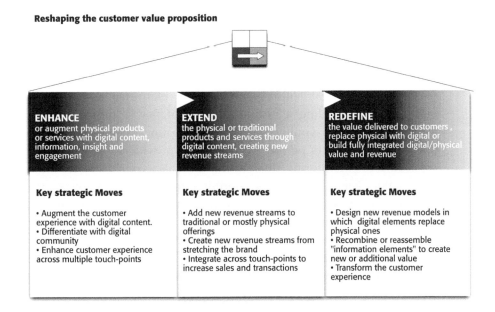

ENHANCE or augment physical products or services with digital content, information, insight and engagement	EXTEND the physical or traditional products and services through digital content, creating new revenue streams	REDEFINE the value delivered to customers , replace physical with digital or build fully integrated digital/physical value and revenue
Key strategic Moves	**Key strategic Moves**	**Key strategic Moves**
• Augment the customer experience with digital content. • Differentiate with digital community • Enhance customer experience across multiple touch-points	• Add new revenue streams to traditional or mostly physical offerings • Create new revenue streams from stretching the brand • Integrate across touch-points to increase sales and transactions	• Design new revenue models in which digital elements replace physical ones • Recombine or reassemble "information elements" to create new or additional value • Transform the customer experience

Figure 6.2.4   Three stages in reshaping the customer value proposition
Adapted—Source: IBM Institute for Business Value Analysis.

on their mp3 files, take phone calls and adjust temperature more safely with integrated voice-control technology.[12] Toy companies are seizing comparable opportunities. For example, WebKinz provides the young owners of its stuffed animals with a code for entering an online world, where they can "feed" and accessorize computerized versions of their pets. In addition to creating satisfying play for kids, the toy company gains revenue by selling aggregated data to other marketers.[13]

Redefine core elements for a radically reshaped value proposition. Seizing the full opportunity of the digital revolution, some companies transform the entire customer value proposition. Often this is a response to technologically innovative new entrants that spur traditional companies to radically reshape their customer value propositions. For example, while paper-based publishers struggled to find sustainable

---

12 MyFord touch defines intuitive driver experience: Advanced capabilities all voice-controlled now. MyFord. (January 7, 2010). [Online]. Available at: http://media.ford.com/article_display. cfm?article_ id=31716.

13 Cory Treffiletti. The wonderful world of Webkinz. MediaPost (April 4, 2007). [Online]. Available at: http://www.mediapost.com/ publications/index.cfm?fa=Articles.showArticle&art _ aid=58184.

business models in an era of free content and citizen-journalists, The *Wall Street Journal* established incremental charges for its online articles. This strategy attracted new customers who preferred reading on PCs and mobile devices. The company created bundles across its portfolio of physical subscriptions, online platforms and affiliated publications, providing a virtual package of news, information and events its customers would pay for.[14] In the healthcare industry, medical device manufacturers partner with medical providers and patients to create disease-monitoring devices that can also communicate critical information about a patient's condition to remote caregivers. This communication service has become more valuable than the medical monitoring device itself.

Redefining the operating model. A focus on new customer value propositions is always dependent to some degree on a new operating model (see Figure 6.2.5). In many cases, the extent to which one transforms the operating model is also correlated to the efficiency and productivity gains that can be achieved.

Create new digital capabilities. Typically, organizations first create the basic structures to engage customers through online channels. Burberry, for example, used its iconic plaid trench coat design to become a high-fashion house. It then created an innovative online channel, designed especially for young customers, and gained over 1 million followers on Facebook. It was a pacesetter in digitally streaming fashion shows, enabling customers to order online during the events. Shoppers can, at any time, easily click on the website to engage a representative by phone or text chat. On the operational side of the business, supply chain investments have compressed order fulfillment time to weeks instead of the months typically required for high-end fashion.[15]

14 *Wall Street Journal* media case pyramid case study. *Mequoda Daily* (September 4, 2009). [Online]. Available at: http://www.mequoda. com/reviews-and-studies/wall-street-journal-media¬pyramid-case-study/.

15 Paloma Vazquez. Burberry's digital moves pay off. PSFK Conference (June 25, 2010). [Online]. Available at: http://www.psfk. com/2010/06/burberrysdigital-first-moves-pay-off.html.

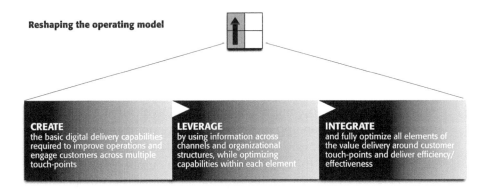

Reshaping the operating model

CREATE
the basic digital delivery capabilities required to improve operations and engage customers across multiple touch-points

LEVERAGE
by using information across channels and organizational structures, while optimizing capabilities within each element

INTEGRATE
and fully optimize all elements of the value delivery around customer touch-points and deliver efficiency/effectiveness

Figure 6.2.5   Three stages in reconfiguring the operating model
Adapted—Source: IBM Institute for Business Value Analysis.

Leverage information to manage across the organization. At the next level of operating transformation, companies leverage information and relationships across channels, business units and supply chain partners. This makes it possible to integrate digital and physical components that provide the most value—to improve speed to market, for example, or to equip employees with information enabling them to surpass customer expectations. Meredith Corporation, best known for its special interest "shelter" magazines and local broadcast stations, leveraged insights about its readers and viewers by creating full-service marketing capabilities for its advertisers and other business clients. The marketing unit has worked with leading organizations from consumer products to financial services on social media and mobile campaigns, as well as traditional publishing.[16]

Integrate and optimize all digital and physical elements. Companies focused on fully reshaping the operating model optimize all elements of the value chain around points of customer engagement. Tesco, the third-largest retailer in the world, has long been a leader in innovative uses of technology—from self-service checkouts to the creation of its "Tesco in a box" capability that enables new stores to be set up quickly anywhere in the world with standardized business systems.[17] Integrated information

---

16 Emily Steel. Meredith builds up a sideline in marketing. *Wall Street Journal* (February 25, 2010). [Online]. Available at: http://online.wsj.com/article/SB100014240527487035102 04575085752704563926.html?KEYWORDS=meredith+m arketing.

17 Tesco to outpace growth at global rivals — study. Reuters (February 16, 2011). [Online]. Available at: http://www.reuters.com/article/ 2011/02/17/tesco-igd-idUSLDE71F1LR20110217.

also benefits Tesco customers who want mobile and interactive shopping. Customers can use their phones to scan barcodes of products they have right at home—instead of sitting at their computers and scrolling through product lists to make selections. The scanned items are added to customers' online shopping baskets for home delivery. Within a month of its launch, this shopping phone app was downloaded 400,000 times. Tesco also provides an app for tracking loyalty points (customers don't have to carry a plastic card to the store), as well as apps for finding stores nearby. Once inside, the app can provide aisle numbers for products on customers' shopping lists.[18] Fully reshaping the operating model requires optimizing the value chain around points of customer engagement.

CHOOSING A TRANSFORMATION PATH

Determining the best path to transformation—whether an extensive reshaping of the customer value proposition, a transformation of the operating model, or a combination of both—requires a thorough understanding and evaluation of several factors:

- Where products and services are on the physical-to-digital continuum in your industry.

- Mobility and social networking adoption levels and expectations of customers.

- Strategic moves by other industry players.

- The degree of integration at every stage of the transformation— between new digital processes and legacy, physical ones.

Transforming operations first, for example, builds customer alignment and efficiency. But if competitors are interacting with customers in new ways, operationally focused organizations may lose revenue opportunities, customer loyalty and market share. Conversely, moving too quickly to transform the value proposition may raise cost challenges if the new offering involves too much complexity or manual intervention. Too narrow a focus on customer

---

18 Mark King. Tesco launches barcode scanner app for online orders. *The Guardian* (October 26, 2010). [Online]. Available at: http:// www.guardian.co.uk/money/2010/oct/26/tesco-app-barcode-reader.

value is also very likely to result in a one-time breakthrough rather than continuous innovation for greater customer value.

IS YOUR ORGANIZATION READY FOR DIGITAL TRANSFORMATION?

Are you reshaping your customer value proposition?

- How are you engaging with customers to understand their needs and expectations—and how are they changing in the digital environment?

- How do mobile and online technologies change the way you can engage with and create new value for your customers?

How will you drive the digital agenda in your industry rather than having it imposed on you by competitors?

Are you optimizing your operations?

- How do you integrate online and social media touch-points, customer information and insights across your entire enterprise?

- What are you doing to make sure you are putting the customer at the center of your supply chain planning and execution every time?

- How are you realizing the benefits of open collaboration—within your enterprise, with customers, and with partners?

- How are you optimizing your digital and physical components across all aspects of your operating model?

ESSENTIAL CAPABILITIES

Businesses aiming to generate new customer value propositions or transform their operating models need to develop a new portfolio of capabilities for flexibility and responsiveness to fast-changing customer requirements (see Figure 6.2.6).

Deliver business model innovation. Foremost among capabilities for the digital age is the ability to design and deliver new business models.

Companies must constantly explore the best new ways to capture revenue, structure enterprise activities and stake a position in new or existing industries. Subscription or per-usage fees? Acquire new skills or outsource certain functions? Collaborate with competitors or break into an entirely new industry? Answers to these questions will help determine flexible new business models suited to the fast-changing era of digital transformation. And as quickly as each question is answered, it must be re-examined again. Only the most disciplined approach to reassembling all the elements of business frequently, even continuously, will enable companies to keep up with customers and ahead of competitors.

Drive customer and community collaboration. Another key competency is finding new ways to engage customers and communities. This requires interaction with customers across every phase of business activities — not just sales, marketing, and service, but also product design, supply chain management, human resources, IT, and finance. Engaging with customers at every point where value is created is what differentiates a customer-centered business from one that simply targets customers well. Customer interaction in these areas often leads to open collaboration that accelerates innovation using online communities. Companies may create their own virtual communities, or use groups already organized by customers.[19]

Integrate cross-channel. The ability to integrate across all customer touch-points is essential for managing digital operations. Online, customers switch back and forth between e-mail and social networks. They change platforms and channels — comparing prices on a smartphone one minute, trying on shoes in a bricks-and-mortar shop the next, and later making a transaction on their PC. During all of these interactions, customers expect consistency and clarity. They want companies to be aware of their past purchases, service calls, and inquiries.

Experiences in one channel raise expectations across all of them. Customers want a toll-free phone number, but have little patience for voice menus. They want a website that gets them to information as quickly and effectively as an iPad application — one or two clicks at most.

---

19 Lawrence Owen, Charles Goldwasser, Kristi Choate and Amy Blitz. The power of many: ABCs of collaborative innovation throughout the extended enterprise. IBM Institute for Business Value (2007). [Online]. Available at: http://www-935.ibm. com/services/us/gbs/bus/pdf/g510-6335-00-abc.pdf.

Digital transformation capabilities

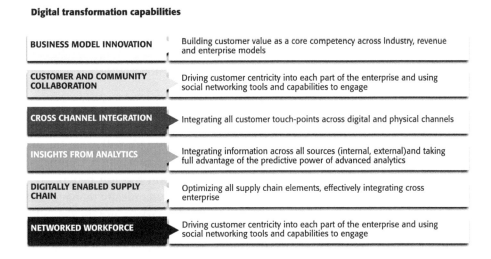

BUSINESS MODEL INNOVATION	Building customer value as a core competency across Industry, revenue and enterprise models
CUSTOMER AND COMMUNITY COLLABORATION	Driving customer centricity into each part of the enterprise and using social networking tools and capabilities to engage
CROSS CHANNEL INTEGRATION	Integrating all customer touch-points across digital and physical channels
INSIGHTS FROM ANALYTICS	Integrating information across all sources (internal, external)and taking full advantage of the predictive power of advanced analytics
DIGITALLY ENABLED SUPPLY CHAIN	Optimizing all supply chain elements, effectively integrating cross enterprise
NETWORKED WORKFORCE	Driving customer centricity into each part of the enterprise and using social networking tools and capabilities to engage

Figure 6.2.6   Reshaping the business and operating model requires a new set of capabilities
Adapted—Source: IBM Institute for Business Value Analysis.

Consistency builds the brand promise and bolsters customer satisfaction. Continuity and context provide seamless experiences across all points of customer contact.

Get insights from analytics. Creating and maintaining a customer-centric enterprise changes the basis for decisions within an organization and among its partners. Insight from analytics brings predictive capabilities to all functions so that all channels can be aligned around customer needs and preferences. For example, electronics retailer Best Buy leverages data and analytics to transform the way it manages its supply chain and engages with customers. Its sales people, equipped with data analysis tools, are able to suggest add-on purchases based on past customer behavior.[20]

The computing power needed for analytics can be local and centralized, or accessible through shared services "in the cloud." Businesses of every size have the ability to develop highly segmented and individualized

---

20 Drew Neisser. Twelpforce: Marketing that isn't marketing. FastCompany (May 17, 2010). [Online]. Available at: http://www. fastcompany.com/1648739/marketing-that-isn-t-marketing.

information that meets individual customer expectations. Top-performing companies are formulating decisions based on facts rather than gut feeling or personal experience and are embedding analytics into all their operations to transform insights into action.[21]

Optimize the digitally enabled supply chain. Physical components of the supply chain, such as trucks, pallets, warehouses, even individual packages, are being equipped and interconnected with sensors and actuators that enable data and analysis for on-the-spot action. Companies that capture and integrate that information gain the full benefits of a digitally enabled supply chain—the ability to dynamically manage costs for serving even the smallest segments of their markets and the flexibility to determine the best inventory allotments based on supply and demand predictions. Using real-time data, these companies can also find the best transport methods by weighing predicted customer service outcomes against impact on their carbon footprint.

Too often, though, organizations are designing optimized supply chains to satisfy partners' and suppliers' needs rather than the newly awakened expectations of customers. Only 53 percent of companies include customer input in their decisions, compared to 63 percent who include that of suppliers.[22]

Enable the networked workforce. All these capabilities require the right people and skills across the workforce. A workplace that fosters social networking among employees, as well as with customers and partners, requires values-based guidelines instead of rigid rules. In companies where business leaders set the example, employee participation in online communities can bring a variety of viewpoints into the organization and create fertile ground for innovation and business growth. And with workforces increasingly mobile and global, face-to-face oversight of work teams is as obsolete as reports submitted on paper. Instead, collaboration, enabled by mobile and online tools, is becoming an essential part of

---

21 Steve LaValle, Michael Hopkins, Eric Lesser, Rebecca Shockley and Nina Kruschwitz. Analytics: The new path to value: How the smartest organizations are embedding analytics to transform insights into action. MIT Sloan Management Review and IBM Institute for Business Value (2010). [Online]. Available at: http://www-935.ibm.com/services/us/gbs/ thoughtleadership/ibv-embedding-analytics. html?cntxt=a1008891.
22 The smarter supply chain of the future: Global chief supply chain officer study. IBM Institute for Business Value (2009). [Online]. Available at: http://www-935.ibm.com/services/us/gbs/bus/html/gbs-csco-study.html?cntxt=a1005268.

the communication mix within organizations and among companies, partners, and customers.

HOW TO GET STARTED

How do companies determine the best strategy for digital transformation? A structured approach allows organizations to engage customers, partners, and employees at every step along the transformation roadmap.

Identify transformation opportunities based on a thorough understanding of digital transformation in the industry. This depends on the degree to which your products and services are—or could be—digitized and how competitors are responding to new and rapidly changing customer expectations. And products and services are directly affected by new technologies, changing how customers engage and collaborate.

Redefine the value proposition based on what existing and prospective customers are likely to pay for going forward. This requires looking at new ways to use technology to differentiate offerings, reach existing customers with new digital offerings or relationships and, finally, redefining entire offerings for digital value.

Design the optimized operating model that combines organizational capabilities and technology requirements. Thinking through the "how" of value delivery requires understanding of current capabilities and opportunities. Operational design should support customer interaction as part of cross-channel integration and supply chain collaboration.

To execute the strategy, redefine the operating model as needed to support the new value proposition. Optimize processes across online and physical interactions, building a new set of digital capabilities for customer engagement, supply chain integration, and a networked workforce.

Continuously evolve using customer insight and advanced analytics. Customer requirements and preferences change as new markets are opened, as customers embrace new technologies, such as location-based applications, and abandon older channels, such as e-mail. With the ability to analyze customer interactions even at the micro-segment level a fresh source of insights is always available for innovation.

All of these transformation paths require clear vision, the right skills in the right place and tenacity to overcome cultural resistance to analytically based decisions across the extended enterprise.

The path to digital transformation will vary by industry, as will customer adoption and an organization's legacy environment. However, every industry is under pressure to change, and every organization needs to have a plan in place. Those that do not take advantage of the new digital age may drastically limit opportunities for future success. Those that are able to overcome the challenge of optimizing both physical and digital elements by implementing new business models based on customer demand can win first choice of talent, partners and resources. As industry leaders, they have the opportunity to distance themselves from new and existing competitors.

Abbreviated version of *Digital Transformation: Creating Business Models Where the Digital Meets Physical* first printed in 2011. Reprinted with permission from the authors and the IBM Institute for Business Value. IBM Global Business Services, through the IBM Institute for Business Value, develops fact-based strategic insights for senior executives around critical public and private sector issues. This executive report is based on an in-depth study by the Institute's research team. It is part of an ongoing commitment by IBM Global Business Services to provide analysis and viewpoints that help companies realize business value.

ABOUT THE AUTHORS

Saul J. Berman is a Vice President and Partner of IBM Global Business Services and the global leader for strategy consulting and innovation and growth services. He has over 25 years' experience consulting with senior management, has published extensively and is a frequent keynote speaker at major conferences. His most recent book is Not for Free, *assessing revenue models for the digital age. He was named one of the 25 most influential consultants of 2005 by* Consulting Magazine.

Ragna Bell was the Strategy Lead for the IBM Institute for Business Value within IBM Global Business Services through May 2011. Ragna has over 10 years of consulting experience with leading clients focused on mergers and acquisitions, strategy formulation, and corporate transformation. She has published several articles and books on business model innovation and enterprise transformation.

7

The Organizational Dimension

7.1 Designing from the Inside Out: Passion Corporation

What if we apply the behavior space template (Figure 1.1.4) to the design of an organization? First let's look at how organizations are designed today. Most businesses organize themselves around a product or a service. Imagine an entrepreneur and his invention. To bring it to market he/she needs capital and to secure the capital he or she will produce a business plan. The plan identifies business milestones, as well as the support structure that will bring about the flawless execution of the tasks. The structure is often a template; in other words the structure of the organization is predicated upon what the investors are looking for in a business plan and not what the invention needs to succeed. This is design from the outside in. The invention on one end, the organization at the other, with no connection in between, as each of the titles on the business plan is more or less a convention, rather than a necessity. And the people populating the corporate tree have no connection with the object of the invention. They did not generate it, and have no intellectual or emotional connection with it. The object is the passion of a single individual, the inventor. The others are connected with it from the outside in.

An organization is put in place around this object, for the purpose of delivering it to the market. They succeed in the first iteration of the company but how sustainable is this organization? What are the chances of this organization delivering another product success to the market, maintaining market share, or gaining new share? The answer depends on how passionate people in the organization are about their work, how connected these people are with the markets for which they work, and how free they are to keep redesigning themselves. Hard to do in an organization run by professional managers rather than originating entrepreneurs. Take a look at Nokia for a case study. Take a look at Yahoo. By contrast, take a look at Google.

Now add to this mix a new empowered generation—a generation that is no longer satisfied to work for pay, *but wants to work for pleasure*. A generation that is more accustomed to asking "Why am I doing this?" seeking reason for every action that they are asked to be engaged in. As the pages that follow will detail, Generation Why is no longer satisfied with asking what should they do, but focus on the *reason for doing*.

Generation Why will demand a redesign of the organization from the inside out; from the passions of the individuals to the output of the organization. Every output will be a manifestation of passion and purpose, in an organization that will perpetually supersede their previous achievement. Is this an ambiguous business? No more and no less ambiguous than any business today as everyone's output is subject to the usual variables and disclaimers. A corporation working from the passion of its employees has at least a better chance of keeping pace with the emerging context.

What professions today are the embodiment of work from passion? Take a look at actors, movie directors, and professional athletes. Take a look at U2. Is U2 not the model of an organization run from passion? Since 1976, four guys from Dublin have produced and performed their form of rock and roll, and tirelessly toured the world; their 2006 tour "Vertigo," grossed an astonishing $389 million in one year, making it the second most successful tour ever.[1] What keeps their fire burning? Two words: *Job satisfaction*.

These two words are the difference between a productive and participatory employee, and one that is quickly looking for the exit door. Writing for *Forbes* magazine (December 14, 2011) Eric Jackson lists the Top Ten Reasons why large companies fail to keep their best talent. Here are some of them:

- bureaucracy;

- failing to find a project for the talent that ignites their passion;

- no discussion around career development;

- shifting strategic priorities;

- the missing vision thing.

---

1   [Online]. Available at: http://www.allmusic.com/artist/u2-p5723/biography [accessed: January 3, 2012].

A group of my students from the MBA program at the Joseph Rotman School of Management at the University of Toronto—Ivan Yuen, Caitlin Storey, Sergey Kovalyukh, and Terence Smith—set out to discover and describe the themes that will influence the ways Millennials will interact with the workplace. They looked at trends, technology, and social methods, in order to develop guidelines for an innovation in organizational design. Through a number of imaginative user scenarios, they described the value and scope of a new possibility, imagining an organization designed from the inside out, from the passions of the individuals at its core, to the products and services they create as outcomes. The group understood that as behavior is a dynamic, the organization must be a dynamic as well, and they allowed for this dynamic by designing business models that change, as the behavior space and the context changes.

They called this organization Passion Corporation. The following pages explore what Passion Corporation might be about.

Vision Statement: Our Purpose, Our Future

We believe that the biggest barrier to achieving greatness is a lack of passion. We exist to remove that barrier. Passion Corporation's vision is to be recognized as the very best at helping individuals exercise their passion. To do this will mean to create a world where each person can understand their own passions, and connect to opportunities that allow them to exercise those passions. The result will be global niche communities organized around shared purposes, to achieve the unimaginable, and levels of personal fulfillment and satisfaction that are simply unattainable today.

In Passion Corp.'s vision of the future, *you will work for a purpose, not an organization.* You will love your work because it was designed for you. And your success will be measured by your social capital, not your material assets. To contribute towards achieving this vision of the future, Passion Corporation dedicates itself each day to decoding the passion algorithm, matching people to opportunities, and promoting a life of passion.

The Foresights

To help you imagine this world, here are three important foresights about the future:

1.   Gen Y will be replaced by Gen *Why*;

2.   Second Life will become just life;

3.   All the money in the world won't buy you a following.

FORESIGHT 1: GEN Y WILL BE REPLACED BY GEN WHY

Generation Y, also known as the Millennials, grew up with advanced technology, social media, and instant communication. This group have used their access to information to demand a voice and open up doors for members of all ethnicities, orientations, and denominations to be treated with equality. Without these barriers in place, the post-Millennial generation was able to focus instead on what they wanted out of life, their own passion. Like a persistent child asking, "Why?" at every turn, this generation will seek nothing more than the purpose behind their actions. Rather than asking what should they do, this new generation will instead focus on the reason for doing. Without a reason, there will be no doing. This will be Generation Why.

Amir, the subject of the first scenario, writes on his blog:

> *There were so many things that interested me, but I knew I wanted to spend my life doing meaningful work, not just chase dollars like my parents used to. I can't blame them though, it used to be really hard to find out what you're passionate about because it took forever to try lots of different things and it was hard to understand where the potential was for a real passion to develop.*

The data set (see Figure 7.1.1) reveals that the future will be characterized by loose ties, collaborative experiences, and a virtual reality that mirrors reality itself. In effect, everything will be digital, and individuals will remain forever connected, such that digital avatars will become pure extensions of themselves, a core part of their personal brands. Managing life and work will be as much about managing digital connections in digital spaces as it will be about face-to-face meetings. Each person will be a part of a myriad of communities, large and small, devoted to the experiences, desires, and passions they share.

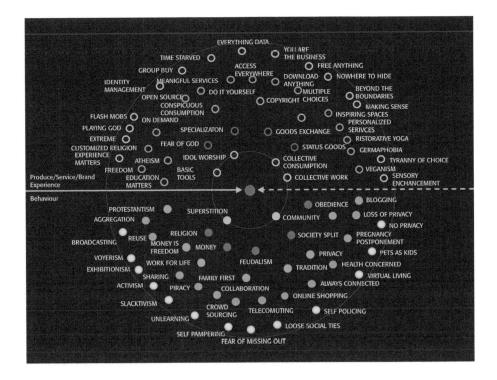

Figure 7.1.1   Emerging behavior data set

SCENARIO 1: LOVE WITHOUT PASSION IS DREARY, WORK WITHOUT PASSION IS NO MORE

I was just reading Amir's post about recruiting individuals to work with based on their Passion Compass readings. I have to say I think it's a great idea! I started using the Passion Compass myself a few years ago when I was trying what opportunities to pursue after I was finished my studies. There were so many things that interested me, but I knew I wanted to spend my life doing meaningful work, not just chase dollars like my parents used to. I can't blame them though, it used to be really hard to find out what you're passionate about because it took forever to try lots of different things and it was hard to understand where the potential was for a real passion to develop.

Now with the Passion Compass, you can continually fine-tune your understanding of what really drives and motivates you. Now you'll know whether the idea of firefighting drives you because you like the excitement or because you like helping people. If you find out it's because of the excitement, you can spend more time collecting data during exciting activities and deepen your understanding of whether it's the danger that gets you going, or the uncertainty of knowing what will come next. With this level of understanding about my own passions, I now have perfect clarity when assessing new potential opportunities to apply my skills in the working world. I also have a foundation from which to form my own brand, which is so important in this world where everyone is broadcasting themselves—like Amir says, it's hard to trust what people say sometimes, but when you broadcast your Passion Compass readings, there's little denying that you're telling the truth (no one can fool those brain scanners).

You know what's funny? I found out a couple years ago that I have a passion for understanding how the brain works, which led me to start working with the University Neuroscience Network, which is an academic-based social cause that contributes to building and refining the algorithms that drive the Passion Compass. Who knew that it would lead me here?! Now I not only contribute to this ground-breaking research, but I also manage the network's partnerships with 3M Health (which provides the personal brain scanning hardware) and eHarmony2.0 (which provides an accessible point of access for people to submit their Passion Compass data for analysis and eventually match with other personalities that share the same passion).

You know, the original intent behind the Passion Compass was to help people find meaningful work so that they could enjoy their lives each and every day. This generation isn't about waiting, it wants to enjoy life NOW and the Passion Compass helps them do that. I'm thrilled to see that people like Amir are finding even more ways to make use of the Passion Compass. Amir—let me know if you ever want to grab coffee to talk about your experiences recruiting for passion.
—Henry

The opportunity: while the Millennial Generation seeks greater control and feels increasingly more empowered, the post-Millennial generation will take their digital capabilities to the extreme. Unsatisfied to live out only virtual fantasies, they will demand a place to work, share, and play as true extensions of themselves. By providing a home for Generation Why to live out their passions with each other, we can be the place where passionate people gather to carry out purpose-driven initiatives.

FORESIGHT 2: SECOND LIFE WILL BECOME JUST LIFE

Although the Millennials played video games all their lives, many were first introduced to the idea of digital life mimicking real life through Tamagotchi digital pets, that they kept alive during school hours in the 1990s. Some of them went on to run virtual cities in SimCity, live out day-to-day lives in the Sims, or dominate the world in massive multiplayer online games such as World of Warcraft. All of it was a fantasy.

With the introduction of MySpace, Facebook, LinkedIn, Twitter, and many other social networks, Millennials grew comfortable sharing and living in the online space. Second Life, a digital world where people can create avatars and interact with each other much as they can in the real world, became a moderate success. Yet, it wasn't until the post-Millennial generation that real and digital life completely merged with one another. Driven by a desire to connect with others who shared their passion and purpose, Generation Why grew frustrated with the limitations placed on them by physical and virtual realities. A new digital avatar emerged, one that went beyond online profiles and beyond online fantasies to become a true extension of the human self. All it needed was a home:

> *If Cornucopia only had a physical office, it wouldn't be possible for them to create new workspaces so easily. If my digital avatar hadn't been walking down the hall towards this new virtual space, I never would have bumped into Talia and wouldn't have received an invite to be a part of this team. Workbook really is a digital hub for the passionate mind — it's a place where you can run into people who you would never meet physically or even think of searching for online. Scenario 2*

The data set in Figure 7.1.2 reveals that the future will be characterized by loose ties, collaborative experiences, and a virtual reality that mirrors reality itself. In effect, everything will be digital, and individuals will remain forever connected, such that digital avatars will become pure extensions of themselves, a core part of their personal brands. Managing life and work will be as much about managing digital connections in digital spaces as it will be about face-to-face meetings. Each person will be a part of a myriad of communities, large and small, devoted to the experiences, desires, and passions they share.

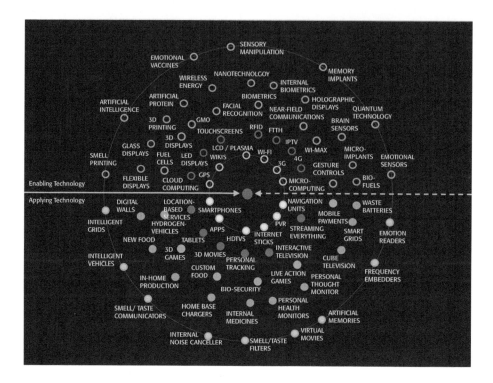

Figure 7.1.2   Emerging technology data set

SCENARIO 2: IMPROMPTU MEETING OF THE MINDS

The craziest thing happened at work today. I logged into Workbook around 7 a.m. and immediately I noticed that a new wing had been added to the Cornucopia Project's virtual office. I wanted to go over to explore, so I directed my digital avatar to walk over to see what was happening. I could tell from my third person view of the office that there was already a big gathering there, including some people I recognized from my Cornucopia orientation the other day.

Along the way, I bumped into a woman who seemed to be heading in the same direction—she introduced herself as Talia and asked where she could find the new virtual office wing. I told her I was just on my way there now, and asked why I hadn't seen her around before. She mentioned that she was visiting from her native project that is hosted on another community hub dedicated to helping endangered wildlife. I've always had an interest in the topic and was curious to hear more, so I prompted a 3D Telepresencing chat with her and she instantly popped up on my 3D Holographic Display. As our digital avatars walked towards the new Cornucopia virtual office wing, I was able to have a face-to-face conversation with her 3-D replica, almost as if we were right next to each other all along (even though I later found out she was based out of India!). Gone are the days of awkward video conferences or instant messaging chats—the bandwidth is so wide now that it can easily support everyone having a streaming 3-D Telepresence. It's as close to life as you could imagine without actually being next to each other.

When we got to the new wing, I found out that it was a dedicated workspace intended to bring together members from other community hubs to tackle one of the biggest problems of our time—I have to keep hush hush about it on here, but boy was it exciting! The only problem was, they were looking for seasoned veterans to be a part of the team and I was only just a beginner. Talia (my new friend from India) was coincidentally heading this new project. You'll never guess what happened next—she invited ME to be a part of the team! Apparently I had made a good impression on our walk over to the new virtual wing. She said it will have to be on a trial period until I prove myself, but it's an opportunity of a lifetime!

It's days like these that make me wonder how anyone got things done before Workbook (which, in case you don't know, is a collaboration between Facebook, Second Life, and Cisco). If Cornucopia only had a physical office, it wouldn't be possible for them to create new workspaces so easily. If my digital avatar hadn't been walking down the hall towards this new virtual space, I never would have bumped into Talia and wouldn't have received an invite to be a part of this team. Workbook really is a digital hub for the passionate mind—it's a place where you can run into people who you would never meet physically or even think of searching for online. Imagine if Talia and I were just visiting the Cornucopia website like other companies used to have back in the day—we never would have met!

Okay, that's all I can write for now, I need to get some sleep because tomorrow is going to be a busy day. Thanks Talia!!

The opportunity: in order to enable Gen Why to live out their purpose-driven lives, a method of measuring passion will be needed. Without a true understanding of what drives them, Gen Why will be forced into an uncertain guessing game about their true passions, leaving many to fall back into roles that satisfy cultural norms of the past.

By helping Gen Why understand their passions, we can enable them to seek out a purpose-driven life that is too uncertain today.

FORESIGHT 3: ALL THE MONEY IN THE WORLD WON'T BUY YOU A FOLLOWING

Traditionally, employees offer up their skills to organizations who promise to pay them money in exchange for their time and expertise. While the Millennials did start to change the employee—employer relationship by demanding greater working flexibility, the core structure of employment remains the same. However, once Generation Why is able to understand their true passions and connect with those who share their passions through a digital workspace, this core structure will change.

Generation Why will be driven far more by the potential to exercise their passion and as such will be drawn to those individuals with the greatest social capital, not financial capital, to employ them. The new working world will run like a movie studio, bringing together carefully chosen experts to tackle a defined area of opportunity for a defined period of time, with each person sharing in the results of their combined efforts. Generation Why will follow those with the greatest determination and inspiration, not the largest bank account:

> When Michael comes up with an idea, he needs to build a team of professionals and inspire everyone to execute it. He creates a digital avatar to broadcast the purpose, the problem and inspiration for his followers to set up the team that will tackle the issue. His digital avatar bonds and inspires the team in their effort to bring the idea to life.

The data set in Figure 7.1.3 Emerging Markets reveals that the future will be characterized by global transparency, ubiquitous work spaces, and worldwide niche communities. Millennials will open the door for new ways of working together to achieve post-capitalist goals driven by sincerity. Credential creep will prompt a new form of evidence for qualifications based on social capital and crowd sourcing. Finally, a new market for work and capital will emerge that is un-pluggable, always on, and driven by a new form of currency that cannot be traded. Social capital will be the engine that drives the next generation to pursue a purpose-driven life while tackling global objectives unimaginable by their predecessors.

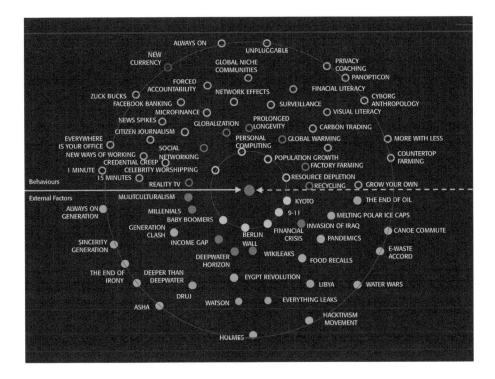

Figure 7.1.3   Emerging markets data set

SCENARIO 3: THE SOCIAL CAPITAL CORPORATION

I'm here to share a story of my friend, Michael and his way of managing Social Capital.

Michael is a person with a purpose. He has identified his passion in 3-D computer modeling many years ago and conducted several successful projects that helped change the world into a better place. He has many followers and people expect from him new endeavors that would shape their lives. He has a great deal of Social Capital. When Michael comes up with an idea he needs to build a team of professionals and inspire everyone to execute it. He creates a digital avatar to broadcast the purpose, the problem and inspiration for his followers to set up the team that will tackle the issue. His digital avatar bonds and inspires the team in their effort to bring the idea to life.

Michael has many digital avatars for specific projects; this allows him to engage with his teams on a very deep level, sharing his social capital with the followers in a very tailored way. This multiplicity creates an organization structure called the Social Capital Corporation, which is an alternative to a corporate structure that was common 10 years ago.

From a technology standpoint digital avatar is a virtual persona wired into a social network with loose ties and ability to connect users based on their interests, professional skills, achievements and passion. A real person sitting behind the virtual persona can be a transmitter or a receiver of information within a group that acts towards a common purpose or passion. These activities can range from flash mobs to collaboration on scientific projects in both physical and virtual spaces with an ability to telecommute and act together as a team. All of this requires a technical solution around social networks, such as Twitter, built up on virtual reality principles. The digital avatar acts as a capacitor for social capital built up over a history of successful interactions within the network.

This project has been created by IBM, a prominent innovation company with its latest R&D in psychology and virtual reality, together with Pixar Animation Studios, Twitter and Facebook, who brought in their expertise in unstructured networks and access to a large customer base.

—Sergey

Passion Corporation: The Opportunity

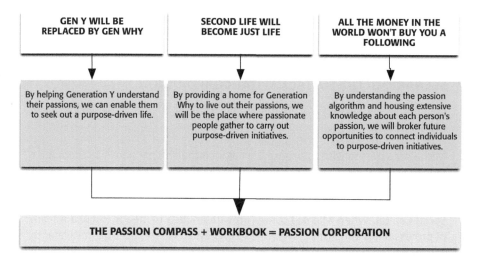

Figure 7.1.4   Passion Corp. opportunity

Passion Corporation: The Evolution (see Figure 7.1.5)

Work from passion is an ultimate motivation that defines behaviors of the Generation Why. The Passion Compass, the Workbook and Passion Corporation, are the paradigms intended to shape the behaviors of people in the decades to follow. Many of the features of these services can be implemented with the technologies that we have at our disposal today.

The sections to follow will show the Now-Ability of these services, their Acceptability, and Viability.

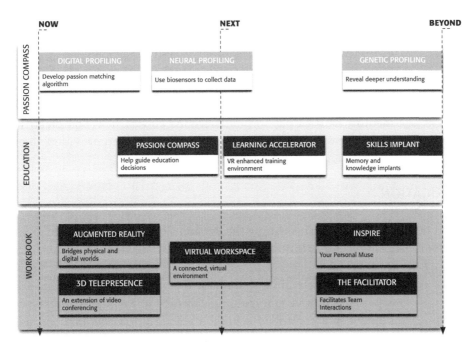

Figure 7.1.5   The evolution

Now-Ability Criteria: The Roadmap

Three milestones are evaluated for now-ability criteria:

- Year 2013 (or 12 months from now)

- Year 2017 (or 5 years from now)

- Year 2022 (or 10 years from now)

PASSION COMPASS

- **Digital profiling.** Using a collection of online and digital profiles (Facebook, Twitter, iTunes, Netflix …) to analyze one's interactions and preferences. An algorithm matches the person's passion to areas of work that will create the greatest level of interest, allowing greater satisfaction and performance.

- **Neural profiling.** Using a series of biosensors to track one's neural feedback in everyday interaction and specially designed sensory stimuli. By assessing the neural response and interpreting the results, this can reveal more in depth information about a person's area of passion.

- **Genetic profiling.** Using an individual's genetic information to identify areas of passion to determine best fit. This complements both expressed desires and biological feedback to provide a more complete understanding of an individual.

EDUCATION

- **Passion Compass.** Apply the Passion Compass algorithm to guide training and education decisions.

- **Learning Accelerator.** A training tool which provides hands-on experience in a virtual reality environment. Facilitates specialized training in a controlled setting, allowing for accelerated learning and skill development.

- **Skill implant.** Memory and skill implants for accelerated training. Suitable for both physical and knowledge based work. Implants can be customized to create personalized experiences, adapting to the method of learning that works best for the individual.

WORKBOOK

- **3-D telepresence**. A visual form of communication that conveys presence, body language, and emotion. This is a natural extension of the voice/video conferencing commonly used today.

- **Augmented reality**. Provides a bridge between the physical and digital worlds allowing a user to interact with both simultaneously.

- **Virtual workspace**. A high-fidelity, simulated work environment that is flexible and stimulates social and ad-hoc interactions. The virtual environment also facilitates the free flow of ideas and self-expression critical to a creative environment.

- **Inspire**. Your personal muse. Works with the Passion Compass to understand a person's passion and experiences. Personalizes a visual and audio sensory experience to inspire creativity. It also incorporates biosensory readings from other people so experiences can be shared.

- **The Facilitator**. A tool that tracks the progress and discussions within a group of people, and is able to extract context and meaning. By combining this data with the individual's profile, this tool facilitates discussion and decision-making, offering suggestions and a resolution process.

Emerging Desires, Behaviors, and Value Proposition, Year 2013

Passion Corp.'s opportunity (see Figure 7.1.6) lies in new products and services that will help a new generation of workers and learners shape and improve their experience of self-discovery.

The current moment is defined by the emergence of a generation with expectations around the concept of "work" that are unlike the expectations of any generation before it. The Passion Corporation acknowledges and celebrates these expectations and provides this generation with an essential tool in their journey of self-discovery. The Passion Compass allows users to continually fine-tune their understanding of what really drives and motivates them.

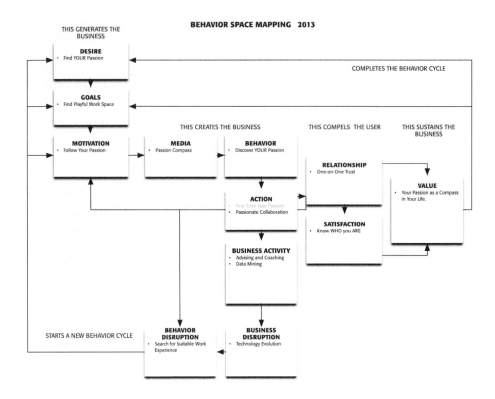

Figure 7.1.6   Passion Corp. behavior space Year 1

Today's latent desire of finding passion is fulfilled with the Passion Compass which provides a medium through which users can let their passions guide them—in effect a "compass for life."

Emerging Desires, Behaviors, and Value Proposition, Year 2017

Tomorrow's latent desire is exercising passion and finding a suitable work environment that will help Gen Why achieve a 100 percent ROP (return on passion). This desire is fulfilled by the Workbook, which allows users to engage in collaborative activities with those who share a similar passion. Workbook empowers participants to share and apply their passion in various work projects. Ultimately, this leads to an accumulation of social capital and an associated behavior disruption: wealth becomes less about money, and more about the ability to be a mentor, leader, and architect of action (see Figure 7.1.7).

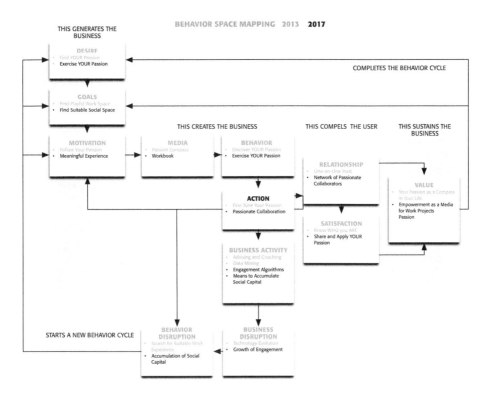

Figure 7.1.7   Passion Corp. behavior space Year 5

Emerging Desires, Behaviors, and Value Proposition, Year 2022

The latent desire of the social capital age is exercising social capital by leading other people towards a meaningful goal. When people become part of a larger "passion force," they will want to feel engaged, and connect with larger passion groups, in order to feel the enormity of the change that is being brought to life. Passion Corporation allows users to accumulate social capital in the form of achievements, followers, and skills to lead other people. It shapes passion forces into a universal passion stream, and provides a platform, space, and media, in a joint effort to change the world (see Figure 7.1.8).

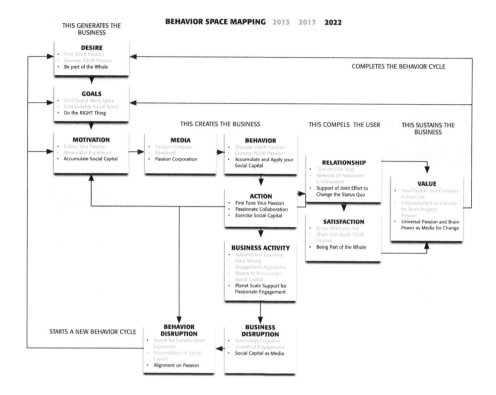

Figure 7.1.8   Passion Corp. behavior space Year 10

Business Model

VALUE PROPOSITION

Passion Corp.'s opportunity lies in breakthrough products and services that will help a new generation of workers and learners shape and improve their experience of self-discovery (see Figure 7.1.9).

The value proposition allows users to:

1.   discover passion

2.   exercise it, and

3.   accumulate social capital

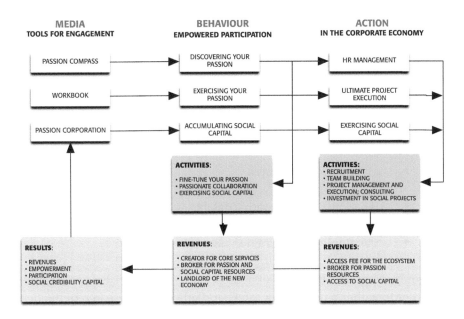

Figure 7.1.9   Passion Corp. business model

For organizations, this new economy leads to the following value proposition:

1.   natural HR management

2.   ultimate project execution

3.   exercising social capital

Core passion services are free for the users of the system and paid for by enterprise customers. As a result, Passion Corp operates primarily as a *broker of passion resources*.

VALUE ACTIVITIES

In order to deliver this value to customers, Passion Corp. must constantly refine the Passion Compass tool and develop the most effective and comprehensive service delivery distribution network.

Key value activities will include:

- data mining

- developing and refining passion algorithms

- neuroscience research

- behavioral science research

- virtual reality research

- developing collaborative databases

- developing a distribution network

Ongoing research in the fields of neuroscience and biosensors will be a priority in order to gather a user's data safely and efficiently. Research in the fields of neuroscience, motivation, and organizational behavior, will help analyze the user data efficiently and accurately.

Passion Corp. will develop expertise in collaborative databases (wikis) in order to keep information about occupations and companies current, and highly relevant to users.

The ultimate goal of these activities is to build an unrivalled collection of information relating to the passions of individuals. Passion Corp. will use this data to match people with purpose, as a main business activity, thus contributing to the creation of a dramatically different approach to how work is organized.

Guiding Principles: the central goal of the organization is to enable kindred spirits to *"work from passion."*

- When working *for a purpose* individuals are more creative and productive than when working just for a "company."

- Everyone has a right to find their passion, and act their life out of it.

Conclusions

Corporate organizations based on social capital are new forms of business expected to appear within the next decade. Their evolution is based on disruptive behaviors of the Generation Y during its transformation into a meaningful society of Generation Why. Current trends in behaviors, technology, and markets support our hypothesis of growing importance of passion, intelligence and social capital. As individuals become more accustomed to their passion, fine-tune their ability to feel it and live to it, the society overall becomes more self-aware and actualized. The basic needs and desires of the majority of population change to accommodate new perspectives.

Passion Compass as media satisfies the desire to identify one's passion answering the question: "Who you are?" The next question: "How to become who you truly are?" is synonymous to exercising your passion. A question like this supported by the persistence of an individual who has found his passion imposes a behavior disruption that brings down the concept of conventional corporate structure. The answer to this question is Workbook, a medium that empowers collaboration based on passion and social capital that becomes a repository of passions of millions of individuals. In the new era of social capital the evolution of Workbook becomes a platform for an innovative organization structure—the Passion Corporation.

The business opportunity of Passion Corporation stands out by its unique value proposition that accommodates disruptive changes in the behaviors of the Generation Why. Provided the potential scale of the market—the increasing numbers of Gen Why individuals reaching the workforce— and the platform-ability of the system, this model represents the creation of a pre-competitive form of organization.

Acknowledgements

Ivan Yuen is a technology entrepreneur and has worked with Internet and mobile technology for over a decade. He is the co-founder of Wattpad, the largest online community for reading and sharing stories.

Caitlin Storey works as an executive assistant and heritage building enthusiast at a real-estate investment company. The rest of the time she calls herself a watercolorist, a balcony gardener, and a student of human behavior.

Sergey Kovalyukh has been an industrial engineer, a project manager, a business director, and an entrepreneur in Canada and Ukraine. His current focus is innovation in heavy industries through design of computer simulation tools. Sergey is a proponent of personal development and self-actualization applied to a business environment.

Terence Smith is Partner and Co-Founder of Blue Guru Consulting, a firm specializing in Design Thinking for Business(TM). He started this firm out of a desire to change the way the world does business, by applying new ways of thinking to the problems and opportunities facing today's organizations.

7.2 Redesigning the Experience of Work: The FEED-R3 Model

TERENCE SMITH

There is a growing base of research in motivational theory that suggests "if-then" contingent rewards (that is, if you do this, you get that) work most effectively in a narrow band of mechanical tasks and can actually have a detrimental effect on performance in tasks involving higher degrees of cognition.[2] For these higher-order tasks, performance is influenced more by intrinsic rewards, which many believe are driven by the autonomy, mastery, and purpose an employee is given in his or her employment experience. While opportunities for autonomy and mastery can be negotiated between managers and employees, instilling employees with a sense of purpose requires an experiential strategy that moves employees to feel the fire inside each of them. A manager can provide an employee with opportunities for training, and can allow him more leeway to manage his own projects and work streams, but a manager *cannot* simply give an employee a sense of purpose. A sense of purpose has to be felt emotionally for it to be engaging:

> *Our newest brain, our Homo sapiens brain, our neocortex, corresponds with the "what" level. The neocortex is responsible for all of our rational and analytical thought and language. The middle two sections make up our limbic brains, and our limbic brains are responsible for all of our feelings, like trust and loyalty. It's also responsible for all human behavior, all decision-making, and it has no capacity for language.[3]*

2   D. Ariely et al. 2009. Large stakes and big mistakes. *Review of Economic Studies*, 76, 451–69. © 2009 The Review of Economic Studies Ltd.
3   Simon Sinek. 2009. TED Talks, How great leaders inspire action, filmed September 2009 at TEDGlobal200.

Sinek (2009) suggests that to connect to employees in a powerful way, an organization needs to go beyond the rational bucket list items that are commonly discussed in employment descriptions, such as salary and benefits, and attempt to impact the way those employees feel. It's not enough to simply convince employees that this is a great employment opportunity; in order to truly engage employees with an organization, the organization has to make the employees feel something. When employees feel an urge to be a part of an organization not because their neocortexes tell them that it's a rational alliance, but because their limbic systems tell them that they want the pleasure of being a part of that organization, a purpose-driven organization is born.

What is the value of a purpose-driven organization? According to Kenexa, a leading global human capital consulting firm, engaged employees work harder, perform better, and are more motivated to succeed.[4] Aon Hewitt, another leading firm in the field, goes one step further to claim that organizations with high levels of engagement outperform on the stock market and those with low levels of engagement underperform on the stock market.[5] These are not simply self-serving claims by consultants looking to earn a few dollars. In a meta-study published in 2002 in the *Journal of Applied Psychology*, Harter, Schmidt, and Hayes found that across almost 8,000 publications on the topic of job satisfaction, employee satisfaction, and engagement were positively correlated to productivity, corporate profitability, customer satisfaction, and both customer and employee loyalty.[6]

The benefits of a purpose-driven organization can be gained only when the organization pays full attention to the experiences of its employees. As Lewis Carbone and others have said for years about designing customer experiences, customers are already having experiences, so an organization is better off trying to manage them than to simply let them happen.[7] Similarly, employees are already having experiences, so rather than ignoring them, an organization is better off trying to design them in such a way that they ignite the fire within

---

4   Kenexa Research Institute. Driving Success through Performance Excellence and Employee Engagement. 2009.
5   Aon Hewitt. Trends in Global Employee Engagement. 2011.
6   James K. Harter, Frank L. Schmidt, and Theodore L. Hayes. 2002. Business-unit level relationship between employee satisfaction, employee engagement, and business outcomes: A meta analysis. *Journal of Applied Psychology*, 87(2), 268–79.
7   Lewis P. Carbone and Stephan H. Haeckel. 1994. Engineering customer experiences. *Marketing Management*, 3(3).

and make employees feel a connection that can serve as a source of energy and inspiration in their work.

An organization's ability to design these experiences to instill a sense of purpose in employees and truly connect with them on an emotional level will be a source of competitive advantage in the future. As information becomes more quickly diffused and intellectual property increasingly muddled, the emotional connection forged between an organization and its employees may be the one thing left to help an organization separate from the pack. To help organizations begin designing experiences for their employees, I propose a new model for employee engagement, called FEED-R3. The FEED-R3 model encourages organizations to feel, desire, rehearse, rekindle, and review:

- **Feel**: the organization must connect emotionally with its employees by developing a purpose-driven vision, that aims to resolve a grand conflict in the world and create a better future.

- **Desire**: each employee must be given a taste of success so that they can truly desire fulfillment of the organization's vision.

- **Rehearse**: work itself must be constructed as a cast of roles, rehearsing a deep and inviting narrative in front of an engaged audience.

- **Rekindle**: variety must be designed into the system, to enable new perspectives, capture new imaginations, and rekindle the fire that burns within.

- **Review**: the success of employee engagement initiatives must be measured by the progress of the organization, the temperature of its employees, and the quality of the overall performance.

FEEL

The first element of the FEED-R3 model is Feel. As mentioned earlier, a purpose-driven organization is born not when employees agree that the organization is providing all of the rational benefits needed to prevent employees from leaving their posts, but when employees want *the pleasure of being a part* of that organization. To achieve this, an organization must decide why it exists in the first place and communicate this to employees so that they know what it means to be a part of this organization. It is the "why" that matters for connecting with employees, and to design an effective "Why," an organization must consider three elements:

1.   A grand conflict to resolve

2.   A chance to become immortal

3.   An engaged audience as witness

A grand conflict to resolve

The first step to building a strong purpose-driven vision is to identify a grand conflict to be resolved. Humans are driven to action to resolve conflicts in their own lives (for example, "I am hungry" is an internal conflict) and can be driven to action to help resolve conflicts that require the combined efforts of a larger social group, such as a corporation or other organization.

The framing of a conflict requires a current state, or status quo, and an envisioned state that surpasses the status quo. Consider Google, whose mission is "to organize the world's information and make it universally accessible and useful."[8] This mission identifies a conflict where the status quo is unorganized, inaccessible information and the envisioned state, the resolution, is a world where all information is organized and accessible. In a simple one-line statement, Google has invited potential employees to contribute to the resolution of a clear conflict that manifests in greater and greater ways, the deeper and deeper you look. Looking at the progression of Google Maps from ordinary street maps to satellite maps and eventually street views demonstrates the potential of framing a vision this way. A grand conflict resolution such as "all information organized and accessible" prompts employees to imagine what information exists that isn't currently being captured, and how can it be captured so that it can be organized and accessed. The inclusion of birds-eye imagery and street-level views comes from an attempt to organize new information in an accessible and useful way, inspired by the company's vision.

A company that fails to paint a picture of a better world that can be created will fail to tap into the source of energy that humans have to resolve conflict in their lives. Without a desire for a change to our present condition, we have

---

8   Google. Corporate Information – Company. [Online]. Available at: http://www.google.com/about/corporate/company/ [accessed: December 2, 2011].

no desire to act. If I am okay with exactly how things are right now, if I am not thirsty or hungry or bored, then I do nothing to get out of my condition. Because desire for change prompts action, a purpose-driven organization benefits from designing a vision that helps people see the change they can create in the world, by contrasting the current inadequate status quo with the superior, desirable future state. When done well, the framing of this conflict can spark an emotional response from employees, and make them feel an urge to contribute to the larger effort to resolve this conflict.

A chance to become immortal

The second step to building a purpose-driven vision is to provide a chance for those pursuing the resolution of a given conflict to become *immortal*, or at least get closer to it. The human desire for immortality manifests in three ways. First, we invest in products and services that promise an extension to our own lives, so that we may be physically present in the here and now for just a little bit longer. Second, we reproduce and pass along our genes, thus securing at least another generation of life for our genetic material. If we cannot live on, then at least someone carrying our genes will live in our place. Third, we work tirelessly to leave an impression in the minds of others so that even if we cannot be physically present, we can at least occupy a space in the cultural narrative that persists beyond our physical existence. It is this third manifestation of the human desire for immortality that organizations can tap into, as a source of energy for designing a purpose-driven vision. Tapping into this source of energy requires a vision that seeks to be one of three things: *First, Best,* or *Only.*

First: When John F. Kennedy declared that the United States would put a man on the moon, he tapped into the human desire for immortality by inviting Americans to be a part of the first-ever moonwalk. Not only did the moonwalk symbolize progress in resolving a conflict with the Soviets, it represented an immortal achievement that would persist for generations. If the United States could reach the moon before the Soviets, it would forever be the first nation to land a man on the moon, generating a tiny piece of borrowed immortality for each American citizen to wear with pride.

When framing a vision around "First," it's important to remember that there are a lot of firsts that are not immortalized because the conflicts they resolved were too easily imitated. First to pick up a pebble? First to hurl humans at thousands of miles an hour into the vast emptiness of space to land on a rock a fraction of the size of the one they left? Now that's something to remember. And something to be a part of.

Best: being "Best" comes in many forms. Some bests are officially documented, such as Guinness World Records, Superbowl champions, and even annual entertainment awards such as the Oscars. Other bests are unofficial and often up for much debate and interpretation, such as the best CEO, the best hockey player, the best car company, and so on. Some would argue that even the official bests such as the Oscars are up for debate, as awards are given based on the subjective judgment of the Academy. With so much subjective judgment at play, it is more difficult to own the title of "best" than title of the "first," for the simple reason that you can be bested. You can be bested by someone who actually performs better than you, or you can be bested because the perception of what constitutes "best" changes from person to person, or from one point in time to the next, as values and context change. In the end, being best is a fleeting achievement. That is one advantage to being first—while you can (and probably will) be bested, you can never be *firsted*.

For an organization, being best could be framed around meeting a market need, performing a particular task or process, achieving a certain quality standard, or some other worthwhile goal. An advantage to framing a vision around best is that there is always room to improve, either because of pressure from the competitive environment or because of new unrealized potential generated from new processes, new innovations, or technological discoveries. There has not been much excitement over the Moon since the first man walked on it, but there continues to be discussion about who produces the best car, computer, and smartphone each year. Each year a new company has the potential to emerge as the best, displacing last year's top contender.

Only: the final way to look at immortality is in terms of "only." If an organization is the only one to do something, it has a chance of becoming engrained in the cultural narrative simply because of its uniqueness. Unfortunately, once imitated, there is a diminishing value to the original achievement. When China will land a man on the Moon, as they are now considering attempting[9] they will not get the benefit of being the "first"; however, they will diminish the immortal achievement of the United States, who would then be the first, but not the only, nation to land a man on the

---

9   AFP. China hails spacewalk "heroes" and sets eyes on moon. (September 28, 2008). [Online]. Available at: http://afp.google.com/article/ALeqM5iIB4lnTfrgyge8JLLlBwamdRZfsw [accessed: December 2, 2011].

Moon. If, in a hundred years, humans are landing on the Moon left, right, and center, the immortal nature of the first moon-landing will continue to diminish in value. The moon-landing is iconic because it captures the first and only time someone has been to the Moon. As the number of nations that successfully land a human on the Moon increases, the value of the achievement decreases.

One way to avoid the diminishing value of *only* is the do something that simply cannot be done again. It is here that we see the power of conflict resolution discussed earlier. To do something that cannot be done again requires large-scale change. If the achievement set out by an organization is truly oriented to resolving a conflict, to changing the status quo, then success will be inimitable. Once the status quo has been changed in a certain way, it cannot be changed in that way again, making change unique. And it does not matter if things are changed again. Once a significant change is made, a mark in time is drawn to separate *before* and *after*, and the cause of that mark will be immortalized to some degree.

An audience as witness

The third element required for a purpose-driven vision is a large and engaged audience to witness the organization's journey. Why does an audience matter? Because pop stars sing for the fans, basketball players play for the crowd, and Broadway actors perform for the audience. Because an audience is a source of energy. The arts and entertainment industries recognize the importance of an audience to delivering an engaging performance, but regular businesses have failed to adopt this into corporate practice. Would the goal of sending a man to the Moon have been as motivating if JFK kept it a secret from the general public? It was the public declaration that turned this vision into a *vision with an audience*, which provided a source of energy for those involved to truly engage in pursuing the goal.

In typical business terms, "audience" might be considered synonymous with stakeholders, but it really goes beyond that. The audience not only has a vested interest in the actions of the firm, but they want to see the journey play out because they are engaged in the conflict being resolved. Think of Martin Luther King and the civil rights movement.[10] There is a huge racial conflict to resolve, there is a chance at immortality by being the first generation of African-Americans to be considered equal citizens, and there is an audience the size of

---

10 This example appeared in the Simon Sinek Ted Talk and was borrowed here for further exploration.

the entire United States of America which is affected by and engaged with the outcome. This large audience highlighted the potential importance of resolving this conflict, which no doubt inspired those involved to continue.

This potential importance is even greater the longer into the future the resolution persists. So long as we consider flight to be the most advanced form of travel, the Wright brothers will remain immortal. However, once (or if) we learn how to teleport, they may be quickly forgotten. Every purpose has its time and place, and is eventually displaced by something better. Purpose-driven organizations must realize this, and frame their resolutions in such a way that they are not easily displaced. Fulfillment should be a state of being rather than a one-time achievement.

These three elements — *conflict, immortality*, and *audience* — can be combined to create a purpose-driven vision that sparks the fire inside of employees, and serves as a calling to be a part of the organization. The grand conflict describes the "Why" that is important to connecting emotionally with employees, the chance at immortality appeals to internal desires to live forever, and the audience brings to the forefront the significance of the conflict, and potential for significant change should the conflict be resolved.

DESIRE

Once an employee feels some sort of connection to the purpose-driven vision, the organization must work hard to make the employee desire fulfillment, which is why Desire is the second element of the FEED-R3 model. The limbic system of the brain, discussed earlier, is also involved in many drug addictions, by prompting the release of dopamine to motivate an individual to seek out the neural reward provided by the drugs. The nearer the substance that can provide that reward, the more dopamine is released, and the more engaged the person becomes in seeking out that substance.[11] In order for this to happen, the person must first experience the pleasure of that neural reward. There is a reason that people who have never taken drugs do not seek them out in the same way as someone with an addiction. Their brains are unaware of the potential pleasure, so dopamine is not released to motivate that individual towards the goal of obtaining the substance. Without experiencing the pleasure, they do not desire its fulfillment.

---

11 Marc Lewis. 2011. *Memoirs of an Addicted Brain*. Canada: Doubleday.

Similarly, in an organization, how can someone be truly engaged and motivated to pursue fulfillment of the purpose-driven vision when they have yet to experience its pleasure? And once they get that taste, how can they be motivated unless they believe their actions will bring them closer to experiencing that pleasure once more? Building a purpose-driven organization requires not only defining a purpose-driven vision, but *giving employees a taste of success* and helping them see a path to future fulfillment, both at the organizational level and within their own careers.

An orientation hook, much like a story hook, can be used at the start of an employee's tenure to engage and excite them in the prospect of fulfillment. It can be as simple as a small project that allows an employee to test the breadth and depth of the employment experience. By giving the employee ownership/ accountability and allowing him the opportunity to experience achievement early on in his employment, the employee may be more likely to feel the desire for fulfillment of the organization's purpose, leading to heightened levels of engagement compared to someone who did not have that first taste of success. This model is sometimes used in professional sports, where newcomers are put on the field early on in their professional careers, before being sent back down to the minors to better develop their skills. The experience of playing in the big leagues is meant to motivate them even further to work hard, so that they may one day taste success once more.

In building this hook, it is important to consider the breadth and depth of the experience being provided to employees. According to Schmitt (2006), there are five different types of experiences that a customer can go through: sense, feel, think, act, and relate.[12]We can see here how each of these can be applied to the employment experience to add richness to the organizational hook:

1. *Sense*: What senses are being engaged? Has consideration been paid to the visual and auditory environment in which the employee is operating? Is the environment itself comfortable to walk in, sit in, work in? A multi-sensory experience will be more engaging than one that doesn't consider senses or only considers one sense.

2. *Feel*: What feelings are desired as a new employee? This could change from one employee to the next, but some combination of

---

12 Bernd Schmitt. 2006. How to build your customer experience framework in five steps. Marketing Virtual Seminar. Transcript of original viewing from May 18, 2006.

acceptance, achievement, and importance are likely to resonate well with an employee starting a new post.

3.   *Think*: What challenge is being proposed to the employee? A challenge that forces the employee to consider the breadth of issues facing the company and allows him to exercise both the analytical and creative sides of his brain will be more engaging than a one-dimensional task.

4.   *Act*: What actions will the employee engage in during this project? Again, a challenge that allows the employee to execute a variety of actions relevant to fulfillment will be more rewarding than a one-dimensional task. For a consultant, this could mean research, analysis, ideation, client management, presentations, and so on. For another occupation, it could be completely different.

5.   *Relate*: What relationships will be formed during this project? A project that isolates the employee from colleagues or customers will not be as engaging as one that introduces that person to the key actors that will be a part of the continuing experience.

Once employees taste success through the organizational hook, and desire the pleasure of fulfillment, they need to believe that the organization can provide fulfillment to them on an ongoing basis. To do this, the organization must be prepared to demonstrate how the business model will lead the organization towards fulfillment and how the employee's personal career path will enable them to be a continuous part of it. Failure to do this may result in employees that desire fulfillment, but do not believe their current path will take them there, leading them to feel disappointed or disillusioned.

REHEARSE

To enable employees to pursue a purpose-driven vision to resolve a grand conflict, an organization must help its employees suspend their beliefs about the reality that surrounds them, the perceptual status quo, and pretend to be something greater. It can do this by framing the work experience as a production for which every day is a rehearsal. For this reason, the third element of the FEED-R3 model is Rehearse.

Consider the Four Seasons, whose vision is "to be recognized as the company that manages the finest hotels, resorts, and residence clubs wherever we locate."[13] With a vision like this, each and every day becomes a role-playing exercise where employees put on a luxurious performance for their guests. The uniforms, the beautiful properties, and the scripts they are taught, are all props and directions for one big production, where each day is treated as a rehearsal.

It is important to clarify that a rehearsal is not an attempt to let people play AT work, but instead an attempt for the work TO BECOME play. The concept of "pretending" is significant here—if an employee is told to go sit at the concierge desk, and *perform the duties* of a concierge, he would produce different actions than if he was told to go sit at the concierge desk and *"pretend" to be the best concierge* in all of New York city. The employee is not a concierge, he is Chris, he has a family, probably kids, may play video games in his spare time. What matters is whether he can do a really great job at pretending to be a concierge, for the time that he works at the hotel. What matters is that his employment experience is framed less around job tasks, and more around *role performance*. When a job is framed around role performance, Chris can become more engaged in producing results, because he has suspended his belief in the current state, the status quo, and has imagined a future state where *he is his role*.

In order to frame a job around role performance and treat each day in the organization as a rehearsal, rather than as work, an organization must pay careful consideration to the elements that are common in any production, such as *cast, narrative, stagecraft,* and *audience*.

Cast

In an ideal world, an organization would be able to find a perfect match between a vacant role and a prospective employee, one who has a passion for performing that role. In some cases, such as professional sports, it is easy to identify passionate individuals, because there are many opportunities in one's life to develop a passion for a particular sport. But, what do you do when you are trying to fill a marketing role in a biotech firm? It is quite unlikely to find someone who spent his playground hours as a child composing positioning statements for tech start-ups. Rather than trying to find exactly the right person who has precisely the passion needed to match a role, an organization can

---

13 [Online]. Available at: http://www.preview.fourseasons.com/about_four_seasons/service-culture/ [accessed: December 2, 2011].

instead look for someone who is likely to develop a passion. To do this, three questions should be added to the *casting interview*:

1.   **Is this person easily ignitable?** The degree to which someone can get excited, or "psyched," about something suggest the potential to become engaged in fulfilling the purpose that the organization is looking to achieve. In interviews, recruiters at Google will ask the questions, "What do you own that you love?" and, "What's the coolest thing you've seen in the last six months?"[14] Asking these questions helps Google learn what each individual gets excited about, and allows the interviewer to witness the degree to which the employee can get excited. Someone who cannot become engaged in answering questions about their own lives, will have difficulty becoming engaged in daily rehearsal.

2.   **Does this person share our values?** On many levels, diversity should be praised and even sought after in an organization for very good reasons. Cognitive diversity is bound to generate different approaches and solutions to problems, social diversity will help develop empathy, and generational diversity will blend experience with fresh ideas. However, for a purpose-driven organization, diversity in values should be avoided. A conflict in values will generate negative conflict in an organization that is difficult to resolve. For example, if an organization values collective performance, but a prospective employee values individual contribution, there will be a clash of values that can produce negative, destructive results.

3.   **Is this person playful?** Playfulness encompasses being open to new experiences, being able to unlearn the old way of doing things, and being able to just "go with the flow." Scripts, props, and cast members can change unexpectedly, and if a cast member cannot adapt, he will fail to contribute effectively to the performance. Someone who is not open to doing things in a new way, and who is not able to adapt, will find it stressful to live in this type of environment.

---

14   Available at: http://techcrunch.com/2011/12/08/marissa-mayer-googles-de-nero-reveals- what-she-asks-job-candidates/ [accessed: December 8, 2011].

Narrative

Once a cast is assembled, a narrative must be created to provide directions for the performance. To examine how a narrative can be created for a rehearsal, let us look at the Volkswagen Transparent Factory in Dresden, Germany, where final assembly of the Phaeton takes place. The Phaeton is a special kind of car. It is a handcrafted car, creating a new luxury class that links innovative construction to traditional values, where the finest of details have been attended to with the utmost precision.[15] But Volkswagen did not just tell people that this was a very finely detailed car, they instead developed a deep and compelling narrative, which created a unique space for the car to occupy in the minds of consumers, while also elevating autoworkers to the status of craftsmen.

The screenshot in Figure 7.2.1 is from an online video that reveals the Phaeton narrative. By invoking images of ancient Japanese china, detailed wooden instrument construction, and the intricacies of watch making, the narrative positions the autoworker as a craftsman, carrying on generations of tradition of high-quality, precision handiwork. The story is one of creation, breathing new life into a machine, one tiny detail at a time. The atmosphere created by the video is sacred and honored, something to invoke pride in tradition. The video is accompanied by music that exemplifies a sort of class and tradition that only comes with something truly special. The general feeling one is left with is assured quality and authenticity. Hard work, done right.

The initial intention of this narrative may have been to speak to the customer, but it is just as valuable, if not more, for its ability to speak to employees by putting them at the center of attention. An employee watching this video understands the role he is to perform is not autoworker, but auto craftsman. He is to pay attention to detail and care about the quality of the output. He is to view the subject as a piece of art rather than a hunk of machinery, and give it the attention it deserves. This narrative gives the employees roles to play and invites them to live up to the standards it sets. It quickly turns what was once a dirty job to be tackled, into something that can be performed with pride and dignity.

---

15 Volkswagen. A car factory in the centre of town. [Online]. Available at: http://www. glaesernemanufaktur.de/en/idea [accessed: December 12, 2011].

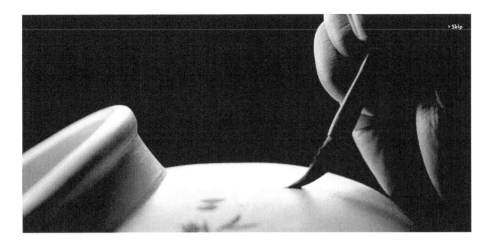

Figure 7.2.1   Volkswagen
Source: http://en.volkswagen.com/en/models/phaeton/highlights.html

Stagecraft

In theatre, stagecraft refers to the technical aspects of the performance, such as costumes, scenery, makeup, lighting, props, and anything else required, enabling actors to live out the narrative in an authentic, convincing manner. In business, this refers to the physical environment in which work takes place, and the tools and costumes given to employees to act out the narrative that they have been given. For a flight attendant, the uniform is part of the stagecraft and can provide clues to employees about the type of role performance they are expected to deliver. Consider the different uniforms of Singapore Airlines and Air Canada, Lufthansa, British Airways. Where the Singapore Airlines uniform embodies tradition, class, and delicacy, the other uniforms stress business and efficiency. Because of the narrative constructed around Singapore Airlines and the expectations that are set for role performance, flight attendants would probably have a difficult time rehearsing in Air Canada uniforms. They could try to behave the same way, but it would lack authenticity because the uniforms conflict with the narrative.

Returning to Volkswagen's Transparent Factory, we find that it is located in the middle of the city of Dresden, rather than on its outskirts, like many auto factories. This decision to locate the work environment here sends another message to employees: that their performance must be worth the premium real-estate it has been given. Inside the building one finds organized and clean layouts, with hardwood floors, bright lights, high-tech equipment, and plenty of space to rehearse. This is not a dirty auto plant, this is a high-tech assembly facility, like something you would imagine for a biotech company. Employees are dressed entirely in white, signaling the clean nature of the operation and the expected care that employees should take in their work. Overall, the stagecraft effectively enables employees to carry out the narrative of combining innovativeness with traditional values.

Audience

Finally, what is a production without an audience? We discussed earlier the importance of framing a vision so that there is a large and engaged audience to witness the pursuit of the organization. The audience comes into play again in rehearsal, where an organization must find a way to let the audience physically or digitally see the performance. Once again, the Transparent Factory provides a great example of a rehearsal in action. The public is welcomed to attend tours of the factory, to witness the production process and can even tour with an individual customer manager to see the process from start to finish. This audience helps transform these factory workers into performers in the Phaeton production spectacle. What better way to engage employees and instill pride in a job well done than to say, "We're so proud of what you're doing, we're going to give you this magnificent space in which to perform your craft, and we're going to put it on display for customers to give you the credit you deserve." That's exactly what Volkswagen has done with the Transparent Factory, and in doing so they have instilled pride and dignity in work that is often characterized otherwise in North America.

To properly rehearse, an organization must provide its employees with a compelling narrative that supports the purpose-driven vision, proper stagecraft to deliver an authentic performance, and an audience from which to draw energy and encouragement. With these elements combined, work becomes a play-space where employees can suspend belief in the status quo, and behave as actors performing roles defined by the narrative of the organization and intended to lead them towards fulfillment of the vision.

REKINDLE

There is sometimes worry that a purpose-driven engagement strategy will generate excitement early on, but that the fire will die out over time. It's a risk worth considering, and planning for, to ensure that efforts are not wasted. There are two main ways in which an organization can proactively rekindle the fire in its employees so that the sense of purpose does not die out over time.

The first way is through a *renewal of purpose*. It is vital that the organization's purpose remain relevant to employees and the surrounding context. For example, in its pursuit of making all of the world's information organized and accessible, Google can rekindle the fire each year by asking three questions:

1. **What information can be collected?** As technology advances, the types of data and information that can be collected continues to evolve. With GPS tracking of Twitter posts, we can now collect a new type of information that was previously unavailable. Technology opens up new possibilities for Google to pursue in collecting information to organize.

2. **What information is relevant to organize?** With more possibilities emerging for what information can be collected and organized, Google must prioritize which information is relevant to organize. To do this, it must maintain a pulse on what its audience values and have the foresight to predict what could create value for its audience in the future.

3. **What does "accessible" mean?** In the past two decades, the definition of accessible information has changed from hardcover books to floppy disks and CD-ROMs, to online websites and even mobile apps and location-based services. Keeping up with these technology changes is vital to ensuring Google's vision remains relevant. Accessible could also mean different things in different regions that have varying levels of access to technology. It can also mean making information accessible to people who have difficulty with traditional information sources, possibly because of a hearing or visual disability.

The second way to rekindle the fire is by *evolving the rehearsal*. Looking to the arts and entertainment industries again for inspiration, we can see how the show *"Lost"* kept the fire burning by changing its cast, narrative, stagecraft, and audience throughout its six-season run. Although the premise of the first season involved a single plane-load of passengers being stranded on an island, the show's use of flashbacks enabled the introduction of other important cast members, which kept audiences interested and engaged. New characters introduced each season, such as Benjamin Linus and The Others, Charles Widmore, The Dharma Initiative, and so on, opened up possibilities for new storylines. The narrative changed and evolved on many levels, from diving deep into different characters each week through the use of flashbacks, or by changing the way in which the story was told from one season to the next (for example, transitioning from flashbacks to flash-forwards). The physical environment, an element of stagecraft, also continued to evolve. A natural island habitat emerged into a scientific test facility, with the discovery of the Hatch, and developed further into island suburbia, with the revelation of The Others occupying the abandoned yellow houses once occupied by the Dharma Initiative.

The same principles used by *"Lost"* to entice and engage viewers can be applied to an organization to rekindle the fire in its employees and re-engage them in the pursuit of the organization's purpose. In an organization, this could mean many things, such as bringing in a new capability/resource, providing employees with a new set of tools, or experimenting with a new product or market. Using the Transparent Factory as an example, we can see how this practice applies:

- **Phaeton cast**: the cast of employees can evolve by bringing in employees with unique perspectives, or different skill sets, to complement the existing cast. This could be on a permanent or temporary basis, such as a month-long visit by a world-class watchmaker who can observe the auto craftsmen and provide suggestions to improve their trade.

- **Phaeton narrative**: the story that has been so carefully crafted can be evolved by finding new examples of handcrafted excellence to inspire the auto craftsmen. These can be woven into the existing story fabric, or introduced to employees in another way, such as having an Indian clothing designer visit the factory to talk about the intricacies of the embroidery in her work.

- **Phaeton stagecraft**: the tools and environment in the Phaeton production can be updated, so that the employees are working with the very latest. Revamping the workspace for employees can help refresh the organization's commitment to delivering an authentic rehearsal.

- **Phaeton audience**: Volkswagen can physically bring in new customers to see the production, or broadcast the assembly journey of the Phaeton over the web. Continuing to put the auto craftsmen on display for the world to see, sends a message of pride and appreciation for the work being done, which can generate a renewed source of energy for employees. Whether through a renewal of purpose or an evolution of performance, or both, efforts to rekindle the fire in employees should be recurring and proactive. It is too late to wait until the fire is gone, an organization must have a rekindling strategy to ensure that employees are continually engaged in the pursuit of the organization's purpose.

REVIEW

A common question among organizational stakeholders when considering investment into a new initiative is, "How do we measure success?" A great idea that is difficult to measure or review may encounter difficulty gaining support, adoption, and resources in an organization. But funding is not the only reason to measure success. It is also important to ensure the good intentions of the plan are being effectively achieved. Two well-known employee engagement models are produced by Kenexa[16] and Aon Hewitt. Both models emphasize a balanced set of inputs that drive employee engagement. As shown in Figures 7.2.2 and 7.2.3 these inputs include work and balance, total rewards, and opportunities for growth, among others.

These metrics, which are backed by many employee surveys, are certainly positive things for an organization to invest in, and the FEED-R3 model is meant as an addition, not a replacement, to these drivers. When considering how to measure successful progress, these models propose measuring employee engagement by asking questions of employees, such as:[17]

- Are you proud to work for your organization?

- How satisfied are you with your organization as a place to work?

- Would you refer a good friend or family member to your organization for employment?

- Do you think about looking for a new job with another organization?

---

16 Kenexa Research Institute. Driving Success through Performance Excellence and Employee Engagement. 2009.

17 Ibid.

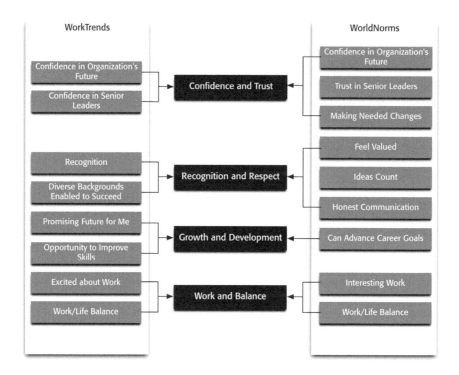

Figure 7.2.2   Kenexa engagement model
Adapted—Source: Kenexa Research Institute. Driving Success through Performance
Excellence and Employee Engagement. 2009.

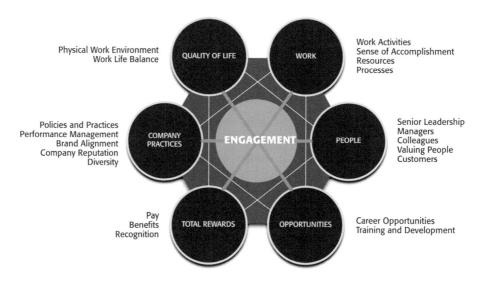

Figure 7.2.3   Aon Hewitt engagement model
Adapted—Source: Aon Hewitt. Trends in Global Employee Engagement. 2011.

These are great things to measure, and certainly metrics that you would want to see your organization trending upwards on, but they fail to capture the fire that defines *purpose and passion*. The question around pride starts in the right direction, but for a purpose-driven organization, these questions are like trying to measure the heat of a fire with a yardstick instead of a thermometer. Is it 12 inches hot? 18 inches hot? What does that mean? To measure fire, heat, passion, a thermometer is needed, not a ruler.

Similarly, a new way of measuring is needed for the FEED-R3 model. There are three key questions to track in measuring the heat of an organization:

1. **Is the organization resolving its grand conflict?** The purpose-driven organization is formed, as we discussed earlier, to resolve a grand conflict and change the status quo into a better-envisioned state. If an organization is failing to make progress on resolving this conflict, the conflict itself will fail to continue as a source of energy for employees. To measure this progress, benchmarks must be established at the outset and then tracked over time. Take Google's "organize the world's information" as an example. Google should be assessing what information is and isn't organized now and how accessible it is, and then track over time how much more information is organized and accessible. As employees see the progress the organization is making towards resolving its grand conflict, they will continue to feel the energy and drive towards fulfillment. With no evidence of conflict resolution, employees may become disillusioned and fail to believe that the business model of the organization can be successful at leading them to fulfillment.

2. **Do employees still desire fulfillment?** It's one thing to ask whether employees still want to work for an organization, which implies that they are comfortable in their posts and willing to stick around for the time being. It's another thing to ask whether employees truly desire fulfillment of the organization's purpose-driven vision. A loyal employee that has lost a connection to the overall purpose of the organization is not an engaged employee. Enjoying a high salary and benefits is not the same as enjoying the pursuit of a grander purpose. Observing the degree to which employees get "psyched up" about the organization and asking employees about the extent to which they believe their personal paths will lead them towards fulfillment within the organization will provide clues

of the degree of desire that exists internally. Ideally, the ratio of happiness to salary + benefits should be high. Higher-than-average happiness and lower-than-average salary + benefits is the ultimate indication of a strong desire for fulfillment.

3.   **Is the performance any good?** The final way of measuring success is by the quality of the organization's rehearsals. The Academy doesn't award Oscars to the movies that make the most money, and movie critics do not judge the quality of a movie by how efficiently it was filmed. It is not that profits and efficiency do not matter to the survival of the organization. They just do not matter to an employee's feelings of engagement. A purpose-driven organization knows the importance of profit, but understands that this is no way to motivate and engage employees. An employee will not feel engaged by being a part of the most profitable performance, but they will feel engaged by being a part of the most moving performance, the most memorable performance, or the most exciting performance.

Consider the language used by movie critics, as posted on RottenTomatoes. com, and imagine if this was used to describe your organization's latest rehearsal. Would you feel more engaged? *"A triumph of craftsmanship over material," "Brilliantly acted and strangely appealing," "Beautiful and intense," "A guilt-free thrill ride," "A highly impressive technical and visual achievement," "Deeply personal storytelling done with enormous conviction."*

Applying the FEED-R3 Model

Although the desire for feeling a sense of purpose is universal among humans, the varying contexts in which we are placed can make it more difficult for some organizations than others to implement the FEED-R3 model. Here we consider ways in which context can change for a purpose-driven organization based on business setting and cultural setting.

BUSINESS SETTING

With regards to business setting, factors like business size, life cycle stage, and industry are all important considerations when attempting to develop a purpose-driven organization. Some questions that will help determine how easy or difficult it will be to implement are:

- **How easy is it to frame an engaging conflict?** Some industries, like health care, may lend themselves more naturally to an engaging pursuit than others because they are easily connected to emotional feelings for most employees. Industries that are not so easily connected to emotional feelings, such as mining or packaged goods, will have to dig deeper to find the emotional connection that will spark feelings of engagement.

- **How easy is it to engage an audience?** The auto industry has a large and engaged audience because of the number of people that buy cars, the relative cost of cars compared to other purchases, extensive media coverage, and the mere fact that every time someone steps outside, they are likely to be within a few feet of roads with cars whizzing by. For a smaller market or a market that is more invisible to everyday life, it may be more difficult to engage the audience.

- **How easy is it to change?** Established organizations with long histories may find it difficult to bring all of the employees through a purpose renewal   process. A new start-up can much more easily attempt a purpose-driven strategy because it can bring in a cast that is likely to be engaged. Initiating a purpose-driven strategy at a large and public company may be met with resistance from entrenched employees and shareholders who joined the organization for other reasons.

- **How much coordination is required?** Smaller businesses with fewer employees, a single office location, and little variance in the types and backgrounds of its employees, may find it easier to join a purpose-driven initiative than larger companies with multiple offices, and many different types of occupations.

- **How easy is it to play?** Some industries and roles lend themselves better to the concept of play than others. Roles with archetypal characters that have common descriptions and uniforms, such as doctors and nurses, are easier to pretend than roles without these things, such as marketing interns. An organization with less playful roles must work harder to give their employees performance guidelines, and build an understanding of what it means to pretend to be great in that role.

CULTURAL SETTING

Two important cultural considerations are the regional and generational variances. What works well in one region, may not work well in another, and what works for one generation of employees in the same region, may not work well for another generation in the same region. Some questions that will help determine how easy or difficult the FEED-R3 model will be to implement in a cultural setting are:

- **What do people value?** People in different regions or from different generations may find different conflicts worthwhile to resolve because they value different things in life. If the members of a region or generation do not value the conflict resolution proposed by the organization, it will be difficult to engage them.

- **How playful are they?** Some cultures are more likely to produce people that are open to new experiences, and are more social and uninhibited, which are important elements of play. Assessing the playfulness of a cultural setting will help predict how willing employees will be to suspend their beliefs in the status quo and put on a compelling performance.

- **How much is the collectivist attitude valued?** Some regions are more collective in nature, valuing group pursuits over individual ones. These regions, and generations, are more likely to find it easy to contribute to a purpose-driven initiative than cultures that place relatively more value on individual achievements. Being a part of a purpose-driven organization means desiring the resolution of a larger conflict that can only be completed through a united effort. Cultures only interested in acting alone will find it difficult to prosper here.

Conclusion

When attempting to engage employees, it is important to consider both the mind and the burning fire inside each individual. Kenexa and Aon Hewitt have done much work to codify the ways in which the organization can engage the employee's mind, but nothing to suggest how an organization can engage an employee's "fire." The FEED-R3 model (see Figure 7.2.4) is intended to spark the fire within, and to measure its heat with a thermometer, not a ruler. This model is in its infancy, and much work remains to be done to help organizations understand how to ignite employees within, and engage them in being a part of the organization for *the pure pleasure of it.*

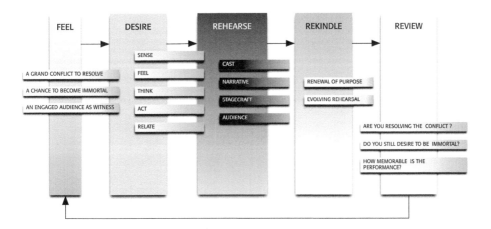

Figure 7.2.4   The FEED-R3 model

Acknowledgement

Terence Smith is Partner and Co-Founder of Blue Guru Consulting, a firm specializing in Design Thinking for Business(TM). He started this firm out of a desire to change the way the world does business, by applying new ways of thinking to the problems and opportunities facing today's organizations. Prior to this, Terence worked at Satov Consultants, where he led engagements in telecom, financial services, health care, and retail industries. Terence holds a BBA from Wilfrid Laurier University and is currently completing his MBA at the University of Toronto's Rotman School of Management. Terence believes

that the biggest barrier to achieving greatness is a lack of passion. He proposes
the FEED-R3 model to help remove that barrier.

> *Every idea which is formed in the human mind, every activity and*
> *emotion, has some relation, direct or indirect, to pain and pleasure.*[18]

---

18 George Santayana. 1896. *The Sense of Beauty*. [Online]. Available at: http://www.gutenberg.org/
    ebooks/26842. Released 2008.

8

The Marketing Dimension

8.1 New Behavior Space: The Internet is Just Beginning

You might recall the movie *Inception* in which Leonardo De Caprio plays Dom Cobb, a specialist in extracting secrets from peoples' subconscious mind, by invading their dreams. Cobb accepts a new assignment, this time premised on the reverse of stealing an idea; he has to plant an idea in the subject's mind. His assignment is summed up as *"How to transform a business strategy into an emotion."* His task is to plant the idea of breaking up a corporate empire which the son inherited from the father, but to do it in a way in which the idea seems to his subject to have been originated by himself. To accomplish this task, Cobb and his team need to construct three distinct dreams, at three layers of the subconscious, and skillfully jump from one to the other. We have all experienced this in our state of dreaming: we are in the middle of a dream, with no memory of how we got there, and then we find ourselves in the middle of another dream, again, with no memory of how we got there. And this second dream has *absolutely no connection to the first*. Each dream has a unique landscape, unique actors, and unique conflict resolutions. No lesson learned in the first dream is applicable in the second.

I feel the same way about the Internet: we are entering the third dream of the Internet age—the fully addressable cyberspace—an era with its own landscape, own actors and unique opportunities. And there is no connection between the Internet age of 2012 and the Internet age of 2000, as recent as 12 years ago. The actors have changed—both behaviorally as well as at the level of the corporations that service the behavior. Nothing today compares with how things used to be. We are now ready behaviorally, technologically, and organizationally, to take full advantage of the opportunity of the Internet, connectivity, information on demand and the potential of networked individuals. Organizations have updated their infrastructure and are now fully digital. Relationships between people and organizations are now conducted digitally as well. Old Content has been transferred on to digital formats, and new content is generated digitally. Indeed, we are ready for the Internet now more than ever, so it is appropriate to declare that in effect the Internet is just beginning. And this is both a challenge and an opportunity.

The challenge is not dissimilar to the one faced in the conversion to the Industrial Age; product development's role was to extend the limits of technology—by improving how things were made, what they were made of, and to also extend the capabilities of the machines that made them. These were technical limitations, and they were eventually transcended by technological invention. In the current cultural and technological paradigm, the development model calls for something different. It calls for understanding and mapping of behavior—understanding the current limits of knowledge and wisdom, as well as the limits of people and their environment. This is not a technical challenge, nor is it a tactical one; *it is a strategic challenge* to our limits as humans, and to our desire to transform them into possibility. This is a challenge limited by imagination only. If technology is a medium into the possibilities of any experience, what experiences do we want to make possible now? And how are we equipped to deal with this challenge intellectually and emotionally.

These are hard but exciting questions as we live in hard but exciting times. Hard, because choices need to be made. Exciting, because of the same thing, choices need to be made. Every company wants to know "Where do we go from here?" "Where will future revenue come from?"

On one hand we have people—their desires, motivations, and goal driven behaviors—and on the other we have technology—the way we can address our world in this moment. Who translates one world to the other? As mentioned in other parts in this book, it is high time that we return marketing to its roots: the creation and delivery of a standard of living. This is the true role of marketing, a role that will see marketing being the bridge between people's desires and the possibilities of technology. When various individuals pejoratively call Apple "a marketing company," they unwittingly spell out precisely the fact that Apple is the living proof of marketing as the creation and delivery of a standard of living. The delivery of the experience of life, in the age of the Internet.

What is different in this age, and how does this difference force organizations to redesign business models? Let's just look at a few behaviors that did not exist prior to the Internet, and thus do not have an archetype, or a case study—which is why the present is so confusing to corporations.

Humans were never networked on a massive scale. Networked individuals have value as media for marketing communication, but they also have value intrinsically, as a group holding social capital that did not exist before. Social capital refers to those stocks of social trust, norms, and networks that people can draw upon to solve common problems. Social capital is the structure of relationships, the mutual trust between participants in a social network. Social capital is formed by each new group that sets itself up with a Facebook page, and social capital is also formed when we expand the notion of social networks, to include entities previously not engaged, namely objects and spaces enabled to store, transmit, and receive data. When places become your friends on Facebook and your contacts in LinkedIn, the social capital of both your Facebook page and your LinkedIn page increases.

Networked individuals + networked objects + networked places = Power. This power comes from real-time communications, and the freedom to broadcast comments, likes, dislikes, and links. If this is the human behavior space today, what new behavior spaces will we create tomorrow?

ON DATA AS MATERIAL FOR THE NEW DEVELOPMENT BRIEF

Product and service design and development underwent a profound shift of focus after the introduction of the World Wide Web in 1991, and its unprecedented acceptance as a tool for daily use. The reason for this shift was the creation, amalgamation, storage, transmission, and transfer of a new material. Pre-1999 the design and development brief was centered around problems, and the necessary capability required was that of *problem solving*. Every product or service which performs in a competitive category has multifaceted problems: features vs price comparisons with its closest competitor, performance comparisons, aesthetic comparisons, and so on. These are problems rather easy to identify by asking standard qualitative or quantitative questions. Once answers are obtained, they become the "problem to be solved" and a development brief is drafted to reflect the scope of the work to be done in order to solve the "problem." This is all good and easy, and one can plan for it with a reasonable expectation that the problem will be solved, the product or service redesigned, and the share in the market recovered. All of the inputs into this process deal with known factors: the demographic, the technology, the material, and the behavior in which the product or service fits. Post 2000, a new material starts to become part of the development brief. This material is DATA.

While vast amounts of data was collected before the wide spread use of the Internet pre-WWW, the Internet world allowed individual users to create, manipulate and consume data at an unprecedented scale and rate. And once Google released their search algorithm, this data became searchable, collectible, and thus usable in a beneficial way. After all, in a data transfer behavior space (say Earth, mid 2011) all we do is data-centric; it is all we gather, research, and create. So now we have the data, but it does not have any value; it must be transformed in information. Information is comprised of the way we organize data, the way we present it, and the way we design its architecture (the framework of data that is most relevant to the questions we are asking). Information is:

- the organization of data

- the presentation of data

- the architecture of data

This simply means that data is the new material we are shaping by design. Data is the resource. Transformed into information, data becomes a Product. No different than forged steel that becomes a blade. A blade that tells—thus informs—wood, flesh, any matter: SPLIT!

Knowledge, on the other hand, is data transformed into facts, ideas, truths and principles. Sharper at times than the blade; knowledge allows one to create the blade for different purposes. Knowledge gives purpose to the data embedded into the piece of steel: you are a knife, or you are a sword.

The last embodiment—or use—of data is *Wisdom,* which is the accumulated knowledge needed to make a decision or to pass sensible judgment. Do I use this knife, or the other one? Which knife is most appropriate for my task? What are the consequences of this task? Knowledge and wisdom are services. Both operate in a minimum of three contexts: local, global, and personal. "Am I committing an illegal act while using my sharp blade" is a matter of context (where am I and what am I doing, what are the threats, what are the consequences, what are the laws of the land, what are my own values).

In the Internet age the development question became "what can we use this data for?" Music? Poetry? Video Motion? Image? Opinion? Profiling Preferences?—or the "database of our intentions," the repository of humanity's curiosity, exploration, and expressed desires, as John Batelle[1] has called the current role of the search engine in his 2006 (*The Search: How Google and Its Rivals Rewrote the Rules of Business and Transformed Our Culture*). The opportunity for massive retrieval and consumption makes data a new material for the design and development of products and services. This material changed the development paradigm; no longer focused on "satisfying need" or at providing a solution to an identified problem, but focused on the creation of new business platforms.

This is the opportunity of data as material and it leads to a new type of organization: the data enabler organization.

THE DATA TRANSFER BEHAVIOR SPACE: DATASPACE

The data transfer behavior space, or Dataspace,[2] is the distributed and interconnected physical, digital, and human network of places, spaces, and relationships. In a dataspace, information is embedded in objects and spaces, creating a new world of addressable spaces in which devices know where they are. In this new embedded sensory world, all devices incorporate context awareness and emotionally intelligent capabilities and established social forms change in fundamental ways. Intelligent devices recognize the context of the user; once the context is recognized, the device will process, communicate, and retrieve appropriate information. This capability means new opportunities for people, organizations, and markets; opportunities that may lie beyond the current business models of organizations. Business success in the next decade will be tied to understanding the impact and nature of this transformation, and taking advantage of it by providing new services, understanding the resulting new values, opening and taking advantage of new channels of communication.

A PRACTICAL DEFINITION OF DATASPACE

A dataspace is any perimeter containing communication and data enabled devices, fixtures or structures. A prerequisite for dataspace is that it contains a minimum of one of the following: enabled objects/fixtures or enabled spaces. Your smartphone is an enabled object. The mall you shop at is an enabled space. Your home, and any other place where you wirelessly connect via WiFi is also

---

1   John Batelle. 2003. [Online]. Available at: http://battellemedia.com/archives/2003/11/the_database_of_intentions.php [accessed: June 22, 2011].
2   A. Manu. 2006. *The Imagination Challenge*. Berkeley: New Riders, p. 184.

an enabled space. So dataspace does not describe science fiction or some long term foresight scenario: *it is your life right now.*

A third element of a dataspace is enabled people, which can be defined as users in possession of a device that enables them to retrieve or transmit data to the objects or spaces in their proximity, as well as to objects and spaces outside the immediate proximity (through a carrier). The presence of an enabled individual in proximity to an enabled object or space, creates the final component of dataspace which is *enabled data.* Enabled data is a descriptive term for data that has been filtered through personal parameters, and has been transformed in information of distinctive benefit to the user of the retrieving device. The address book on your mobile device is enabled data. As an example of use, imagine you are shopping for new golf clubs at your favorite specialty retailer. While in proximity of the club section of the store, data stored in clubs as well as in the retail display structures, is transmitted to your enabled device. The device contains information of a defined nature—personal filters such as preferences—which combined with the data received from the object becomes knowledge for the individual. Once knowledge is acted upon—a decision being made, a recommendation being followed, a new set of clubs being purchased, and so on—it becomes wisdom, or what we can refer to as *enabled data use.* Enabled data use is the management and collection of all transaction or location data that can further result in a user benefit.

Once enabled to do so, people will reveal their needs and wants through their very interactions and behaviors. In an emerging world of omnipresent data, the role of technology will shift radically; technology will become an essential element of the ecosystem, determining its very nature. When places and objects are data enabled they take meaning from people. When meaning is enabled it becomes *benefit.* Every possible action, observation—twitting, blogging, email, SMS— has become data readily available for analysis. Every different combination of people, devices, and places will create a wealth of unique social capital possibilities. Every setting and every interaction will determine a one of a kind ecosystem of opportunity. Presence is proximity, and data transfer is a potential marketing opportunity.

Where does this opportunity come from?

1.   **Propagation of information**. The self is the viewpoint from which we create a perspective of the world. This is why what we want to propagate by broadcasting *our information.* This explains blogging,

Twitter, Facebook, Flickr, as well as very personal YouTube videos. They are the means by which we fulfill our hunger to inform others about ourselves. Social Networks are about how *our information* relates to others in a given group. Value in information is always related to the self. The information that has value is only the information that teaches, speaks, refers to the self, or to the ones the self is protecting or cares about. Social networks are not ends in themselves; *they are conduits for the larger purpose of self-expression in the service of self-propagation*.

2. **Me on a massive scale**. The data of Person A is attached to Object B, in proximity of Space C; the opportunities of this information are so abundant that it means nothing, unless the question it was answering was already understood. The data itself yields no new knowledge. How do you sell it? How does it become useful? Whom would this data ultimately benefit?

What is the shape of the organization that can undertake this challenge? Here is a possible vision.

8.2 Marketing in Dataspace

THE DATA ENABLER ORGANIZATION

What is this organization after? Defining, collecting, transforming data into information and knowledge into wisdom at specific locations. Four critical contexts frame the opportunity of the data transfer behavior space:

- People's actions and engagement in life or commercial activities expressed as data will become a new form of currency.

- Location-based structured data will become the marketing communication media of choice.

- Any company with an audience will be in the granular broadcast business as a curator of the experience of place.

- Every company is in the business of creating content.

The data enabler organization operates from two essential premises that are returning marketing to its roots of creating and delivering a standard of living. The first is the belief that in the dataspace of the networked mobile society "standard of living" extends beyond the sale and use of branded goods and services, embracing all of the activities of everyday life. The second premise is related to the trust people place in the brands they favor; a trusted brand is well positioned to monetize this trust by brokering transactions—or the entry into experiences—which are part of the whole that defines standard of living.

Critical to creating and delivering a standard of living are the following tenets:

- You have to be part of the cultural life of the user.

- You have to be part of the emotional life of the user.

- You have to be part of the intellectual life of the user.

- You have to create culture, not products.

- You have to be in touch with the culture of the user.

- You have to engage the user on multiple platforms of experience.

Three strategic elements are required for marketing in dataspace:

- a brand value platform strategy

- a proximity/location engagement strategy, and

- a mobile device strategy

I am using the consumer-packaged goods (CPG) sector as an example, as this is the sector that spends most on marketing its products. P&G was the largest advertiser in the world in 2010, spending $8.68 billion dollars.[3] The old-fashioned way to do brand-building was by vertically expanding products and strengthening core brands. This seemed like the right strategy for growth, and growth was tied to product sales. The first challenge for consumer-packaged

---

3   [Online]. Available at: http://hbr.org/product/procter-gamble-marketing-capabilities/an/ 311117-PDF-ENG [accessed: January 6, 2012].

goods companies is the realization that growth based on sales is a finite business, which neglects the real opportunities afforded to trusted brands. In the old wisdom, a brand did not become a brand until it offered something spectacular. And the best of the CPGs got very good at delivering spectacular value to consumers, by leveraging core strengths—consumer understanding, brand-building, innovation, go-to-market capability, and scale. By mid 2010— as the penetration of smartphones and mobile apps reached the mainstream— this was no longer enough, as it became clear the brands needed to play a new role in this emerging context.

In the emerging context *a brand is not spectacular unless it enables a new experience*. Behavioral realities are changing the structure of business, by enabling new forms of engagement and participation. Twitter, Facebook, LinkedIn, YouTube, Google Buzz, Google Earth, were just some of the early manifestations of the transformation in progress, transformations that required consumers actively engaged in actions. These actions of daily life were actually expressed as data (IBM was one of the companies that understood this early in the decade), and it is clear that data in this context becomes a new form of currency. It is also clear that the Internet is becoming location-based and location-centric—my friends, my stuff, my places— and that structured data— what we know about the brand's consumers and their preferences—will become the marketing communication media of choice, engaging consumers at the granular level, one on one, with the potential of individually enhancing one's experience of one's location.

On the technology side it is also clear that "Places" will communicate data—maps, navigable attributes and content— about themselves actively and passively to people, objects, and other places. Bandwidth and mobile device limitations (memory, screen size, power, and so on) will no longer be relevant; in this context, users will expect perfect information of what is around them, and how to navigate to what interests them. When every place on Earth will have a location profile, can a large brand afford not to be there? The emerging context calls for a new ambition:

> **Navigating Life.** This means that brands will become more valuable as a trusted brand/partner for consumers to "navigate life," by providing a comprehensive suite of tools, applications, content, and mobile services; a trusted brand can now become a *granular broadcaster*, transforming the *consumers* of its products into an *audience*. With this understanding, large advertisers must reframe the role of Marketing Communications: it is

not about what a brand wants to talk about with their consumers, *but about what the consumers want to talk about*. It is about their life, in all its dimensions. And what they want to talk about is connected to where they are; to a location.

What new experiences can a trusted brand enable? If location is proximity "to something" in the "context of something else" then three opportunities open up:

- to become a "proximity *conduit* expert"
- to become a "proximity *context* expert"
- to become a "proximity *content* expert"

The first — *conduit expertise* — is a strategic shift that requires answers to the question: *how can the brand make money because it is?* In other words, how can one of your brands leverage the trust consumers have in it by becoming the broker of the experience consumers have at specific locations, and further on, by brokering possible transactions that enhance this experience?

The second — *context expertise* — will leverage one of the core competencies of CPGs which is consumer understanding.

The third — *content expertise* — will leverage open innovation by enlisting as location content alliance partners products and services that people use and rely upon on a daily basis, and whose value profile matches the values of your brand. These partners are value markers in people's lives, offering location-based content, the products and services consumers are interested in at a specific geo-location.

The *disappearance of the mass market* and the emergence of the micro and individual markets are the next cultural wave. In the old model of mass communication, *interruption* was the norm (Figure 8.2.1): content was placed at locations likely to be visited by the target demographic. These were virtual locations — TV shows, radio programs — as well as physical ones such as newspapers, magazines, outdoor displays, and so on. The content of the location was responsible for the emotional context of behavior; a sporting event on television will see the placement of advertisements that fit the charged emotional context of someone watching a particular sporting event, whereas a midnight comedy series will provide a different emotional context, and hence

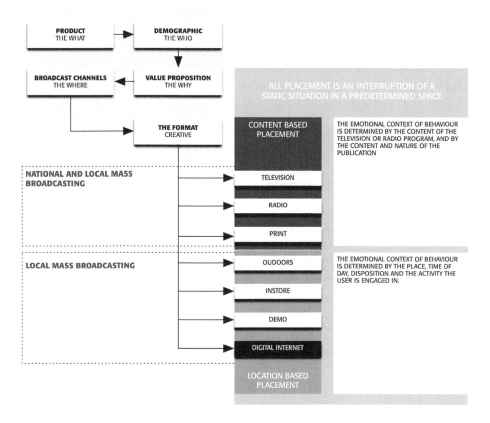

Figure 8.2.1   Mass broadcast model

the placement of a different brand message. This placement was an *interruption of a static situation, in a predetermined space and in a predetermined emotional context*. How different is marketing in dataspace from this picture?

Firstly, it is likely to take place *on a single platform*, your mobile connected device, and in a creative format that is native to the platform. No more TV spots, no more radio, no more print creative formats. Secondly, the broadcast of the message will be triggered by three equally important attributes: one's geo-location, the specific activity one is involved in at the time, and the personal preferences set on the device. The activity will set the emotional context of behavior—you will receive a different broadcast if you are shopping for wine, than if you are picking up your daughter at the daycare— while the location and individual preferences will determine the content of the message and tone (Figure 8.2.2). This is the *un-mass granular model of brand broadcast*, characterized by *engagement with multiple layers of experience in a dynamic situation*. There is a large increase in the numbers of people who want, and are willing to pay for everything from news and entertainment, food, and clothing—products and services focused and tailored specifically *to them*. The new role of the brand in the un-mass broadcast and marketing reality of dataspace is that of *aggregator and curator of the everyday life experience, and the provision of customized value information in everyday places*. (See business model in Figure 8.2.3).

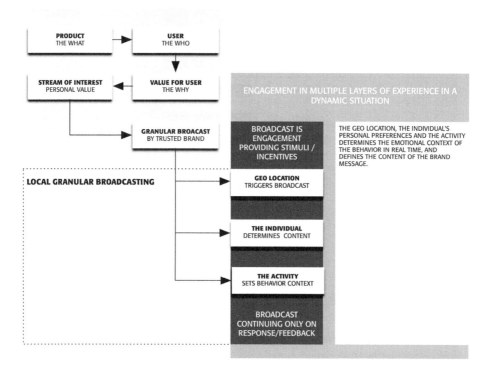

Figure 8.2.2   Un-mass broadcast model

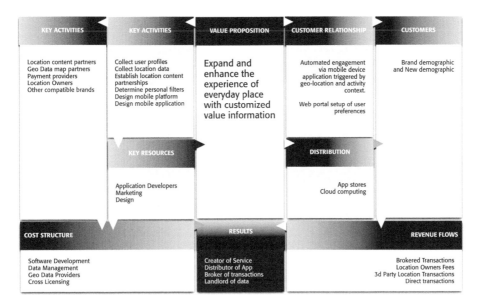

Figure 8.2.3   Data enabler business model

9

The Future Dimension

Keeping an Eye on the Future: Redefining Strategy through Scenarios

A key tool in the ability to interpret signals in the emerging context is scenario building. Scenarios help the leadership team prepare a strategic and imaginative response to emerging market conditions, and implement changes faster. Used at their best, scenarios create pathways for change out of sets of signals directly affecting the organization, and reveal the dynamic of the behavior space in which an organization functions. Scenarios provoke thinking and analysis; they define methods that engage an organization's ability to shape the future, to create options of possibility and link any future activity to *action today*.

Business in 2020: The Normative and Strategic Scenarios

FUTURE SCENARIOS AS STRATEGIC TOOLS

In this environment of continuous transformation—the world at this moment—emerging contexts are the constant, and business the variable. Change is not permanent, nor is it continual: change occurs only as a voluntary act, when one reacts to emergent forms of technology or behavior. What will prompt us to engage in change? As mentioned in various parts of this book, a vision of possibility is a powerful attractor image for change. A change strategy needs to be based on courageous foresight scenarios, scenarios that explore the nature of human beings at the intersection of technology and behavior. *Humans are the ultimate medium through which technology manifests itself.* And scenarios are the ideal platform to explore these manifestations and make strategic choices for change.

Foresight, uncertainty, and ambiguity

It is common for executive groups to express discomfort around strategic foresight scenarios, seen by many as full of uncertainty. It is important to note here that foresight scenarios are no more and no less uncertain in their outcomes than any forward-looking statement regularly disclosed by public companies. A foresight scenario is *an assumption* derived from *information currently available*. In other words, not dissimilar from any other assumption made currently; all public companies place disclaimers in regards to "forward-looking statements" prominently on corporate communication materials.

Forward-looking statements are typically full of words such as "might," "should," "estimate," "project," "plan," "anticipate," "expect," "intend," "outlook," "believe," "expect," "foresee," "plan" "seek" "forecast," "anticipate," "intend," "estimate," "goal," and "project" and similar expressions of future or conditional verbs such as "will," "may," "should," "could" or "would" and variations of such words and similar expressions are intended to identify such forward-looking statements. These statements are not guarantees of future performance, and involve assumptions, risks, and uncertainties that are difficult to predict. There is little difference in the degree of ambiguity at hand between a regular future operations plan (which is a scenario by another name) and a foresight scenario. Both are based on informed assumptions. But only one will deliver a new competitive space …

Any strategy is as good as the scenario that informs it. A scenario is the story built upon the operating platform of a narrative that explores how a latent behavior becomes manifest. These stories describe new product concepts, services, or business models from an experiential first-person perspective, for the purpose of incorporating a signal behavior—a trending behavior that is observed—into existing behavior models. A scenario is a compelling platform in which to explore the experience, and allows for a deeper understanding of events, user roles, actions, and objects used in the performance of tasks, as well as the role of support systems (services and businesses). Scenarios do not forecast technology but foresight human behavior. What would humans do if the technology *was* at their disposal? How would we change? What else will change, and will these changes impact the continuity of life and business on Earth?

How do we discover within ourselves the capability allowing our latent behaviors to emerge? First and foremost, we must allow for the opportunity of story. When you engage in any form of narrative, you imagine anything is possible; your mind is at play and does not worry about the constraints of reality as you enter the temporary play space of a story. In this space we all become narrators of the possibility of a technology. Through free play we become storytellers and performers, we became full participants in the unraveling of the story. The potential for any kind of latent behavior to become manifest is a current capability within all of us. A scenario assumes that everything is possible as far as technology is concerned. Arthur C. Clarke writes in 1961's *"Profiles of the Future"*:[1]

> *Without going into technical details (of interest largely to those who can already think of the answers) the time will come when we will be able to call a person anywhere on Earth, merely by dialing a number. He will be located automatically, whether he is in mid ocean, in the heart of a great city, or crossing the Sahara. This device alone may change the patterns of society and commerce as greatly as the telephone, its primitive ancestor, has already done. Its perils and disadvantages are obvious; there are no wholly beneficial inventions. Yet think of the countless lives it would save, the tragedies and heartbreaks it would avert. No one need ever again be lost, for a simple position—and-direction-finding device could be incorporated in the receiver on the principle of today's radar navigational aids.*

For Clarke the behavior space of the telephone was very clear—humans will demand an extension of the space in the mobile realm; it was just a question of "when" and not a question of "why." Clarke uses narrative to describe a world in which the behavior space of mobile communications extends as far as people can reach.

When using future scenarios, perspectives can shift from one location to another, behavior sets are modified and signals acquire new and unexplored meaning. We can imagine anything in these stories, and we can glimpse futures not yet invented. Future scenarios lessen the abstraction and invisibility of current technologies by moving our focus away from ideas of tangible, mechanical devices in need of possible technological improvements (an industrial-age hangover) towards devices that are driven by behavior. Scenarios allow us to shed the social constraints of rationality, by creating a space where the imagination can run wild and providing a venue to learn and incorporate new meaning and implication into cognitive behavior. The

---

1   Arthur C. Clarke. 1962. *Profiles of the Future*. London: Orion Books, pp. 175–6.

premise of the narrative establishes a new set of dispositions and expectations that allow for the our latent behavior to emerge. Future scenarios are not about what technology will achieve in the future; they are about what *we want to do* in the future. Scenarios are people-centered.

By creating a compelling platform in which to explore the experience, we gain a deeper understanding of events, user roles, actions, and objects used in the performance of tasks, as well as the role of support systems (services and businesses).

Humans in their own lives, as well as in organizations, aspire to understand how the future will shape itself, as soon as a new emerging context is observed, and what is likely to happen in their personal and business environment. The future is about choices made by individuals and organizations. It is about choices made by groups that may have at times different interests. Scenarios are the ideal tool to explore and pass judgment on the possible forms of change: what will happen to technology? What will happen to our business? How do I play a significant role as a business in this emerging context?

Scenario typologies: two types of scenarios, each one holding value from strategic to tactical are presented in the next section.

Normative scenarios

Normative scenarios have no immediate strategic value, but inform about the possible shape of the economic, cultural and political space in which the other scenarios would operate. What is described in normative scenarios is the answer to: *How is the Landscape Changing*? The answer often takes the form of *"when this technology happens, this is what society will become!"*

Strategic scenarios

A strategic scenario has two advantages: it discloses the big picture in which any user experience scenario operates—which allows the organization to plan strategic approaches that deal with the emerging context—and it can be used in turn as a point of departure for user scenarios, as it describes a new behavior, a new opportunity and a new attitude. What is described in a strategic scenario is the answer: "Because this technology and behavior happened, this is what our organization has become!" In other words, answers to the strategic questions: *What is the meaning of value in the mobile society? What do Millennials consider essential and important? What desires do they need fulfilled? What are the characteristics of the market? What, therefore, are the characteristics of the organization that will best respond to this dynamic?*

The normative scenario that follows is a compilation of technological themes from "The World in 2025: A Normative Scenario" which presents a scenario based on the inputs of 550 futurists, scholars, business planners, and policy advisers from around the world. Millennium Project participants identified and rated norms that formed the core of a number of normative scenarios. Their views on global developments were distilled into a range of issues, opportunities, and actions to address. These have been woven together into a scenario based on achieving norms by 2050 that were identified by Millennium Project participants from around the world.[2] The Millennium Project's mission is to improve thinking about the future, and make that thinking available through a variety of media for feedback, and to accumulate wisdom about the future for better decisions today. Their vision is to function as a global foresight network of nodes, information, and software, building a global collective intelligence system, recognized for its ability to improve prospects for humanity ....[3]

A Normative World in 2050: The Technological Theme

JEROME C. GLENN AND THEODORE J. GORDON

By 2050 the Internet has become a right of citizenship. Businesses give free accounts to all customers; employers give them as an employee benefit. The connection of virtually all people to the global information and communications systems accelerated the pace of scientific research and the introduction and diffusion of new technology. Biotechnology, nanotechnology, and closed-environment agriculture fed the world. New and improved sources of energy made cleaner economic growth. Brain-like intelligent systems used neural networks to augment human intelligence and improve decision-making. Molecular manufacturing (nanotechnology) lowered manufacturing unit cost, requiring less volume of materials and energy usage, and hence lowered the environmental impact of a population that had almost reached 10 billion. Vaccinology and genetic engineering eliminated most acquired and inherited diseases further reducing the need for more frequent pregnancies to have a

---

2   [Online]. Available at: http://www.millennium-project.org/millennium/normscen.html.
3   [Online]. Available at: http://www.millennium-project.org/millennium/overview.html.

similar-sized family. This was a factor in further lowering fertility rates, even though generational mini-booms have continued from the great population explosion in the mid-twentieth century. Cyberspace had become a major medium of civilization creating a constantly growing, non-zero-sum economy and had changed day-to-day life as significantly as the industrial revolution had changed life 200 years earlier. The success of the International Space Station had led to other orbital habitats, the lunar base, and the pioneer communities on Mars. Nearly 250,000 people now work in space communities in orbit, on the moon, and on Mars, giving a new frontier for human imagination and advances in civilization.

Breakthroughs in the unified theory of matter and energy have led to a deeper understanding of mass, inertia, gravity, and quantum behavior. Experiments have begun in the field of anti-gravity and faster-than-light communications through the use of quantum phenomena. There are perhaps a hundred scientists who are studying possibilities of extracting intrinsic, resting energy from space and using it in various forms of propulsion. Cosmologists are adding more rigor to their theories of the origin of the universe and have duplicated the earliest time in computer simulations that seem almost exact, but the search still continues. Some signals of apparently extraterrestrial origin have been detected but debates continue over whether they are truly extraterrestrial or human artifacts, and if extraterrestrial, over their precise meaning.

The debates about the potential of extraterrestrial contact have forced us to think beyond our geographic and ethnic boundaries. Additionally, scientific breakthroughs, the ease of international and near-space travel, and the constant global communications among people of different views on Earth and near-space have also helped broaden our perspectives. As a result, people began replacing their more parochial views and consider global ethics more seriously. Not all people value love, truth, fairness, family, freedom, and belonging, but far more than in the twentieth century and enough to keep a relatively peaceful world. The field of conflict-resolution, which has made great progress since its earliest applications a hundred years ago, recognizes these simple points and its councilors build on them in resolving disputes. Interestingly, the Great Cyber Games played by one out of every three people alive today were instrumental in the identification and acceptance of these global ethical norms which provide much of the common ground for today's global cooperation. Although ethnic prejudice still exists, it has been held in check more effectively than in the previous century.

Progress in information technology has been astounding. Microprocessors have continued to increase in capacity; they are speedier, smaller, and less expensive. Today computers are built into and integral with almost everything we make from machines and appliance to buildings and artificial eyes with zoom lenses. Computer elements are molecular in size, and their operations utilize quantum behavior.

Much of the computing capacity today makes machines simpler to use. Rather than requiring everyone to learn to use them, the machines have been taught to listen and act to needs and wishes of their users. The digital world's vast amount of data has been translated into computers and related technologies with access so easy and natural, people use them without even knowing it, making them seem truly transparent.

Health is a widely accepted human right; equity in coverage and accessibility to quality health services and health information exist regardless of capacity to pay, culture, race, geographic location or social ascription. Tele-health and tele-medicine is widely available and easily accessible. Health-care providers adopt new paradigms to forecast and prevent potential health problems through personal and public health approaches and early detection through bio-monitoring and management of problems that do occur.

Some people used to believe that computers would regiment us by forcing us to conform to their specifications in order to use them. Today computers and the machines that use them have supported diversity through mass-customization. Manufacturers make very short production runs of products that are tailored to the specific needs of very small segments of consumers, differing in detail, but matching their criteria. The software technology that uses one's body as passwords has eliminated toll-booths, credit cards, and passports, since people can be recognized by machines. Shopping is now augmented by personal databases of everything from your buying history to clothing measurements allowing the online or in-person to say, "This jacket will match the slacks you bought last month," or "Don't you want to get some matching clothes for your niece's doll for her birthday next week?

All of these improvements in information technology have resulted in an intricate system of communications that some have called a "global brain" and planetary "nervous system" which has improved the prospects for humanity. As access expanded, diminishing costs of educational software (edutainment), any motivated person could obtain a college education and continue to learn about everything they wanted. Individuals cross political and corporate boundaries in pico-seconds forming new alliances unknown to traditional power structures. Rich and poor have nearly equal access to cyberspace almost anywhere and anytime. The old distinctions between First and Third Worlds are meaningless in cyberspace.

The old one-way media tended to be conflict-oriented; audiences were held by the drama of disagreement. Interactive media tended to be cooperation-oriented, users were held together by the satisfaction of collaboration. Cyberspace distributed the new wealth of information more democratically than previous systems. As a result, anyone can get the training, market research, planning, credit, and other resources to start their own unique businesses and sell to the global cyberspace market. Over the past 50 years, this development has been major factor in reducing unemployment worldwide.

The invention of secure electronic money revolutionized retail transactions, international trade, and provided extraordinary growth of employment. Individuals felt confident to create businesses and sell worldwide. While retail use of the Internet got most of the early publicity and attention, business-to-business transactions have grown phenomenally. Today, businesses of any size identify suppliers and partners worldwide, barter, order, and track order status simply and instantaneously around the world. Rules preventing wild currency fluctuations limited financial crises and allowed small business growth with security around the world. A fee-based system for central banks made currency transactions transparent with online prices, information on counterparties, and purposes of trades reduced speculation.

The synergy of telematics and micro-genetics provided a jump in human evolution eliminating many diseases and increasing human capabilities. Robots, both giant and nano, do the dangerous, repetitive, and precision work in surgery, security, health-care, space industrialization, house cleaning, sewer pipe clearing, bridge inspections, mining, laboratories, and even the preparation of fast food. These robots are, for the most part, adaptive to their environments, single-purpose, and employ biosensors that are derived from both living cells and manufactured microprocessors.

Telecitizens, born in poorer areas but working in richer ones, helped their original countries as tele-volunteers, accelerating the development process. The development of artificial intelligence and its use in communications provided individuals with needed and timely medical, financial, and other information.

Software for multi-language translators increased communications among different language groups.

The image of people walking by vending machines, reaching in their pockets, but finding no coins and walking on, drove distributors in the early twenty-first century to create voice-activated machines that billed at the end of the month on people's cyber-game accounts. The televendors had a simple voice-recognition and synthesis program that let people speak to the machine, use their body patterns as their password, order their sandwich, soft drink, communications, and play in the Great Cyber Games while they drank or ate alone or with friends.

The Great Cyber Games contained links to databases that described global problems, opportunities, challenges, strategies, and tactics. Players received points as they identified answers that matched or improved on those in the database, or identified new problems judged to be critical enough to add to the database. When a person scored enough points, they won "reality." They got a prerecorded message from a policy-maker working on the issue in which the player had received the highest score. The message challenged the player to play in the "real world game." The current real world situation was given to the player by the policy-maker, researcher, or potential employer. When the player came up with something that was considered valuable, the player got connected live to discuss their insight. Winners got to play in the real global game with real actors and many got new jobs and careers.

The Great Cyber Games were attractive to policy or other kind of decision-makers because it filtered out all the noise of computer conferences, journal articles, and got right to the person with the ideas. The players liked it because they had the potential to see their ideas realized and earn a living at meaningful work. Basic research labs used it to identify the young scientists with the greatest potential to participate in their research. An unintended bi-product of the game was a global personnel selection system that today is credited for contributing to the phenomenal growth in new theoretical principles that have led to many improvements. Another surprise was that it performed the role of a global employment agency.

The Great Cyber Games also became an informal way to prevent some of information warfare's destruction, by promoting more precise, honest, and compassionate thought around the globe where it was needed, when it was needed, and in the form that was needed, so that constructive action has had a chance to keep ahead of destructive action. Granted, it continues to be a software race to keep ahead of the bad guys.

When it was scientifically demonstrated that certainty of discovery was the most effective deterrent to dishonesty and crime, means for improving certainty of discovery and positive identification, based on voice analysis and cross-referencing global databases were created and the crime rates fell. International protocols were established for sharing police data-banks and the use of non-lethal weapons such as sticky foams and aerosols that induce sleep.

Nanotechnology transceivers with voice-stress software were incorporated into clothing and jewelry; these systems alerted the user when people were lying or becoming aggressive. Although counter software will always be a problem, requiring constant upgrades, people have become more honest, or at least behave more honestly than in the last century. It is difficult to imagine a return of dictatorships and to the organized crime networks of the past with today's global connectivity and honestware universally available.

The field of miniaturization has been extremely important to the success of our world. Nanotechnology helps produce low-cost and custom-designed food. As nature breaks down dirt, air, and water and re-assembles the molecules into potatoes, nanotechnology "universal assemblers" break up materials into molecules or atoms, then follow the instructions from custom-designed food molecules to manufacture food. With nanotechnology, whatever we can design, we can build. The same technology that had been used to produce integrated circuit chips was used to produce tiny machines. For example, a mass spectrograph, complete with all valves and analysis apparatus was made on a silicon chip. Motors are now constructed with diameters of less than a millimeter; accelerometers used in automobile air bags are too small to be seen with the naked eye. It is commonplace to use biological materials in such chips now to sense the reaction to various contaminants or initiate actions based on their presence. Technologists have learned about forces that occur uniquely at this scale (for example, lubricants can have molecules that are too large to work properly in such machines) and have developed special molecular forms (fullerines) that have desired properties.

All of this activity has had a great affect on materials science. After a plateau that lasted for several decades, superconductivity is being experienced at higher and higher temperatures; now thin film superconductors exist at −100 degrees Celsius. The developments in this field included bio-molecules, low-pressure diamond coatings, ultra-light solids that float in air, and composite materials strong and light enough to form the skin of a large-scale rocket designed to enter orbit with a single stage.

New forms and mechanisms of the distributed global economy began to emerge in the early twenty-first century. A whole new lexicon was developed to describe the digital life forms that built cyber culture and the collaborative economies of today. Software agents assisted our transition. They sought new opportunities for collaboration, alerted us to synchronicity to discover the value of new and counter intuitive ideas, and coached us in new forms of self-organization. They even produced images of fields of people, places, and opportunities of cooperative intent. Such "fields of cooperative intent" are one of the new units of social organization and entrepreneurial effort. Knowledge and wisdom have become added measures of wealth and value.

Global idea management systems were integrated into the Great Cyber Games, further accelerating the progress of more environmentally friendly economic and technological development. Common data protocols for unconventional science and an international registry of new and unconventional ideas with national copyright protections was connected to clearinghouses that reported success, failure, and inconclusive research. Use of software that prompted the user to see potential synergies of their work with research in other fields, that they might not have otherwise considered, has now become a useful protocol in all fields.

Biotechnology has created high-yield plant species that are disease and pest-resistant, use less fertilizer and are more tolerant of drought and brackish water. More recent applications of biotechnology are completely changing the 10,000-year traditional use of seeds, water, and land to grow crops. Today large-scale production of food in factories using genetic techniques produce much of the world's food. Food factories use genetically altered micro-organisms to organize raw materials into nutritious food. The inputs are primarily sunlight or other energy forms, carbon dioxide, water, and nitrogenous materials. The output is amino acids and directly consumable food. In another approach, cells from natural foods such as carrots or meat are cloned and the outputs of the food factories are edible replications of the parent cells. Such techniques make agricultural production possible without land. It is also beginning to reduce the need for farmland for meat by producing novel protein, substituting meat from cows and chickens. Such meat substitutes for fish has promoted the recovery of ocean fisheries and the establishment of ocean plantations. Perhaps equally important, inventions in this field have also produced the current counters to biological weapons and removal of pathogenic microbiological agents from food.

The mapping of bacterial, human, and plant genomes, provided knowledge of genetic processes and to some extent, information about how to control them. The tiny interior robots of nano-medicine repair cells, tissues, and organs. Some of the diseases that have been eliminated or controlled are cancer, cystic fibrosis, hemophilia, rheumatoid arthritis, AIDS, hypercholesterolemia, and some forms of mental illness. Monoclonal antibodies, sometimes mounted in bio-chips, are being used in sensitive diagnostic tests and in drug delivery systems that pinpoint specific sites in the body. Techniques in this field have led to genetic medicine in which the genetic properties of humans are modified *in vivo* to cure or ameliorate diseases caused by genetic anomalies. Disease-diagnosis based on the analysis of one's genetic material is routine; these diagnoses not only relate to existing diseases, but also the propensity to future disease and in some cases, the propensity to abhorrent behavior.

The traditional view of human reproduction is still undergoing changes simultaneously with the increasing progress toward self-determination, equal rights, economic autonomy of women, and the evolution of male and female roles. Some of the more controversial advances have centered on long-term male and female contraceptives, the ability to select the sex of a child before conception, and the ability to influence genetics and biochemical processes. The world became quite alarmed in the early twenty-first century when low-cost and portable methods for determining the sex of a baby before conception became commonly available. Many feared that parents in some cultures would only select males, distorting the future demographics of human race. After several years of intense debate, threats of international sanctions, interventions of leading personalities, and a short but rapid increase in male births in some countries, the number of female and male births returned to balance. This left many uneasy about unforeseen consequences of new technology. As a result, technological forecasting and assessment has become a normal part of the work in advanced institutes today.

The World Energy Organization, created in the early twenty-first century, coordinated research and helped improve policy leading to today's safer mix of sources that have reversed the greenhouse effect. These include hydrogen, third-generation fission plants, solar-power satellites, and renewable energy sources. Hydrogen has become a major source of energy for automobiles and medium for transporting energy from origin to use. In its gaseous form it was stored at high density in metal hydrides and later released by a modest amount of heat. In addition to extracting it from natural gas, it is also produced from water by electrolysis (the focus here was on a new form of catalysis) and by high-temperature disassociation of water, processes that use a great deal of electricity or very high temperature. The former method of extraction from water has provided the basis for an argument to build second- and third-generation nuclear plants and solar satellites, while the later for large-scale solar-thermal plants. An additional benefit of the production of hydrogen from seawater has been desalination to produce fresh water, and hence preventing water conflicts in the Middle East and other potential crisis regions.

The synergies of advanced research in biology and physics necessary for human space flight has generated an extraordinary number and range of inventions, stimulated thought about the meaning of life, history, and our common future, and created many opportunities for peaceful international cooperation. International R&D cooperation led by INSPACECO (the international public-private consortium) lowered launch costs to under US$500 a pound making it possible for an individual to move to a space community with a basic support package for a quarter-million dollars. This, plus the growing space tourism and space lottery business (winners get a free visit to an orbital space vacation center), has opened a political debate on space migration. Some argue that migration from Earth is inevitable; it is in the myths of many cultures. People advocate accelerating the construction of alternative habitats in space as insurance for the human species, should an earthly catastrophe threaten life on Earth. Others argue that life always moves to new niches and our curiosity will drive use one day beyond the solar system.

Space-related inventions have created new industries, tax sources for social programs, improved living standards, expanded access to tools by miniaturization and production processes that have lowered the costs of many technologies from satellite communications to medical diagnostic techniques. Income from satellite communications, solar-power satellites, orbital energy-relay satellites (orbital electricity grid), lunar and asteroid mining, weightless manufacturing, and space tourism has led to an enormous growth of private sector ventures in space. This acceleration of the privatization of space applications has avoided the public cycles of interest and disinterest in space support, so common in the last century.

Hierarchical institutions of the twentieth century have given way to network organizations and a plethora of short-term, task-oriented, individually initiated teams made possible by intelligent software agents in cyberspace. Cyber-UN and other international organizations can only be understood in cyberspace, because "employees" are not concentrated into one building or geographic center from which they operate. Instead people are connected around the world under the cyber umbrella of the international organization, but they may also be working for other institutions such as NGOs, corporations, universities, other UN systems, and traditional systems like nation-states and regional organizations. These cyber organizations are better thought of as executive information systems, with knowledge visualization, that are available in cyberspace for improved decision-making by a user or group of users. This is the medium through which harmonization of global standards was achieved and through which accountability, transparency, and participation in the range of human enterprise today are reinforced.

Despite the technological progress and scientific insight in which today's society is based, most scientists and engineers believe that there is still more to come, that the future holds further excitement, progress and discovery.

Acknowledgement

Excerpt from 1999 State of the Future: Challenges We Face at the Millennium *by Jerome C. Glenn and Theodore J. Gordon. First published: August 1999. Reprinted with the permission from the authors.*

Experience Opportunity: What New Behavior Spaces Does This Scenario Foresee?

Scenarios explore experiences with devices, applications or methods that might be employed in the course of daily life, at a set moment in time, and based on a set number of assumptions. The scenario is in effect a canvas of the mind, on which we can sketch and explore any number of images of opportunity. Experience opportunity is the parsing of scenarios for the products, services alliances, and collaborations that that are described within. Parsing this normative scenario, the following potential new behavior spaces are noted:

- **The Internet has become a right of citizenship**. Businesses give free accounts and corporations have made the Internet an employee benefit.

- Biotechnology, nanotechnology, and closed-environment agriculture fed the world.

- **Intelligent systems use neural networks** to augment human intelligence and **improve decision-making**.

- **Molecular manufacturing** lowers manufacturing unit cost.

- Vaccinology and **genetic engineering** eliminates most acquired and inherited diseases.

- Cyberspace had become a **major medium of civilization**.

- The Great Cyber Games are played by one out of every three people alive and are instrumental in the identification and acceptance of these global ethical norms which provide much of the common ground for today's global cooperation.

- **Computers are built into and are integral** with almost everything we make from machines and appliances, to buildings and artificial eyes with zoom lenses.

- Computer elements are molecular in size, and their operations utilize quantum behavior.

- The machines have been taught to **listen and act** to needs and wishes of their users.

- **Health is a human right**.

- Tele-health and tele-medicine is widely available and easily accessible.

- Health-care providers **forecast and prevent** potential health problems through early detection through bio-monitoring.

- Manufacturers **make very short production runs** of products that are tailored to the specific needs of very small segments of consumers, differing in detail, but matching their criteria.

- Shopping is **augmented by personal data bases**—everything from your buying history to clothing measurements.

- Rich and poor have nearly **equal access to cyberspace** almost anywhere and anytime.

- **Secure electronic money** revolutionized retail transactions and international trade and allowed individuals to create businesses and sell worldwide.

- **Robots,** both giant and nano, do the dangerous, repetitive, and precision work in surgery, security, health-care, space industrialization, house cleaning, sewer pipe clearing, bridge inspections, mining, laboratories, and even the preparation of fast food.

- **Voice-activated machines** that bill at the end of the month on people's Cyber Games accounts.

- **Televendors** have a voice-recognition and synthesis program that let people speak to the machine, use their **body patterns as their password**, order their sandwich, soft drink, communications, and play in the Great Cyber Games.

- The Great Cyber Games contain links **to databases that described global problems**, opportunities, challenges, strategies, and tactics.

- **Players receive points** as they **identify answers** that matched or improved on those in the database or identified new problems judged to be critical enough to add to the database.

- Winners got to play in the **real global game** with real actors.

- The Great Cyber Games are **attractive to policy- and decision-makers** because they filter all the noise of computer conferences, journal articles, and got right to the person with the ideas.

- Players liked it because of the incentive to see their ideas realized, and earn a living at **meaningful work**.

- An unintended bi-product of the game is a **global personnel selection system** that performed the role of a **global employment agency**.

- **Nanotechnology transceivers** with voice-stress software are incorporated into clothing and jewelry.

- **With nanotechnology, whatever we can design, we can build.**

- **Software agents** seek new opportunities for collaboration, alert users to synchronicity in order to discover the value of new and counterintuitive ideas, and coach people in new forms of self-organization.

- **Knowledge and wisdom have become added measures of wealth and value.**

- **Global idea management systems** are integrated into the Great Cyber Games.

- Hierarchical institutions of the twentieth century have given way to **network organizations** and a plethora of **short-term, task-oriented, individually initiated teams** made possible by intelligent software agents in cyberspace.

- Cyber-UN and other international organizations can only be understood in cyberspace, because "employees" are not concentrated into one building or geographic center from which they operate. Instead people are connected around the world under the cyber umbrella of the international organization.

- Cyber organizations led to the **harmonization of global standards**, and to accountability, transparency, and participation.

Business in 2020: Strategic Scenario

> *The best way to predict the future is to simply tell somebody something*
> *about a present-day reality that they haven't yet been informed about.*
> *If it's new to them, it's new in the most critical way. They really don't*
> *know. And you won't be caught dead, because you're simply telling*
> *them the truth about something objective and obvious that they simply*
> *had not gotten their heads around.*
>
>   *(Bruce Sterling, lecture at Era 2005 Copenhagen, Denmark,*
>   *September 26, 2005)*

A back-casting scenario describes a desired future situation and the actions
that allowed an organization to achieve them. It is the ideal navigation tool,
allowing the leadership of an organization to explore future strategy based
on desired qualitative results. It paints the picture of a possible state of the
business, identifying the variables that needed mastering, the actions taken
as well as the actors involved. The following scenario describes the state of
the public gaming industry—state lotteries—in 2020. In most countries, public
gaming is a major contributor to the revenue base of the jurisdiction in which
it functions, and one of the industries immediately affected by the emerging
mobile networked context.

The First Five Years of the Great Global Cyber Game

21 NOVEMBER 2020: SPEECH BY THE CHAIRMAN OF THE BOARD, GLOBAL CYBER GAMING CONSORTIUM

I am going to offer you a couple of observations about how we got here, less
of a history lesson and more of a reflection on the sets of decisions that led us
here. A few years ago we realized that the life our players was undergoing
profound changes in expectations. At the turn of the millennium, gaming
reached new heights globally. This was due to a change of mentality and a
change of generations; by 2011 the majority considered gaming as an ordinary
entertainment, and that many brands employed gaming as part of their
promotional strategy. We also understood that certain parts of the gaming
market were developing without any form of regulation or control, as the
Internet facilitated the development of a global gaming market completely
beyond state control. Interestingly enough, while more people were playing

games, numbers confirmed the steady decline in participation rates in traditional lotto games, across all jurisdictions. In some, the decline was in the double digits. A small but statistically significant decline of 8 percentage points in overall participation rates, coupled with a small but statistically significant decrease in overall average individual monthly expenditure, made it clear that if this trend was to continue, a significant portion of our industry will cease to be sustainable. To achieve growth, a new demographic needed to be attracted to our offerings; so we looked at the 18 to 44 crowds as our target.

We focused on the millennial generation.

The developments I just mentioned at the beginning were challenging the old definition of "gaming" to the point that a number of fundamental questions had to be asked by regulators and operators in the market space:

- Where is the division between public and private gaming?

- How do we compete with the ever increasing number of G3 (gaming, gambling, and games) applications now available and new operators in the space?

- How do we compete with unregulated gaming entertainment?

- How do we leverage the trust people placed in our brands over the past half-century with a new generation of players, the Millennial?

As mobile devices were transforming our relationships with people, events, and places, and everyone was empowered to produce and share entertainment, what role can we play? At the same time, global audiences are revolutionizing the size of the gaming marketplace; so the natural question became "are we Global enough in scope and ambition?"

By 2012, it was clear that Marshall McLuhan's insight into the laws of media was based on reality: indeed, *"Any powerful new medium modifies existing media"*. Over the past decade we have witnessed the migration of electronic hardware from being disconnected and immobile, to being increasingly networked and ubiquitous. Most adults in industrialized countries had mobile phones. This was particularly powerful for games-based entertainment, since the very nature of most game play was enhanced in a networked environment.

Playing games for money has also been affected by shifts in technology and consumer expectations. In most jurisdictions, online gambling was legalized by 2013, which meant that remote gambling was now seen by the majority as a legitimate, mainstream entertainment choice, and new technology allowed players to indulge freely in it. With over 1 billion users by 2013, Facebook became the main supplier of gaming entertainment worldwide, and the natural platform for the convergence of remote betting, lottery games and casino gambling. For our organizations to prosper in this new environment, we needed to think beyond competition. Competing with Facebook would have been foolish and counterproductive. So we decided to embark on a new strategic direction, one that capitalized on the trust people already placed in or brands at the local level, as well as the understanding that new forms of gambling were likely to emerge, forms particularly suited to delivery by *remote means and at specific locations*.

Our early understanding of location-specific gaming was our first breakthrough. Jurisdictional fears did not matter anymore, as we discovered that geographic location is jurisdiction. And location is unique: there is only one Fifth Avenue, only one Avenue des Champs-Élysées, only one Tower Bridge ... And this is how *Square Mile Lotto*, the first mega game success of our consortium was born.

The story of the Great Global Cyber Game and Square Mile Lotto is the story of multiple organizations having a common vision, and a common understanding of the opportunity at hand. It is also the story of courageous executives and wise policy-makers, people who were not afraid to unlearn frameworks that seemed for a long time to serve them well.

THE OPPORTUNITY BACKDROP

As gaming was moving from the fixed location of the gaming terminal onto mobile consoles in everyone's pocket, "play here" became "play anywhere." The image of people walking by lotto terminals, reaching in their pockets for the cash necessary to purchase a lotto ticket, is inconceivable today. We have long moved from location-specific terminals to *individual cyber gaming accounts*, where players are billed at the end of the month for their activity. This created an expansive new strategic direction, where we needed to think beyond the conversion of existing games to mobile platforms, to new forms of engagement in the space in which the Internet resides. And that is cyberspace. Cyberspace had become a major medium of civilization creating a constantly growing, non-zero-sum economy and had changed day-to-day life as significantly as the industrial revolution had changed life 200 years earlier. We understood early on in this business redesign effort, that while culture cannot survive without gaming entertainment, what was changing was the profile of the players, and the play interfaces: from an analogue mindset accustomed to a printed ticket to the digital mindset and its new technological platforms. What was also changing was purpose and intention: the "Why" of public games.

The only sustainable source of value creation is via consumer demand driven growth, and consumer demand driven growth is delivered through the gaming entertainment that people choose. And the Millennial's choices were not accounted for. The Millennial is a creature of purpose and intention. The intention is to participate, within a group of like-minded individuals, in the reshaping of society. The games we needed to design for them must make their purpose easily achievable and most of all, fun.

BREAKING THE WALLS

In the recent past, the job of the state gaming authority was to build walls around the games people play within a defined territory. Walls that were high enough to retain our players within, walls high enough that the player had to jump a long way in order to choose the next best bet. So we got hooked on the monopolies that came with our control. But as we witnessed the shift toward Internet gaming, these were not monopolies we dictated or owned anymore. Once the Internet became part of daily life—and thus part of daily gaming entertainment—our strategic choices were limited to:

- lobbying for the suppression of the technology and the legislation of the behavior, or

- leading proactively in the redefinition of gaming, games, and gambling in cyberspace.

The track record of those trying to suppress technology was not giving us too much reason to proceed in that direction; the recording industry failed abysmally in its efforts to suppress the MP3 technology in the late 1990s, and the P2P streaming that followed. Technology-suppression and legislated behavior has proved futile in our sector as well; the nature of the technology being what it is, providers could operate from—or outside—any jurisdiction they choose. So option one was not an option at all.

LEADERSHIP

Embarking on a path of leadership in our industry was a logical choice, and a choice that gave our consortium stakeholders a common strategic purpose. Our strategic intent was clear: to create and own a *new gaming model* that will achieve a worldwide following. A strategy defining ambition. The model had to take advantage of new technologies as well as protect jurisdictional interests, while maximizing the opportunity of specific geographic locations. And this is what led to LSG, *location-specific gaming*, which is now the standard in all geo-location games.

The key lessons of this transformation? Ask "What If?" questions and ask them soon and often. Here are some of the questions we asked:

- What if we evolved the composition of the Global Cyber Gaming Consortium to involve cross-jurisdictional alliances? (This led to Square Mile Lotto being simultaneously rolled out on five continents.)

- What if we jump early on technology experiments?

- What if we invented gaming formats for massive scale location-based gaming experiences?

WELCOME TO THE MOBILE SOCIETY!

We recognized a few things at the outset of the Mobile Society: that we needed to become experts in understanding value, and that in order to add value in people's experience of everyday life through gaming, we must first understand where new value resides. So we set out an ambitious program of unlearning the old paradigms and relearning new ones. Along the way, we transformed the challenges into opportunities. The key was to recognize the nature of the challenge posed by the mobile society.

Let us deal first with the terminology: mobile media, digital media, and the digital landscape stand as descriptors of both a technology—digital data and the devices that transmit and receive it—as well as a behavior, a user engaged in retrieving or creating data while being mobile. The innovation was the fact that data was now mobile and digital. Mobile digital data could be transferred from one user to the other, from multiple entities to one, and from one to multiple. It is fair then to term the environment in which this activity takes place a mobile digital behavior space—the expectations of the users and the deliverables of organizations, being tied to the understanding of the "mobility of data" as a cultural outcome, and one that results into new sets of relationships, new community structures, and new forms of organization, all leading to a new society, the mobile society.

The challenges of doing business in the mobile society were not about technology, but about business strategy. One challenge was the fact that mobile digital media is not a channel; media are not channels, they are modes of individual action. Aside from short-term challenges of technology and infrastructure, the second challenge was posed by our ability to engage and mobilize the community of players around common interests, and the ability to initiate and sustain a meaningful dialogue with them. These were the new measures. This is what we needed to learn: how to initiate a participatory dialogue with our players, and empower them to directly affect the distribution of proceeds towards social programs, education or infrastructure, in the communities they care deeply about. The seeds of Square Mile Lotto were planted here.

THE LOCATION EXPERIENCE IMPERATIVE

Behavioral realities were changing the structure of business, by enabling new forms of engagement and participation. Twitter, Facebook, LinkedIn, YouTube, Google Buzz, Google Earth, were just some of the early manifestations of the transformation in progress, transformations that required consumers actively engaged in actions. At the same time, the Internet was becoming location-based and location-centric and what we knew about our players and their preferences was the critical asset used in transforming mobility and location in the *gaming media of choice*, by engaging players at locations they care about, at the granular level, one on one, and giving them the opportunity to make difference. Was this not the originating purpose of lotteries, to make a difference in the local community? This was our second breakthrough: we understood that by connecting location with a cause we will return to one of the earliest archetypes of public gaming: the hope of winning balanced by the desire to do good.

A New Gaming Audience and the Rise of Social Gaming

Empowering participation by players was a signal that we were now ready to attract a new demographic, the Millennial. But to fully be able to do so, we first needed to understand how is the Millennial different from the baby-boomer. In as much as the Millennial is an empowered individual who acts on this empowerment by participating actively in the shaping of his/her own world, the baby-boomer was empowered in thought but not in action. The majority of the baby-boom generation did not change the world, but witnessed it being done by rebels from their own midst, in the garages of Silicon Valley. And this was the key in understanding the gap between the two generations: the millennial wants to have fun as *a life attribute*, while the baby-boomer has *fun as entertainment*. Programmed fun, within its time limits and specific formats and places.

The marketing of public games to the Millennial demographic had to change as well. For the millennial words are not actions; they are a generation that needs to transform feelings into reality, and they have the means, the desire, and the will to do it.

From individually focused campaigns that emphasized the riches of a life in the winning circle, we shifted to a marketing communication strategy based on outcomes. The outcome of the player's participation; this is what your participation has accomplished, this is how your community of interest has benefited. We successfully transformed an individual reward message into a *social object*, with the power to attract communities and their demographics.

Transforming our brands into a social object was a long and delicate process, but a process that needed to take place before any social media application could be used in our new games. The concept of "social objects" helped in understanding the formation of, and the activity in social networks online and offline, and it has been advocated by numerous experts in the fields of social media, and Internet-powered collaboration, as a key issue when considering community engagement. The underlying premise behind the theory of object-centered sociality is that community and communal action doesn't happen simply because people have the possibility for it. Communal action happens only if one has an intrinsic reason to do it, if one is attracted to do it. The relationships and links between people are not the central element in communities and social activity. Instead, the crucial building blocks are the social objects: common shared objects of interest for a given group of people, that gather those people around them to share stories about, discuss issues concerning them, celebrate them, or in some other way manifest their relationship to them. Various contexts give rise to various social objects: an earthquake in Haiti in early 2010 created one of the social objects of the same year, with millions of people registered on the over 30 Facebook pages dealing with relief for Haiti. Relationships between people, then, emerge as links that revolve around the same social objects, and it is the social objects that are key in the forming of communities and social activity.

And this was our third breakthrough: *we recognized that within each square mile of a city there were issues that people really cared about, issues that were waiting for the spotlight and the transformation in a social object in proximity to a user.* We realized that this is about the school their kids goes to, about the hospital their parents are treated in, about the roads criss-crossing their community. What if we could connect a player's number selection directly to a social object of interest to them? What if we can connect the 49 numbers on a lottery selection board, with 49 deeply cared for issues in the community near you?

We purposefully chose not to be reactive in our strategy, but rather to be proactive. To succeed in Cyber Gaming, we needed to engage in new ways, for a better and more expansive relationship with the player, on new and multiple platforms of experience, and on the player's terms. Our ability to move swiftly from one platform to the next, and from one compelling theme to another, is due in no small part to the *fact that we are now longer observers of change, but we live it and we initiate it.*

We are now an intrinsic part of our players intellectual and cultural life.

> *... pleasure must not be in the consequence of the utility of the object or event, but in its immediate perception; in other words, beauty is an ultimate good, something that gives satisfaction to a natural function, to some fundamental need or capacity of our minds. Beauty is therefore a positive value that is intrinsic; it is a pleasure.*[4]

---

4   George Santayana. 1896. *The Sense of Beauty*. [Online]. Available at: http://www.gutenberg.org/ebooks/26842. Released 2008.

Afterword: Getting Started

John Sutherland

Now what? No matter who, or when, or where you are, you have almost reached the end of this book and somewhere during this read you may have reached a number of conclusions. *This book explains the heart of product and service design and development. This book posits a new way to think about how the world works: why products succeed and fail, why businesses succeed and fail.* But somewhere in the back of your mind you are also wondering *what do I do with it? How do I use this new learning? Now what?*

We are creatures of habits. We connect with all other living things through a common trait: we all consume energy. That truth holds for trees, bacteria, lions, and to us. And when we die, we stop consuming energy. For animals, this biological law caused the emergence of habits as a survival mechanism. Adopt a habit and you consume less energy. Consume less energy, and your chance of survival increases. We can no more stop behaving habitually than we can stop breathing. Now you know why it is so hard to follow through on New Year's resolutions. Habits are hard to break. We are working against millions of years of genetic evolution.

This book described the mechanism by which new habits are formed. A new medium is introduced to an individual—or a demographic—and it allows new behaviors to emerge, and over time, new habits to form. We have learned in this book that we do not so much *need* the iPhone as much as our instinct to express our desires in new ways drove us to experiment with it, and find a new personal behavior space to occupy. In so doing, we developed new habits around communication, socializing, playing, and so on. The behavior space we develop as individuals is unique to us. But, the desire to experiment with new media to create new behavior space (and so a new habit space) is universal. And that same genetic law drives it. We cannot escape it. So what?

Well, this book is medium for you. What is presented here is not a technology; rather it is an idea, a new way of thinking about the world, a *Be Different* philosophy if you will. Until you adopt this medium, this idea, these concepts as your own, there can be no relevance for you. Only when your behavior changes, when new habits form, will this book and its ideas have meaning for you. Only then will it change your personal behavior space, and in so doing, change your relationship to your world.

That is the *now what*.

There are thousands of potential new behaviors you could adopt to incorporate these ideas into your life. Where should you get started? And so, where should we get started? At the beginning, of course. But where is that?

Life is full of patterns. When it comes to success in business, we have watched a pattern repeat itself again and again. *It is about leadership.* Compared to other organizations, leadership teams in great organizations demonstrate four capabilities exceedingly well. These teams:

1. See more clearly, and interpret with greater insight, the technological and behavioral changes outside their industry norm. They see beyond what is to what could be.

2. Translate those insights into new behavior space for users.

3. Determine faster and with greater precision how to best shape their business to exploit those new behavior space experiences.

4. Implement faster the resultant change with less risk and greater rewards.

It all starts with the skill of leaders to *See more clearly, and interpret with greater insight, the technological and behavioral changes outside their industry norm.*

That was the failure of RIM and Nokia in their response to the launch of the iPhone in January 2007. That was the failure of the analyst community in April 2007, when they did not ask questions about the impact of the iPhone during the earnings call. None of these people saw it. Why did they not read the signals of what was coming? These are bright people. They have built billion-dollar organizations. They have analyzed thousands of industries. Why didn't they see? It is not stupidity or intelligence, so there must be something else at play here.

There is something else. *It is language!*

Not English, or German or Chinese or any other dialect, but the language of ideas. Mathematics has its own language. So does physics, biology, finance, marketing, and so on. They all have terms with definitions that mean something. $E=mc^2$ has a specific meaning that transcends time and space. It does not matter what century it is, what business you operate, or who you are. $E=mc^2$ is a universal truth that applies in all circumstances across all time. That is equally true for ROI in finance, or DNA structures in biology. These are examples of universal truths expressed in a *technical* language.

But what about value creation? What are the universal truths about that? How many universal truths can you name—with terms and definitions—that explain value creation across all times, and in all environments? Exactly. We cannot. That is fundamentally *why we cannot see*. It is not about intelligence or skills, but because we lack a universal frame of reference. We lack the terms and their definitions about value creation, that are as true today as they were 200 years ago, 2,000 years ago, 200,000 years ago. In the absence of these universal truths, we are left with explaining value creation from our own perspective. We have no choice but to filter everything through our own experience. For RIM and Nokia that experience was about secure information technology systems. For the analysts it was about units sold and subscriptions signed. But it is not just them. It is true for everyone. For a beverage bottler, it is about cases sold. For hospitals, it is about patients helped. For car manufactures, it is about performance and brand positioning. For you it is about—<*insert your specific terms here*>.

In the end, RIM and Nokia were right in a sense. Until now, value creation has been about those things that are unique to the industry. That is what blinded them to the shifts. That is what blinds *us* to shifts. More tragically, that is what blinds us to becoming the creator of a shift. In the absence of a universal truth we are all blind. We are all trapped in our own language. Until now.

Value—Creation of

This book is not just about iPhone or any other technology and the behavior space it creates. It is about a universal truth about value creation. Take a look in the *Oxford English Dictionary* and you will find 13 different definitions for value. None of them deal with the *creation of value*. We propose a 14th definition specific to value creation.

> *14. Value—Creation of: The expansion of relationships from new behavior(s) enabled by a disruptor/media.*

Let us unpack this definition.

Life = Relationships

All of us exist in time and space. As we move through time and space we interact with the things around us. So at its most fundamental, our lives are comprised of all the many and varied relationships we have with:

1.   time (when we are)

2.   space (where we are)

3.   self (who we are)

4.   people (by themselves and in groups)

5.   objects (inanimate and living)

6.   ideas (how and why we are)

If we could add up all our relationships, taking into account the good and the bad, we could conceptually measure the size and quality of our lives. We could compute for ourselves our relationship space. So what creates value for an individual at the point of use? Value is created when an interaction with a media improves the size and/or quality of our relationship space. The direct impact the iPhone contact app has on me, or you, is dependent upon how, at the point of use, it changes our relationship with those factors: time—can access any time, space—can access anywhere, people—have all data available.

What is the characteristic of the interaction with the object or an idea that makes the improvement in relationship space? It is the enabling of a new behavior within the existing behavioral norm for that individual. For the iPhone contact app the new behavior of accessing *"contact data anywhere at any time and applying it easily to make a connection"* is what improves our relationship space.

Universal Pattern

We feel the world and judge our happiness in it by our relationships. How we interact with the world—our behavior—affects our relationships. When the interaction with an object or an idea allows us to behave in a way we could not do before, then our behavior space grows. Finally, if this new behavioral addition to our behavior space improves our relationships, we feel satisfied and seek to interact with it more frequently.

That is the universal pattern that has existed since *Homo sapiens* first walked the earth. In the beginning the first media were fire and language. Those inventions/media disrupted the existing behavioral norms, allowing new behavioral norms to emerge—build fires, describe plans for hunting. These new norms changed their relationship with the world: warmth in cold climates, more efficient hunting. This pattern has continued ever since. It was true 200,000 years ago and it is true today.

Products, services, ideas, offerings, all work the same way through behavior change, and its impact on the user's relationship space (see Figure A.1).

Figure A.1   The universal pattern

Take a simple example of wishing happy birthday to a friend. Prior to the invention of writing, the postal service and the telephone, we only conversed with family and friends when we were face to face. If your friend was two miles away, you had to physically move yourself to where she was located to wish her happy birthday. With the advent of mail in Persia in 55 BC, we could *send* a letter instead. The invention of the telephone in 1876, allowed us to wish her happy birthday over the phone, with only our voice traveling. These two inventions, mail and the telephone, allowed new behaviors to emerge: writing letters and phoning people. The invention/medium, acted as a disruptor to existing behavioral norms, causing new behavior spaces to emerge, and over time, a new behavioral norm.

Below is a list of media and their approximate date of invention. Each one gave us a new behavior we can use to solve the problem of wishing our friend happy birthday when she is out of shouting range.

Mail	55 BC
Bicycle	1839
Subway	1863
Phone	1876
Car	1881
Email	1971
Cell phone	1979
Instant messaging	1990s
Skype	2003
YouTube	2005
Twitter	2006
Facetime	2010

Some of them involved different ways to transport ourselves, some transported the messages, and some transported the electronic representation of our voice. Each one of these added to our behavioral landscape. As these new behaviors became normative, we changed as well. Our culture, what we find acceptable and unacceptable, changed to adapt to the new behaviors that emerged. If you were born at the dawn of Homo sapiens, you only had one choice if you and your friend were two miles apart. You walked. That was it. Your desire to wish your friend happy birthday—presuming ancient man did such a thing—could only be expressed one way. You walked, and then you said "Happy Birthday." Of course, having made the effort to walk that distance it is highly unlikely that you would say happy birthday and then leave. The energy expenditure was too great for so little an interaction. And you certainly would not express your thoughts in the equivalent of 140 characters, then turn around and walk back. The culture would not allow it, because it never happened. We accept it now, because *it happens*. Culture follows behavior, not the other way around. New mediums create the new behaviors that drive culture. Ancient man lived in a behavioral desert. By comparison, today we live in a jungle of behavior space possibilities. I mentioned 12 different ways to say happy birthday, but there are likely hundreds more, thousands if you count combinations.

Perhaps you are not convinced. Perhaps you are wondering about a specific item, or object, or idea and cannot see how this pattern works in that particular case. If that is the case, do the following exercise. Walk outside and stand on the soil or grass somewhere, and look at a building and the roads and vehicles that surround it; 5,000 years ago none of what you see existed. The asphalt in the road did not exist. The metal in the light standard did not exist. The idea called magnetism that led to the electricity that runs the street lamp did not exist. The cement in the sidewalk did not exist. The phone in the building did not exist. The ballpoint pen that someone is using inside did not exist. The synthetic materials that are used to make the clothes you are wearing did not exist. None of it existed. None of it! And the millions of ways in which we laugh, have fun, learn about each other, communicate with each other, travel, eat, play, rest, and relax did not exist either. All of those behaviors came from those inventions, and the ideas in mathematics, physics, medicine, and material science that made them possible. Five thousand years ago most of the words in this paragraph did not exist either. We had to invent them, so we could talk about our daily life.

Media (in the form of products, services, ideas, platforms, technology, whatever) disrupts the existing behavioral norm allowing new behaviors to emerge. People interact with media in the universal search to express themselves, to become better selves. In doing so, they create new behaviors for themselves. They benefit from these new behaviors in the expansion and improvement of their personal relationship space. The form the medium takes is irrelevant. Product, service, idea—it does not matter. All that matters is whether it allows new behaviors to emerge. Here are a few examples.

THE PRINTING PRESS C.1439 (PLATFORM)

With the advent of the printing press people *published* books. By comparison to copying books, a slow and cumbersome process full of errors, printing ensured each book was an exact duplicate and cheaper to produce. Exact duplicate books enabled the dissemination of fact-based books, starting with masonry. Now masons could try others techniques and learn which worked and which did not. This behavior of *sharing techniques beyond your local area* became widespread. The new behavioral norm created by the printing press was so pervasive that for some, Gutenberg was credited with launching the renaissance and the modern scientific era.[1] Think of how that new behavioral norm changed the relationship space for every person who followed over the last 1,000 years. Time, space, ideas, objects, people, self. We all changed as a result of the renaissance and what followed. Our lives are immeasurably different since the advent of printing.

TELEPHONE 1876 (PRODUCT)

With the advent of the telephone people conducted voice to voice conversations over long distances. This new behavior, *long distance verbal communication* dramatically improved our relationships with other people and ourselves. Space was shortened, time spent traveling was reduced. We could have more frequent conversations with people we wanted to talk to. Overtime, we sped up our conversations as we shortened them. We are now down to tweets of 140 characters.

---

1   American journalists in the book *1000 Years 1000 People* voted Gutenberg as the "Man of the millennium."

FED-EX 1971 (SERVICE)

Overnight shipping from here to anywhere guaranteed. Prior to Fed-ex we posted mail and waited. We shipped goods by truck and train and waited. In rare cases we put people on planes with packages to get them there fast. Fed-ex changed our behavior. Our relationship with time, space, and objects has changed for the better. Now we ship overnight and don't even think about it.

The value creation pattern is universal. The introduction of new media allows new behaviors to emerge. Those new behaviors enhance and enrich our relationships. When relationship space grows, value *is created*. From fire, to the printing press, to electricity, to phones, to cars, to planes, to insulin, to calculus, to the Internet, to the declaration of independence, to smart-phones, and a million other inventions and ideas that created value for mankind in their day, it is all the same:

1. They disrupt our behavioral norm.

2. They allow new behaviors to emerge.

3. They grow our relationship space.

Now we have a common language for how value is created, independent of time or circumstance. Now we can build tools to help us see shifts occur. Tools independent of your industry. Tools that provide a universal perspective, and so let you escape your language trap.

Earlier in this book we proposed a new cultural norm for organizations. A norm where leaders:

*   Cultivate and stimulate the imagination of others, individually or in groups, and translate it into user value, fitting within the culture of the times.

*   Guide, manage, and inspire others on the path of discovery and learning.

*   Nurture ideas, identify their value, and transform them into opportunities for growth.

To accomplish this transformation leaders need to *behave differently*. To behave differently they will need to be disrupted. To be disrupted they need a disruptor. And they need to start by first seeing the world differently. Seeing it through behavior and not technology, or products, or services, or business models. Behavior.

To help you on your journey, we have included here a signal transformation matrix (see Figure A.2) as a tool that uses the language of value creation. In using the tool, you use the language. And when you use the language, two new behaviors emerge for you.

1.   You *filter signals through a universal pattern* independent of your experience and your industry. In doing so you will understand signals that previously had no meaning for you.

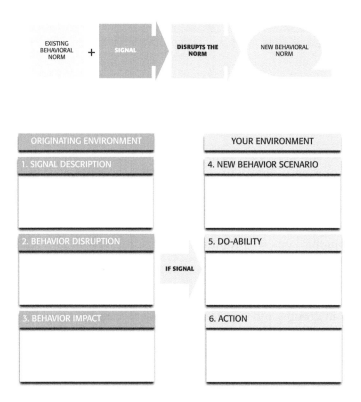

Figure A.2   Signal transformation matrix
Adapted—Source: Ennova Inc. ©2011 Ennova.

2.   This new understanding lets you *apply new signals to your situation*. In doing so, you see opportunities to which you were previously blind.

When that happens, you see more clearly, and interpret with greater insight, the technological and behavioral changes outside your industry norm. You see beyond *what is*, to *what could be*. Your relationship with your world becomes clearer. You lead.

The Signal Transformation Matrix

Signals are information about emerging new behaviors occurring outside your normal frame of reference. The root of value creation is in how fast new behavior signals become understandable by the organization.

ORIGINATING ENVIRONMENT

First, analyze the media/disruptor in its originating environment.

1.   What is the new media? An idea, a technology, a platform? What?

2.   What are the *new* behaviors the media is causing to emerge?

3.   How significant is this behavioral impact?

If the behavioral impact is significant then it has a potential to be a disruptor in your environment. If not, then it is likely just noise.

YOUR ENVIRONMENT

Given the disruptor is indeed a signal ("If Signal" in Figure A.2) and has significant impact, you assess its potential in your environment.

1.   You start by transporting the emerging behavior, not the media, the behavior, to your environment. *How could you use that behavior in your world? What benefit would it provide?*

2.   It may be that the media used to create the behavior in the originating environment, will not work in your environment. If so,

how could you adapt the media or change it to work in your environment. Behavior stays constant. Media changes to suit the environment.

3.   Finally, what are the first actions you will take to test out this idea?

Now What?

We started this afterword by posing the question—now what? All innovations create new behaviors. We proposed here a universal language of value creation, along with a signal translation matrix to help start your journey of transformation, through the creation of new behavior spaces.

Now it is your turn!

Acknowledgement

John Sutherland is the creator of The Own Your Future Program, a leadership behavior-change process that rewires culture for game-changing innovation. A former facilitator at the Xerox International Training Center in Leesburg Virginia, John has pioneered the use of many thought-provoking customer-centric innovation techniques to generate and implement game-changing ideas. John has helped thousands of executives in a variety of industries to implement game-changing as a normative behavior. His life mission is to accelerate economic development by sharing the tools, methods, and the techniques he has developed with entrepreneurs worldwide. Over the past eight years he has been an invaluable collaborator in the shaping of the ideas presented in this book.

> *We no longer mean by work all that is done usefully, but only what is done unwillingly and by the spur of necessity. By play we are designating, no longer what is done fruitlessly, but whatever is done spontaneously and for its own sake, whether it have or not an ulterior utility. Play, in this sense, may be our most useful occupation.*[2]

---

2   George Santayana. 1896. *The Sense of Beauty*. [Online]. Available at: http://www.gutenberg.org/ebooks/26842. Released 2008.

Bibliography

Alexander, F. 1958. A contribution to the theory of play. *The Psychoanalytic Quarterly* (April). [Online]. Available at: http://www.pep-web.org/document.php?id=paq.027.0175a [accessed: January 4, 2012].

Batelle, J. 2003. [Online]. Available at: http://battellemedia.com/archives/2003/11/the_database_of_intentions.php [accessed: June 22, 2011].

Blanchard, K. 1995. *The Anthropology of Sport: An Introduction*. 2nd Edn. Westport, Connecticut: Bergin & Garvey Publisher, Inc.

Burgelman, R. and Growe, A. 1996. Strategic dissonance. *California Management Review*, Winter.

Caillois, R. 1961. *Man, Play, and Games*. New York: Free Press of Glencoe.

Carbone, L.P. and Haeckel, S.H. 1994. Engineering customer experiences. *Marketing Management*, 3(3).

Clarke, A.C. 1961. *Profiles of the Future*. London: Orion Books, p. 9.

Csíkszentmihályi, M. 1979. The concept of flow, in *Play and Learning*, ed. B. Sutton-Smith. New York: Gardner Press, 257–74.

Erikson, E.H. 1977. *Toys and Reasons: Stages in the Ritualization of Experience*. New York: Norton.

Freud, S. 1920. *Beyond the Pleasure Principle*. Standard Edn 1990. London: W.W. Norton & Company.

Glenn, J.C. and Gordon, T.J. 1999. *1999 State of the Future: Challenges We Face at the Millennium*. Washington, D.C.: The Millennium Project.

Harter, J.K., Schmidt, F.L. and Hayes, T.L. 2002. Business-unit level relationship between employee satisfaction, employee engagement, and business outcomes: A meta analysis. *Journal of Applied Psychology*, 87(2), 268–79.

Huizinga, J. 1938. *Homo Ludens: A Study of the Play Element in Culture*. Boston: Beacon Press.

King, M. 2010. Tesco launches barcode scanner app for online orders. *The Guardian*. [Online, October 26]. Available at: http:// www.guardian.co.uk/money/2010/oct/26/tesco-app-barcode-reader.

LaValle, S., Hopkins, M., Lesser, E., Shockley, R. and Kruschwitz, N. 2010. Analytics: The new path to value: How the smartest organizations are embedding analytics to transform insights into action. MIT Sloan Management Review and IBM Institute for Business Value. [Online]. Available at: http://www-935.ibm.com/services/us/gbs/ thoughtleadership/ ibv-embedding-analytics. html?cntxt=a1008891.

Lewis, M. 2011. *Memoirs of an Addicted Brain*. Canada: Doubleday.

Malcolm, P.M. 1968. Marketing and the social challenge of our times, in *A New Measure of Responsibility for Marketing*, ed. K. Cox and B.M. Enis. Chicago: American Marketing Association.

Manu, A. 1995. *ToolToys: Tools with an Element of Play*. Copenhagen: Danish Design Centre.

Manu, A. 2006. *The Imagination Challenge*. Berkeley: New Riders.

Manu, A. 2010. *Disruptive Business*. Farnham: Gower Publishing.

McLuhan, M. and Powers, B. 1992. *The Global Village: Transformations in World Life and Media in the 21st Century*. Oxford: Oxford University Press.

Miller, D.L. 1970. *Gods and Games: Toward a Theology of Play*. New York: Harper & Row.

Neisser, D. 2010. Twelpforce: Marketing that isn't marketing. FastCompany. [Online]. Available at: www. fastcompany.com/1648739/marketing-that-isn-t-marketing.

Owen, L, Goldwasser, C., Choate, K. and Blitz, A. 2007. The power of many: ABCs of collaborative innovation throughout the extended enterprise. IBM Institute for Business Value. [Online]. Available at: http://www-935.ibm. com/services/us/gbs/bus/pdf/g510–6335–00-abc.pdf..

Parasnis, G.A. and Baird, C. 2011. From social media to Social CRM: What customers want. IBM Institute for Business Value. [Online]. Available at: http://www-935.ibm.com/services/us/gbs/thoughtleadership/ibv-social-crm-whitepaper.html.

Pieper, J. 1955. *Leisure, the Basis of Culture*. New York: Pantheon.

Rampbell, C. 2010. Does Michelle Obama's wardrobe move markets? *New York Times*. [Online, October 18]. Available at: http://economix.blogs.nytimes.com/2010/10/18/does-michelle-obamas-wardrobe-move-markets/.

Rieber, L.P., Smith, L. and Noah, D. 1998. The value of serious play. *Educational Technology*, 38(6), 29–37.

Rueter, T. 2010. Macy's offers a virtual fitting room in its NYC flagship store. Internet Retailer. [Online, October 12]. Available at: www.internetretailer.com/2010/10/12/macys-offers¬virtual-fitting-room-its-nyc-flagship-store.

Russell, B. 1921. *The Analysis of Mind*. [Online]. Available at: www.gutenberg.org/ebooks/2529.

Santayana, G. 1896. *The Sense of Beauty*. [Online]. Available at: www.gutenberg. org/ebooks/26842.

Schmitt, B. 2006. How to build your customer experience framework in five steps. Marketing Virtual Seminar. Transcript of original viewing from May 18, 2006.

Sigler, M.G. 2010. Eric Schmidt: Every 2 days we create as much information as we did up to 2003. TechCrunch. [Online, August 4]. Available at: http:// techcrunch.com/2010/08/04/ schmidt-data/.

Sinek, S. 2009. TED Talks, How great leaders inspire action, filmed September 2009 at TEDGlobal200.

Steel, E. 2010. Meredith builds up a sideline in marketing. *Wall Street Journal*. [Online, February 25]. Available at: http://online.wsj.com/article/SB1000142405274870 35102045750857527045639926.html?KEYWORDS=meredith+marketing.

Sterling, B. 2005. Speech at Era 2005, Copenhagen. September 26.

Vazquez, P. 2010. Burberry's digital moves pay off. PSFK Conference. [Online, June 25]. Available at: www.psfk. com/2010/06/burberrysdigital-first-moves-pay-off.html.

Index

For Product Safety Concerns and Information please contact our
EU representative GPSR@taylorandfrancis.com Taylor & Francis
Verlag GmbH, Kaufingerstraße 24, 80331 München, Germany